PROOF OF SPIRITUAL PHENOMENA

"In *Proof of Spiritual Phenomena,* neuroscientist Mona Sobhani, Ph.D., takes the reader through her journey from being a skeptically oriented scientific materialist to realizing there's much more to the Universe. This entertaining and easy-to-read book weaves Sobhani's personal experiences with a diverse body of credible science to demonstrate the desperate need for a revised scientific meta-paradigm. It is this sort of courage and intellectual honesty that will be required for science—and society—to truly evolve."

MARK GOBER, AUTHOR OF *AN END TO UPSIDE DOWN THINKING* AND HOST OF *WHERE IS MY MIND?* PODCAST

"Thank the Universe for Mona Sobhani! Is it any coincidence that neuroscientists, after looking carefully at the brain to answer age-old questions, are starting to turn to spirituality? Nope. It's because they don't find what they are looking for in the materialist paradigm, but they know what they're looking for is real. Sobhani leads the pack with her brilliant and vulnerable take on what it means for her and other scientists to turn the corner from materialism to post-materialist thought—and why it's necessary to explain human experience, including and especially human spiritual experience. By letting us into her journey, she shows us parts of ourselves that are learning a new way of knowing, and then she supports our growing knowledge with her hard-won wisdom."

JULIA MOSSBRIDGE, PH.D., AFFILIATE PROFESSOR AT THE UNIVERSITY OF SAN DIEGO, COFOUNDER OF THE INSTITUTE FOR LOVE AND TIME (TILT), AND COAUTHOR OF *TRANSCENDENT MIND*

"Mona Sobhani is a 'flipped' scientist, a neuroscientist whose mechanical-materialist worldview was turned upside down and inside out by a series of honest life experiences that she refused to deny and instead insisted on thinking through. Her book is a page-turning journey filled with everything from coffee ground divinations, mediums, and intuitives; through past lives, secret government psychical research programs, and the new psychedelic research; to the latest scientific and philosophical visions of a conscious, intentional, and profoundly meaningful cosmos. Her message? The old order of knowledge is passing away. Let it go. The new world is taking shape in and as us. Let it be."

"Like opening a set of nesting dolls, Sobhani takes us on her own journey through the layers of her own mind—from the outermost layer grounded in the physical and empirical world, to the intellectual mind which struggles to make sense of everything, and eventually to the innermost, blissful self, where pure consciousness and *just being* resides. It's a delightful ride along where one can vicariously experience the author's struggle to reconcile science and spirituality, as she comes to rest in knowing that it is fine to accept some things as just a mystery!"

"*Proof of Spiritual Phenomena* is a daring, exciting exploration of the intersection of human consciousness and the intricacies of the physical Universe."

"With *Proof of Spiritual Phenomena,* you hold the key to unlocking a whole new level of experiencing and understanding, not only the world around you that you can see but also the one you can't see. Backed up with easy-to-understand science as well as mind-blowing evidence and interviews, Sobhani achieves what is, in my opinion, the first book to truly unlock the intersection point between science and soul-based spirituality. This book is so outstanding and life-changing, you will find yourself buying extra copies to give to everyone you love so that they, too, can experience the magic that is *Proof of Spiritual Phenomena.*"

PROOF OF SPIRITUAL PHENOMENA

A Neuroscientist's Discovery of the Ineffable Mysteries of the Universe

MONA SOBHANI, Ph.D.

Park Street Press
Rochester, Vermont

Park Street Press
One Park Street
Rochester, Vermont 05767
www.ParkStPress.com

Text stock is SFI certified

Park Street Press is a division of Inner Traditions International

Cataloging-in-Publication Data for this title is available from the Library of Congress

ISBN 978-1-64411-499-5 (print)
ISBN 978-1-64411-500-8 (ebook)

Printed and bound in the United States by Lake Book Manufacturing, Inc. The text stock is SFI certified. The Sustainable Forestry Initiative® program promotes sustainable forest management.

10 9 8 7 6 5 4 3 2 1

Text design and layout by Debbie Glogover
This book was typeset in Garamond Premier Pro with Cover Sans and Gill Sans MT Pro used as display typefaces

To send correspondence to the author of this book, mail a first-class letter to the author c/o Inner Traditions • Bear & Company, One Park Street, Rochester, VT 05767, and we will forward the communication, or contact the author directly at **MonaSobhaniPhD.com**.

Per aspera ad astra.
(Through hardship to the stars.)

*In loving memory of
my sweet and brilliant friend,
Jeff Goad.*

Contents

Welcome to the Public Funeral for 'Old Me'

I really don't want to be writing this book. Sometimes I find myself imagining how my life would have been, had I gone on the way I was before. Sometimes I wish none of this had happened to me and I had stayed on my original path. Nevertheless, like many other things in life, it was unstoppable, it happened, and now I'm here—writing this book I don't want to be writing.

I had a *lot* of trouble sitting down to write this book—a book that would irrevocably change my life. At first, I thought to myself that I could just quietly and privately accept all that I had learned. I thought I could accept both that I had profoundly changed personally and that my view of the world had changed. But the more I learned and thought about what I learned, the more that became impossible.

And here's the reason: At the beginning of this journey, I would have been the least likely person to tell this story. I was vehemently opposed to religion and spirituality because science was my religion. I lived and breathed the wonders of the human brain as a neuroscientist. Then a series of life events led me down a path of investigation that transformed me from an aggressively anti-religious, anti-spiritual, strictly scientific materialist (i.e., believing only matter and energy make up the world) and agnostic neuroscientist into a neuroscientist who believes the interaction between mind and matter are more complicated than we currently understand, and that we are probably all connected through a broader consciousness. I am now someone who is open to the idea of past lives and karma, believes weird things happen all the time that our scientific framework can't explain, and generally finds herself saying things straight out of ancient spiritual texts—and not because I needed comfort, but because that's where the evidence led me. I followed an invisible thread of evidence into the marvelous world of mystery and mysticism, and with this book, I hope to inspire others to do the same.

While that all sounds nice now, the road to the 'new me' was brutal. I would read some evidence—and there was *so much* evidence to be read—and update my thinking but then read something else and change my mind. Scientific materialism, which is the framework that the scientific community currently uses to model the Universe that we live in, was the hammer, and my new beliefs were the monkey in a never-ending monkey hammer arcade game. It took countless books, scientific studies, and conversations with colleagues and experts to update my beliefs. When I finally did open to the possibility of a different worldview—one where *meaning* is embedded in the Universe—in flowed a wondrous feeling of delight and serenity that I hadn't known was missing.

So 'new me' is writing this book for 'old me,' both to process and memorialize my path to one version of me who has space in her life for science *and* spirituality. I'm writing this book also to document the difficulty of altering our beliefs. But I also hope it is helpful for others who find themselves on this twisted, scary, nonmaterialist road. I try to look upon the older version of myself with compassion; and if you find yourself in a similar position, I hope you can do the same. I also try to apply that compassion toward fanatic scientific materialist believers because, boy, have I been there. One thing I hope to never do again is have the audacity to think that we already know all the answers to the mysteries of the Universe.

Another reason for putting the story down into writing is to add my name to the long list of scientists, philosophers, and physicists who think it is imperative that we update the scientific paradigm beyond sci-entific materialism for long overdue innovative breakthroughs in phys-ics, neuroscience, and medicine. In doing that, science may incidentally come to match most people's experience of reality. Scientists and other experts will tell you what they truly think and believe when conversa-tions are had in confidence, but come on! It is too disingenuous that we make one set of statements publicly and a whole different, more hon-est and open-minded set of statements in private cocktail hours. More scientists need to open their minds *publicly*. We need to take an hon-est look at data that doesn't fit our current modern theories of reality, because there is a lot of it. So writing this book is me taking a stand, publicly.

One of the first things we learn in statistics is that you can't just throw away outlying data points. Yet modern scientists do that consis-tently with any data that doesn't fit a scientific materialist framework. Yes, it is important for scientists to be skeptical and try to be unbi-ased. Yes, the human brain is built to believe, and it is a storyteller by design, so we often jump to conclusions and need to check our biases. Yes, many of the things from our past that we believed to be mystical, magical, or religious turned out to be decidedly less so when we had the appropriate ways of measuring them (think viruses and bacteria, for example). All that notwithstanding, the mainstream scientific world has taken these few reasons and turned them into dogma. Just like all religions and cults, mainstream science snuffs out opposing thoughts with stigma, ostracism, indignant condemnation, and condescension. In my opinion, it does it at its own expense. But we can change that!

As I said, I really wish I wasn't writing or living this.

But I am.

Welcome to the public funeral for my former self and to a plea to scientists to muster courage to embrace new ways of thinking.

Acknowledgments

Deep gratitude to the crew at Park City Press/Inner Traditions: Kelly Bowen, Lisa P. Allen, Manzanita Carpenter-Sanz, Sarah Galbraith, Jon Graham, John Hays, Ashley Kolesnik, Jeanie Levitan, Erica B. Robinson, and Patricia Rydle.

To my soul sisters (Chantalle Zakarian, Erica Taghavi, Niousha Nader, Stephanie Friedman, and Tina Farazian), who let me isolate myself because you always knew I'd come back when I was ready—thank you, thank you, thank you! Thank you for coming on the journey with me, helping dissect our psychic readings, and positing theories of the Universe. Thank you for reading drafts of this book, texting me with all your impressions, and being preternaturally supportive.

I must thank Royce Christyn and Solly Hemus for comfortably slipping into my life at the perfect time, and for all the two-hour-long (or more) Zoom calls with inexplicable tech issues! Thank you for the friendship, kind words, hope, coaching, opportunities, and priceless introduction to Inner Traditions. Thank you for knowing that I would write a book, even before I knew, and for encouraging me to do so. Many more coincidences to come!

Ultra-special thanks to Jeff Goad, mentor extraordinaire. In a cruel twist of fate, this "thank you" must now be transformed into an "in loving memory" paragraph. Jeff, thank you for lending your creativity to the initial idea of a podcast, cheerleading the entire way, and leveraging your personal connections to help make this a reality. This project and book definitely wouldn't have happened without you. I miss you and mourn that we can't celebrate the book launch together as planned. I hope it's all true and that you're on the other side.

Thank you to my stellar and sweet colleagues who took time out of their very busy schedules to listen to me try to explain what I was doing and to ultimately throw around commiserations and musings on the nature of life and science. Even though this was a secret project, I also still managed to pick certain other people's brains without their knowing exactly why—sorry, but also, thank you! Special thanks to Dave Herman, Helder Araujo, Glenn Fox, Kingson Man, Katie Garrison, Laura Baker, Jonas Kaplan, Vilay Khandelwal, Shaina Oake, Henry Friedman, Matthew Petros, Chrystal Gill, Amna Vugdalic, Judy Tang, Elizabeth Pendley, Cullen Lethin, Rebecca Ebert, Brittain Bush, Sadaf Bathaee, Laura Garcia, and Brooks DiPaula.

Thank you to the many others who took time to speak with me—a total stranger—about a deeply important common interest. Warm gratitude to Mark Boccuzzi, Julia Mossbridge, Mark Gober, John Alexander, Al Powers, Brittany Quagan, Charlie Hartwell, Maureen Pelton, Vincent Genna, Brandy Walker, Susan Fisher, John Webber, and those who remain unnamed.

I must give a heartfelt thank-you to all the psychics, intuitives, mystics, and psychic mediums from whom I received readings or interviews. Special thanks to Rachel Lee, Dawn Marlowe, Lynda Diane Nichols, and Rosemary the Celtic Woman.

The most glittering thank-you to my parents and brother for making me believe that I can accomplish anything my heart desires and for politely and lovingly listening to all my theories of the Universe.

Thank you to "Event #2" for unwittingly being the lit match to the spilled gasoline of my life.

I bow down to all the scientists and philosophers who paved the way for this book with their curiosity, theories, imagination—and most of all—their open-mindedness.

Introduction

'Old me' would have *hated* 'new me.' As a die-hard scientist, 'old me' would have felt her heart pounding with agitation and contempt as 'new me' discussed mind-matter interactions and differing philosophies of the nature of reality and the Universe. Long after the encounter was over, 'old me' would have kept thinking about how stupid 'new me' was and would have been internally decrying the ignorance of the world. 'Old me' would have, with disgust, told 'new me' that her beliefs were very nice ideas to comfort herself through a difficult life, but that there was no evidence for any of it—never mind that 'old me' had never actually bothered to check if there was any research supporting the claims of 'new me.'

As I prepare to begin writing, I feel constriction in my chest, tightening in my stomach, and that existential pain that dares to try to knock me over. Why? Because it still hurts to think about the journey and the transformation. Maybe it's because all of it is ongoing and fresh, but also maybe it's because of how deeply it tore into me and tore my life apart. That's how deeply our beliefs become intertwined with our identities. It's hard to change what you believe without thinking that you've lost yourself. It truly is like a death and rebirth, and it takes a while for all your neural representations to update and catch up. In any case, an introduction to the former me—or 'old me,' as I will refer to her from here on out—is necessary.

Before I tell you how I had to burn to the ground to rise from the ashes, I need to lay the groundwork by defining a few concepts and explaining a few editorial decisions that I made. This is a book about a personal journey of transformation with anecdotes from my life, but it is also about presenting scientific evidence from multiple disciplines that contributed to changing the way I think about the world. In the midst of an existential crisis, the mystical and meaningful dimensions of life came fluttering into my world, but at first, my scientific mind swatted them away. Looking back now, I can see that at the beginning of the project I was simply curious and wanted to discuss personal experiences with others, and simply play with the idea that science and spirituality could coexist. I thought that a few casual conversations would do the trick and I could move on. You'll hear this in the first few interviews that I did with personal friends. Deciding to fully embrace this challenge and actually try to pursue universal truths by reaching out to the individuals whom I refer to as "the people who know" was an unexpected accident. That accident caused me to examine massive amounts of research materials to come to the conclusions that I made. Luckily for you, I will not be conveying *all* of the information that I consumed, but rather selecting particularly transformative conversations, studies, or books to highlight and share with you the ideas that shook the foundation of my understanding of reality. I do understand that some people will want to do further reading, so a list of recommended reading materials is included at the end of the book. Accompanying the empirical evidence were the transformational personal experiences that dotted my path and ultimately redefined "proof" for me. There, at the intersection of science and spirituality, a new personal worldview emerged, where the Universe is imbued with meaning and there exists a mystical dimension to life.

But before we slip into that story, some logistics. . . .

I thought long and hard about the inclusion in this book of fringe science findings (because what are those other than outliers?) but ultimately decided to include them because the evidence was strong by any normal measure of scientific standards. I have worked long and hard for my scientific training. It is a part of my DNA and of my core identity, and I would die before I let anyone take that away from me. So absolutely zero parts of me were excited to write about all of the scientific findings I discovered on controversial research topics such as reincarnation, precognition, and clairvoyance. Many times, I thought of sweeping it all under the rug, like many others before me have done.

But for me, all we really have is our integrity, and how could I call myself a scientist after ignoring a strong dataset? It would not be authentic or genuine, and worse, it would hurt science and humanity. In the end, I did not want to contribute to the propagation of censorship of data that doesn't fit just one of the many possible models of reality in our Universe.

Language is a beautiful thing, but it can also be a hindrance. How do you describe something that is indescribable? It can be difficult to find appropriate and accurate words or descriptions to convey complex and mysterious topics and experiences. Because of the array of disciplines that I touch on in the book—neuroscience, physics, philosophy, and psychology—there will be complex words and topics, and I will try to break them down in an easy-to-understand way. Most things will be explained within the text, but let's discuss a few here to lay the foundation.

Scientific materialism believes that physical reality is fundamental or, in other words, all that exists. The theory suggests that everything physical would continue existing whether humans were around to observe it or not. There are multiple assumptions that go into this theory that affect the way we do science, but I will tackle those as they come up in the appropriate chapters.

There are other models of reality and the Universe that will be discussed in the book that consider consciousness. *Consciousness* is a tricky little word and concept, but for simplicity let's define it as the awareness of one's fundamental essence, or our inner experience of life. When we study consciousness from a first-person point of view, it is known as *phenomenology*. To examine the *phenomenological experience* of a person is to collect a subjective report of their lived experience—what is it like to be *you*? It is an important research tool.

We will discuss individuals, such as psychics and mediums, who receive information about you and your life outside of the typical five senses. A psychic, also known as an intuitive, reads energy from you and from the Universe to understand your past, present, and possible futures. A medium communicates and receives messages from the deceased. A psychic medium is someone who can both read energy and communicate with deceased individuals. I will mostly refer to psychics or intuitives as "intuitives" to better capture the range of information they provide, unless the source material itself uses the word "psychic." I will use the words "intuitive reading" and "psychic reading" interchangeably, although intuitive reading is becoming the more popular term. If a person is specifically skilled in both, I will refer to them as a "psychic medium" because that is usually how they refer to themselves. A *mystic* might be defined as someone who has direct experience of the sacred and is more of a general term to capture the variety of mystical experiences.

I will refer to any phenomena that are out of sync with scientific materialism as "unexplained phenomena." I will define the phenomena as they arise in the text.

When reviewing scientific evidence in the book for unexplained phenomena, I will mainly outline reviews and summarized findings from multiple studies—rather than individual studies—to focus on findings that have been replicated and are less likely to be a one-off result. Again, this book is not meant to be a comprehensive review of evidence, because other authors have already done a fantastic job of summarizing the evidence.

Toward the end of the book, I will use the words the "Cosmos" and "Universe" interchangeably.

Okay, now that we have gotten that out of the way, it's time to meet 'old me' . . . and you can find out how I joined a little cult called science.

1

Bewitched by Science

On paper, both sides of the family would be considered Muslim. My parents are not religious, although my mom considers herself spiritual. Although I don't explicitly remember any animosity toward Islam from my parents, I'm sure it was difficult to think fondly of the religion given that a radical arm of it had taken over their home country and ripped them from their families. My parents had arrived in the United States in 1976 (two years before the Iranian Revolution) so that my father could attend the University of Oklahoma for a degree in architecture. The Iranian Revolution occurred in 1978 in the name of Islam, and my parents never moved back to their homeland. A study-abroad trip turned into exile.

I grew up in Los Angeles, California—still my favorite place on Earth—with Iranian immigrant parents. I excelled in many subjects in school, but when the time came to think of career choices while applying for college, I initially wanted to be a journalist, or to focus on writing in some way. That changed when I took an AP psychology course in eleventh grade and the chapter on the human brain in our textbook enraptured me. I was enthralled by all the different regions of the brain and how they worked together to produce human behavior, which had always baffled me. I had already found that I loved observing people interact with each other, and I was always curious about why some people got along so well, while others repelled each other. Why did people lie? Why did we care what others thought? How did this blob of cells in our heads direct all these odd behaviors? This seemed like a worthwhile endeavor on which to embark.

I decided to pursue neuroscience when I started college at the University of California, San Diego (UCSD), which housed one of the top neuroscience programs in the country. I also decided to try the premedicine track because, since I'm an Iranian-American, there is an obligation to at least *consider* being a physician as a possible career. (For those unfamiliar, the joke goes that you have two career options as an Iranian-American: physician or lawyer.)

The first two years of college were a menagerie of the basic science courses—physics, organic chemistry, inorganic chemistry, and metabolic biochemistry—and not a lot of neuroscience. I was eager to get to learning about the brain, but as I acquired the foundational scientific knowledge, I was blown away by the complexity of nature. In biology the cascading events that unfolded with precise regularity throughout our bodies and the natural world were nothing short of miraculous. The topics were also extraordinarily challenging with endless pathways and mechanisms to memorize and understand.

The courses that really turned my understanding of the world upside down were physics and chemistry. I had a difficult time with physics and chemistry because, while there were many laws, equations, and rules to memorize and I was great at memorizing, there weren't many explanations about exactly how these phenomena emerged, or why they existed, which did not align well with my learning style. To truly learn and understand something, I need to have insight into more than just the mechanism, like why the mechanism evolved in this particular way and not another way. Due to the fact that the discipline of biology is multiple levels of abstraction above chemistry and physics, you can reach back down for explanations. For example, you may have to memorize DNA replication pathways, but at least you understand the why (cell division) or the how (DNA coming apart, being copied, being rebuilt, and so on). For physics and chemistry, there weren't always neat answers for the why or the how. You would have to memorize that electrons formed a cloud around a nucleus, but there was really no understanding as to why that was the case. You'd have to memorize the equations for Newton's laws of physics, but the textbooks didn't contain any deeper explanation of the forces, how they emerged, why they existed, and why we expect them to be uniform everywhere. I was left with many, many questions about the nature of the Universe, but also with intense awe and respect for these governing forces that we barely understood.

I left UCSD with a good understanding of cellular and molecular neuroscience but realized that I still hadn't been able to dive deeply into the mechanisms of complex human behavior. I had ditched being a pre-med student after an internship at the local hospital, where I realized I really had no interest in being a physician. Instead, I joined a graduate program in neuroscience at the University of Southern California (USC), where I focused on cognitive neuroscience. I was particularly interested in psychopathic traits because I wanted to understand what could go "wrong" in the brain to make a human act cruelly to another. I'm sure my parents were delighted when I informed them that not only did I not want to be a physician, but that I wanted to study psychopathic traits. Hey, you've gotta follow your heart.

As for spirituality, somewhere around the age of twelve, after giving it some thoughtful analysis, I decided that Islam made no sense to me. Praying five times a day seemed time consuming, overly fanatical, and, really, all around nonsensical to me in every possible way. Also, the misogyny didn't sit well with my budding feminist ideals. So I dropped it. Around the same time, I somehow discovered Wicca on the nascent internet and decided that a religion—although I was quickly getting turned off by that word—that worshipped nature and had equal representation for women in the form of a Goddess was the one for me. I was a moon admirer, a nature lover. My Wiccan practice fell to the wayside when I hit high school, though, and I became indifferent toward religion or spirituality, with leanings toward agnosticism.

Until 9/11. The death, destruction, and trauma wrought by the attacks of 9/11 turned my ambivalence into a distaste for religion. It radicalized me into becoming aggressively anti-religious, while simultaneously sparking my interest in international geopolitical affairs. In the first two years of college, we had a core course that required us to read many of the main religious texts and to learn their histories. I remember that somehow everything I learned made me more anti-religious, but in an overly emotional way. Surely it was related to the negative associations between religion and my parents' history. Then the attack on my own homeland fanned the flames.

At the same time that these volatile, combative feelings toward religion were solidifying, I was being armed with a scientific understanding of the world that I used as ammo. Religion aside, I also really didn't see a place for God or any kind of disembodied intelligence in the scientific world. I do not mean that this was my opinion. I mean that I genuinely did not mechanically understand how it could be so. I didn't understand the concept of the soul because I couldn't imagine what it was made of. Carbon? Hydrogen? Oxygen? Where did it sit in the body? When did it emerge during development of the fetus? It just made no sense to me. I didn't even understand what the word "spiritual" meant. I thought people who believed in religion were, frankly, not the brightest crayons in the crayon box; although over time I came to view it as a coping mechanism. Using Darwinian evolution to speculate that religion and spirituality emerged as a coping mechanism for humans to make sense of their environment or to aid the cohesion of a group is a popular narrative espoused by nonbelievers.

BUT WAIT . . . IS THERE MORE TO THE UNIVERSE?

While I was anti-religiosity and anti-spirituality, there was a time, between moving home from studying abroad in Paris during my last semester of my undergraduate studies and beginning graduate school, that I began wondering about the mysteries of the Universe. I'm sure there were events that led to this, I just can't remember exactly what they were. I had always wondered about fate and destiny and coincidences (I was obsessed with coincidences in college), but my science indoctrination was slowly erasing those kinds of thoughts. They had a brief resurgence during this period when I was living at my parents' house. I was particularly interested in the concept of thoughts becoming reality by some unexplained mechanism. Perhaps this is because this was around the time the book *The Secret* by Rhonda Byrne was released, and its topic was in cultural discussions everywhere. The book didn't have a lot of substance or citations, but the concept struck me because it resonated with me, in that I had had eerie experiences where something I thought about obsessively would happen *just the way I pictured it* on multiple occasions. I began reading quantum physics papers and thinking of how it tied to the brain. Alas, graduate school became overwhelming, and I did not have time for extracurricular research, so I abandoned that hobby.

Instead, I was immersed in a deep education of the brain through coursework that took me on a tour from individual neurons to specific brain regions to whole brain network connections and computational models of how the brain works. In addition to coursework, I also got real-world experience with designing experiments, running brain scans, and analyzing the structural and functional connections of the brain using advanced statistical analyses.

I learned a lot of things about the scientific endeavor, but I will reserve those comments for a later chapter. The more I learned about the brain, the more I realized that this organ is really hard to understand and that we don't really know how it works after all! I also learned that, although we feel like we are in charge of our decisions and perceptions, our behaviors are actually driven at a far less conscious level. That kind of revelation makes you question every single one of your perceptions, thoughts, decisions, and actions—looking for evidence that this possibly untrustworthy organ was actually the one in charge.

2

The Untrustworthy Brain & the Religion of Science

"You're wondering if you're on the right path."

"Yes, you are. It had to happen this way for the next thing to come forward. I see the Hand of God. Fate."

Oh, no. She said "God." Barf. I was annoyed but kept listening.

"This is a karmic thing from a past life. God brought it forward to heal it."

Past life?! Karma?? God?! again. That's . . . those aren't real, so. . . .

"The person associated with this situation is one of your soul mates, from your soul group."

Hmm. . . .

I had no idea what she was talking about. I didn't even believe in souls. The intuitive reader's words were even kookier than the notion that she could predict my future.

I would say that neuroscientists are even *more* skeptical than typical scientists because we know how the brain works. Our brains are coincidence detectors, storytellers, and filters of reality. The brain does the best job it can by taking the information that it has and crafting a version of the present moment based on its past experiences and its predictions about the future. Can we trust the brain? I think it might be useful to explain some of the features of the brain that cause us to question its trustworthiness.

Your brain is a storyteller. I do not just mean that our brains can create fictional stories—which is a defining feature that sets humans apart from other animals—but also that the brain is always trying to make sense of all incoming sensory information. The thing is, though, that the stories it crafts are not always based in truth. This is exemplified by what we call the left hemisphere interpreter. The left hemisphere interpreter takes the incoming sensory information that it has, compares it to information from the past, and rationalizes the most likely explanation, or story, for what it is receiving. The best example to demonstrate this feature of the brain comes from experiments with split-brain patients. The two hemispheres of the brain are *normally* connected by a bundle of neurons called the corpus callosum and, for various reasons, some patients in the past have had the corpus callosum severed, disconnecting the two hemispheres and preventing communication between them.

When the two hemispheres are connected, the left hemisphere interpreter has access to all sensory information. This ability is lost in split-brain patients, so their right hemisphere only has access to information from the left side of the body, and the left hemisphere only has access to information from the right side of the body (because the neurons cross over from opposite sides of the body on their way to the brain). In a set of classic experiments (Gazzaniga 1970; Gazzaniga 2005), neuroscientists showed the power of the left hemisphere interpreter's need to reason and explain what is going on in the environment. When an image was presented to the right visual field of a split-brain patient, the patient had no problem naming what they saw because language is contained in the left hemisphere, the same hemisphere that perceived the image (see figure 2.1 on page 12). But when an image was shown to the left visual field, since the right hemisphere does not have the capability to produce language and the hemispheres cannot communicate, the patient could not report out loud to the researcher what they had seen. However, when asked to draw what they had seen, then the patient was able to accurately draw what they viewed in the left visual field, revealing that the brain did, in fact,

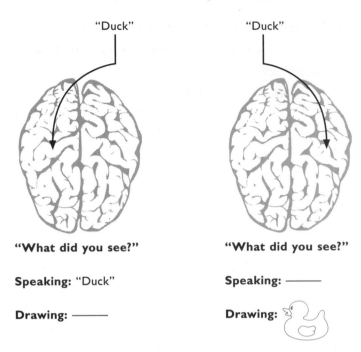

Figure 2.1. This illustration shows a sample experimental setup
for the classic neuroscience split-brain experiment in which the difference
between the functions of the two brain hemispheres are revealed.

receive the information, but just could not communicate it verbally.

When the researchers asked the patient why they drew the picture—let's say it was a glass of water—they reasoned that, "I must be thirsty," unaware that their right hemisphere had actually seen an image of a glass of water in the experiment and that this was the actual reason why they drew it! The correct answer to the researcher's question would have been, "I do not know," but the interpreter's job is to create a story and have an answer, so that is what it did. The researchers found that this effect extended to emotions as well, because when they showed the left visual field an emotional video clip or image that caused a negative mood in the patient and then asked how the patient felt, the patient would respond with "I feel kind of scared. I feel jumpy, I think maybe I don't like this room, or maybe it's you." They felt the emotion but, again, could not report the real reason why they felt that way (the emotional video clip) because the left hemisphere did not have access to the information in the right hemisphere.

When you stop to think about these results, they are so fascinating! Even though these experiments were done with special patients, and our brains do usually have information from both hemispheres, we still typically have at least some missing information because our brains can't possibly process everything. But brains do not like *not* having answers, so they create one however they can.

Our brains are also coincidence detectors and are built to find patterns, even when a pattern does not seemingly exist. This helps the brain make sense of what is going on in the environment and helps facilitate the storytelling. An example of this is when we see faces in clouds or toast, or when Aunt Mildred tells you that she always goes to the casino the day after it rains because that's when she usually wins. This is called *apophenia*, and humans do it all the time. It is not always negative. In fact, people with higher intelligence tend to have better pattern detection abilities (Kurzweil 2013; Lick, Alter, and Freeman 2018), and there is no doubt this brain feature has helped the human species survive. A closely related phenomenon, called the *Baader-Meinhof effect*, also demonstrates this tendency and happens when you start noticing something that you just learned or heard about everywhere. It is typically believed that your pattern-detecting brain is responsible for the repeated perception of the thing, rather than the thing actually being more prevalent. The meaning and significance that one can attach to these coincidental events, such as Aunt Mildred's gambling routine, are personal and thought to only be meaningful in one's mind. Well, that's the popular scientific belief, anyway.

The filtering of incoming sensory information is another of the brain's features. Our brains can only process so much at once so as not to become overloaded with information, so our brains act as filters to limit the bombardment of information. One way it does this is with attention. In the now famous "Invisible Gorilla" experiment (Simons and Chabris 1999), researchers exemplified this effect by asking participants in a study to count how many times a basketball was passed between members of one team in a video of two teams playing. While participants were focused on the task at hand, a person in a gorilla suit walked through the basketball game, nonchalantly. At the end of the task trial, researchers asked participants whether they had noticed anything besides the players, and most participants reported that they had not because they were so focused on the task! That is an example of how your brain filters out irrelevant information. This is called *inattentional blindness* or *perceptual blindness*. A version of this phenomenon that may be more familiar to you is the *cocktail effect,* by which you can attune your hearing by focusing your attention on a person speaking to you at a cocktail party while ignoring the rest of the party's noise.

Information is filtered differently for each person, based on our individual expectations, fears, and desires. Perception really is subjective. The brain enables us to see and experience what we expect and want to see and experience (Schwarz, Pfister, and Büchel 2016; Riccio, Cole, and Balcetis 2013). There are countless examples of how this feature can influence basic perception. For example, how much pain you feel can be modified by what you expect to feel (Anchisi and Zanon 2015; Atlas and Wager 2012; Tracey 2010), and whether you can correctly read the emotion on someone else's face can depend on the context of the situation (Diekhof et al. 2011; Aviezer et al. 2011; Schwarz et al. 2013). If two images are presented to you simultaneously, but too quickly for you to consciously process, you are more likely to automatically perceive the image that has been rewarding to you in the past, for example, an image that is associated with money (Balcetis and Dunning 2006; Balcetis, Dunning, and Granot 2012).

Fear can influence visual perception, too. For example, people who are afraid of spiders judge images of spiders as being closer than do those who are not afraid (Cole, Balcetis, and Dunning 2013). Threats can also direct attention and affect perception. For example, people direct attention to threatening pictures of animals that they fear, like snakes and spiders, more than neutral pictures of flowers (Öhman, Flykt, and

Esteves 2001). Additionally, when people have goals, their goal-setting behavior can direct attention toward objects that can assist in accomplishing those goals. For instance, when primed with mating goals, single participants directed attention to physically attractive members of the opposite sex who represented potential mates (Maner et al. 2007), and frequent cocaine users directed attention to drug-related images to a greater extent than did nonusers (Dunning et al. 2011).

The brain also filters information through beliefs, tending to prioritize and favor information and evidence that support its existing beliefs. One example is *confirmation bias:* If you hold the belief that all people who drive hybrid cars are terrible drivers, you are more likely to notice and remember the incidents when a hybrid car driver cut you off than when a different car did. Humans also have a tendency to believe that after learning an outcome, they could have predicted it all along in something called *hindsight bias,* or the I-knew-it-all-along phenomenon.

In addition to influencing how your brain perceives and processes information, expectations and beliefs can also affect behavior. As one of many examples of this type, performance on a memory task by older adults can be influenced by whether participants were primed with stereotypes of older adults having poorer memory prior to the task (Steele and Aronson 1995; Lamont, Swift, and Abrams 2015). It has been found that using a lucky charm improves subsequent performance in golfing, motor dexterity, memory, and anagram games (Damisch, Stoberock, and Mussweiler 2010)—so don't let anyone make you feel silly for having a lucky charm! It has also been shown that people who stand in powerful poses (think hands on your hips) for a minute or two report feeling more powerful and more tolerant of risk and also had increases in testosterone and decreases in cortisol, showing that belief can affect both behavior and *physiology* (Gronau et al. 2017; Carney, Cuddy, and Yap 2010). We must not forget the infamous *placebo effect* (Colloca 2018; Kaptchuk et al. 2010), when an inert drug or treatment causes a beneficial effect in a patient, such as healing.

One very profound example of the illusions of the mind comes from clinical cases of patients with dissociative identity disorder (DID, formerly known as multiple personality disorder). Different personalities within one DID patient can exhibit physiological differences in visual acuity, levels of pain sensitivity, diabetic status, allergic reactions, and handedness! Expectations can even affect others' behaviors, as has been shown with teachers' expectations affecting their students' academic performance (known as the Pygmalion effect) (Friedrich et al. 2015; Good, Sterzinger, and Lavigne 2018).

That's a lot, so let's review. Your brain uses a filtering process based on your past experiences, expectations, beliefs, desires, and fears to constantly look for patterns and coincidences in incoming sensory information to make sense of the world. If there are holes in the data, don't worry about that—the brain will fill it in with whatever belief, past experience, or other thing that it has available. The big takeaway from getting a Ph.D. in neuroscience was that your brain is not to be fully trusted. This is especially true and exemplified well by implicit biases that require conscious cognitive effort to overcome, such as stereotypical assumptions about other groups of people.

On the other hand, the brain is also a very powerful machine that can actually change physiology, behavior, and performance on belief *alone.* This raises a very interesting question: *Is it always in our best interest to doubt our brain's trustworthiness?*

Another takeaway assumption from the science you learn in graduate school is the concept that "meaning" is constructed in your brain and there is no actual meaning out in the world. The Universe behaves randomly, so everything is unrelated and meaningless. Depressing? Yup, but that's what science says. That dream you had last night that came true exactly as you saw it? Coincidence. Or you remembered it wrong.

THE SCIENCE CULT

By the end of the six years of graduate school, I had been completely indoctrinated into the religion of science, or as I like to call it: The Science Cult.

People would say things like:

"Is there a God?" *Oh, please.*
"Do humans have a soul?" *Geez, get real.*
"Everything happens for a reason." *Seriously, shut up.*

Your brain *wants* you to believe that. Its job is to find coincidences, so of course everything seems related. Of course, it can seem like everything happens for a reason, because given enough time, you can create a nice story about why things happened the way they did that led to the outcome with which you're now okay. I was truly insufferable and not in the least open minded about, really, anything. Ask any of my friends who now admit to editing the things they used to say around me for fear of judgment. But this is how scientific materialism trained me.

At one point I was an atheist, but eventually I became an agnostic because I just truly didn't care whether there was a higher power. Although I didn't care and didn't see how there could be a higher power, I was also always ready to admit that we humans do not have all the answers, including whether there was a spiritual nature to the Universe. After going through rigorous scientific training, I also came to believe that we didn't have the tools or methods to determine whether or not there was a higher power, and, since I didn't care, never thought more of it.

I even had a necklace custom made at one point to have the word *science* inscribed on the bar pendant (which is, yes, I'm aware, very nerdy indeed).

In summary, 'old me' was anti-religious, didn't understand spirituality, did not believe anything happened for a reason, and was pretty hostile and condescending toward people who did believe those things. She was interested in the forces of the Universe and wanted to know the answers to all its mysteries, but she was a devotee of science and believed that was the only way. By the end of graduate school, she brushed off any synchronistic or coincidental personal experiences as lies of her brain, even though prior to that she had sensed meaning behind the coincidences in life. She was pretty happy and self-satisfied with herself for a while . . . until everything lost all meaning.

EXCEPT ARMENIAN COFFEE READINGS

There is one asterisk I have to throw onto the end of the last section. Yes, I was a member of the Science Cult, and yes, I believed more than ever before that the events of life were random and meaningless. However, there is one exception that I have to mention: my mother's Armenian coffee fortune readings. For the unfamiliar reader, some Middle Eastern cultures drink a type of finely ground coffee that leaves coffee grounds at the bottom of the cup. It is customary to flip the cup, let the grounds dry, and look at the patterns for your fortune from an (if you're lucky) experienced fortune teller. It is akin to tea leaf reading. My grandmother apparently had legendary cup-reading skills. Unfortunately, since she lived in Iran most of my life, and the times that I did get to see her I was too young to drink coffee, I never had the pleasure of having my cup read by her. As it turns out, though, my own mother was extraordinarily skilled as well.

These readings had always been going on in the background of our family get-togethers, and I never paid much attention to any of it. The women would usually scuttle off together to a separate table in the house to peek into their futures. I wasn't much of a coffee drinker and didn't need my fortune told. During the time between studying abroad and beginning graduate school, when I was living at my parents' house, my mother began reading my fortune from the coffee grounds. I never asked for it, but we would have coffee together in the mornings, and she would mindlessly and out of habit casually gaze into the remaining coffee grounds in the cup, periodically telling me things about my alleged near-term future. I never took it seriously.

My best girlfriends, on the other hand, would request to come over nearly every Sunday for a chance for a reading. They swore by her predictions. Trading off visits between them was necessary as coffee reading was an energy-draining business. After a short while, I started noticing that the things she would tell me would come true with unusual accuracy.

Now, I know all the criticisms of psychic readings. Please believe me when I say that, even to this day when I get readings, my mind immediately first goes to debunking the information as generic and vague. This is societal and scientific training that runs so deep that I doubt it can ever be fully washed away—and that's probably a good thing. I truly do believe it is important to be discerning and to explore multiple possible explanations for phenomena and observations. Also, at this time, the coffee readings were new to me, and I didn't have any reason to believe they worked, so it caught me off guard. When I say that the things she said started to come true, they were exceptionally specific things to my life at that particular moment that made me stop in my tracks with goose bumps running all over my body. I know you want to hear examples, and I will give a few shortly. Before I knew it, I joined my friends in looking forward to coffee readings from my mom.

My friends and I would drink the coffee, flip the cup, let the grounds dry, and then hold our breath nervously and with intense anticipation as my mother peered into the cup. She has explained to me over the years the way that she reads the cups, and I will share it with you. As her eyes adjust to the grounds, she looks for images that pop out to her and then looks for linkages between the images to tell stories. By the location of the image in the cup, she can deduce if the event is occurring within one's life or is peripheral to it, among other facts. I imagine that for someone who is unfamiliar with this type of fortune-telling you're wondering exactly what she's seeing (see figure 2.2 on page 20). The images are archetypal, and my mom would explain that you translate whatever you see by the characteristics of the object you perceived. For example, if she saw a snake in the cup, she would translate it as somebody who would like to do you harm in a sneaky way, based on a snake's stereotypical behavior of sneaking up slowly on its prey before it strikes. Based on whether the snake's body was black (formed by the coffee grounds) or white (the negative space in the cup), she would deduce whether they were actually capable of pulling off the harm (black meant they could harm you, and white meant they were harmless). She would then look for other clues in the cup to see if it is "in your house" or "outside your house," in order to see how close this person is to you. For example, if it is in a particular place in the cup indicating it is outside your house, that might mean it is someone outside your close inner circle of friends and family that you interact with regularly. Some of the time, she could see additional features, such as other people being connected to the main image, so then she would deduce, for example, that the person associated with the image has a family. Occasionally, she could describe with disturbing accuracy even more detailed information, such as the number of individuals in that person's family, whether one of the family members has an illness, the genders of their children, and so on.

This archetypal manner of reading is what made fortune-telling so hard for me to believe in as a scientist, because what does that really mean? That there are inherent meanings ascribed to images and concepts in the Universe? That meaning is not subjective, personal, and solely constructed by our brains? When you're used to studying electrons and cells, that's a difficult concept to buy into. It just made no sense to me. In science, we utilize the art of reductionism—reducing everything into parts that can be studied further. Pulling back the curtain of symbolic meaning revealed nothing that I could comprehend

Figure 2.2. Armenian coffee grounds from one of my readings

with my scientific training. However, the predictive power of the coffee readings stood on its own two feet, and although the mechanism eluded my understanding, it didn't make it any less real.

At the beginning of graduate school, when I was becoming interested in the underlying mysteries of the Universe, I began having weekly Sunday readings with my mom and documenting them. I took copious notes in an effort to prove or disprove the accuracy of the readings. I used all my science skills. For every prediction, I would wonder whether it could also apply to any of my friends' lives, either at that particular moment in time—or at another time. Or whether the prediction could apply to me at a different, previous time of my life. I wrote them all down for over ten years. My general sense was that the readings weren't 100% accurate, but they were more accurate than not. They were also extremely specific to the person getting the reading, to that time of their life, and with uniquely personal details of the events in their life. Using my newly acquired statistical skills, I deduced that it would just not be plausible for her to be that correct that often by chance. Let me give a few examples that my friends reported as being ones that jolted them and made them believers.

One year before my best friend met her husband, she had a reading with my mom who said that a tall, thin man was going to enter her life and be significant in it, like a boyfriend or husband, and that this man would have a really large family with lots of siblings. My best friend laughed at the time because she said that what my mom described was not her type and thought it highly unlikely. Lo and behold, one year later, she met the man who is now her husband who is tall and thin and has four siblings and a large extended family.

Another friend left my parents' house completely spooked when my mom accurately described an ongoing situation with her partner where the couple was bumping heads while trying to purchase a new business together. She told me that my mom accurately described her feelings, her partner's feelings, the business broker they were working with (physical description and personality!), the broker's relationship to the purchase, and the uncertainty of the situation as well as the possible outcome. Even I had not known that they were trying to buy a business or having a small spousal battle.

Yet another friend was completely shaken when my mom, who didn't even know my friend had a brother, accurately described the brother's physical appearance, relationship to the family, and the secret fact that his favorite pastime was hoarding money!

I know you're probably running through all the other possible explanations we are so used to throwing at these kinds of stories. One that we can immediately throw out is a *cold reading,* when intuitives use behavioral and external cues, such as race, age, and a client's reactions, to make high-probability guesses. I can assure you that my mom wasn't trying to impress us. Also, she wasn't guessing things about our lives at all. She was quite literally reading the cup out loud to us, telling us what she saw, pointing out the images to us, and trying her best to interpret them. She was often reluctant to do the readings, in fact. Another explanation you might be thinking about is that my mom knew me and my friends intimately, and that even if we thought we were not telling her a lot of details about our lives, some bits of information inevitably made their way into her consciousness through our interactions. While I can't dispute that, I can guarantee you that I was not updating my mom on all of the life events of my friends, including details on relationships with their significant others, work colleagues, families—all of which she would somehow just know. It would also not explain how she was correct most of the time about outcomes of these life events in *advance* of their happening.

I will tell my most profound coffee reading story shortly but also want to mention another story here. This is one of the stories that really made me wonder what was going on. It also addresses the possibility of my mom's obtaining information by my accidentally giving it away. In Iranian-American culture, we do not update our parents on our dating lives until we have found the person we will marry, and I inherited a subscription to this tradition. I was always mum about dating and would vehemently deny I was ever seeing anyone (it just was not worth the headache). So when I say there is no chance I would have mentioned this in any way to my mom, it's true. In my twenties I was dating a guy for a few months. He was sweet and cute, and if you had asked me what my favorite feature was of his I would have said his long, feathery eyelashes. I never thought this out loud or told anyone, not even my friends. It was just a personal thought that I had. While reading my coffee cup one Sunday, my mom said, with a surprised tone, "It looks like there's a man in your life." My heart started pounding and I got nervous, but I didn't say anything. By the way, yes, that is one of the downfalls of having your mother read your fortunes—it's hard to hide things. She continued by describing his height (how much taller he was than me), his hair (how much and the style), and his demeanor (easygoing, calm, casual person), all perfectly accurately. She also knew he was in some sort of graduate program. Then she said, "and he has really long, beautiful eyelashes." I almost fell off the kitchen chair from the shock of having her say a private thought of mine out loud. *I just could not believe it.* And no, I am not a well-known eyelash obsessive.

I don't know why this shook me so much more than any of the other validations I had over the years. Yes, it was a fact that he had long, gorgeous eyelashes, but it occurred to me that it probably showed up in the cup because it was significant *to me*. I know that it may seem like an odd thing to be weirded out by, because wasn't the whole point of the reading to get information about you and your life? But since it was so specific and detailed it felt like *someone* or *something* was watching the situation closely—closely enough to know about the eyelashes. That really convinced me that she was getting information from somewhere, somehow. But how was she getting the information? Where was this information coming from? What was the mechanism that prioritized information in accordance with what was meaningful to you, the person receiving the information? And why can we know the *future*? And does that mean it's set in stone? Is there destiny? Fate? Does anything we do or think matter?

These questions would be put on hold while I diligently labored through graduate school. The reemergence of them was the burning dawn of transformation.

3

The Two Events
That Changed Everything

MY MOTHER'S WARNING

There are two pivotal events in my life that led me down this path of questioning the scientific materialist and meaningless version of the Universe. This is the first: In November 2016 I was three and a half years out of graduate school and beginning a new job. It was a typical warm and sunny Los Angeles Sunday afternoon when I popped over to visit my parents in the San Fernando Valley the week before Thanksgiving. My mom and I sat down for our usual Sunday afternoon coffee reading in their sunny breakfast nook. After explaining a few of the images she saw in the cup, she stopped speaking and started fidgeting in her seat.

After a few moments, somewhat exasperated, she succumbed to whatever decision process was going on in her head and finally said, "I have to tell you something. I feel like I have to warn you. I've been seeing this in the cup for a few weeks and didn't mention it before because I was hoping it was a mistake. But since it keeps coming up, I need to warn you. You will be receiving some *very* bad news. Very bad."

I got chills from head to toe and froze; then I started a barrage of questions. "What is it? What is it about? What are the details? What do you mean? When will it be?" But she wouldn't say anything more, even though I knew she saw more. I don't like hearing bad news, and like her, I was hoping she was wrong or that something would change, so I chose not to focus on it. We moved on.

After nine years of tracking the accuracy of these readings, I had a method of taking them seriously, though tempered with caution. I didn't know the mechanism, but whether it was her intuition, channeling, or guesswork, they were not bad guidance to have as I navigated through my life. I took it seriously enough that if she told me she saw a "possible loss of money," you better believe I made sure all my bills were paid or that I wasn't charged extra on something. So I was a little rattled by her reading but soon forgot as the day went on.

The following week, however, I went home for a few days for Thanksgiving, and the dire prediction was in every single coffee reading that I had over those days. In terms of coffee reading accuracy, the more times something comes up, the more likely it is to occur and be accurate. She and I both were becoming nervous. I still didn't know what it was—she wouldn't tell me, which was very unusual. My nerves were frayed by the end of that ominous week. Whatever it was, I just wanted it to be over so I could know and end the uncertainty. I even asked my group of friends on our group chat, "Which of you has bad news?"

EVENT #1: THE DEATH THAT MADE ME QUESTION DESTINY

One week later, on Friday, December 2, the mystery would finally end, when a former classmate from graduate school, with whom I periodically caught up, reached out. The G-chat bubble on my phone popped up, and I read, "Not sure if you heard the news?" I was hosting a holiday gift exchange for some friends at my place when I received the text, and my heart immediately dropped. I knew this was it. I just knew. Someone we both knew had been murdered that day. Not just killed or died . . . but *murdered*. It was one of our professors from our graduate program who had graciously and patiently helped me with one of my dissertation experiments. It was completely surreal. A fog descended on my brain immediately that would linger for weeks. In the confusion of the moment, I couldn't find the words to repeat the news out loud when my friends asked what was wrong, so I passed them my phone in silence so they could read it themselves. Not only was the news itself devastating, but the events of the prior few weeks of coffee readings hung over me, dripping with darkness, mystery, and sorrow. I was *scared*. I wondered what kind of Universe we lived in where such unspeakably terrible things could occur. I couldn't sleep that night and many nights after because I kept thinking about how coffee grounds warned me of impending sorrow weeks before the event itself, while the person I knew had dinner with their family on Thanksgiving, completely unaware of their pending fate. It shook me to my core. It would have chilled me to my soul, if I had believed I had one.

The next day I called my mom and said, "I know what the bad news is." I told her, and she said, "Yes, it was a death. A violent one. I didn't want to say it out loud in case I was wrong. I'm so sorry."

I asked so many questions about fate, destiny, and the Universe, but she could only give me her guesses. I became a little bit afraid of life. I felt watched, like a pawn in a game. I felt mortal. I felt unmoored. What unknown thing was written in my fate that I was unaware of? In all our fates? Was it his destiny? Or did something go terribly wrong? What if he had been warned? Could the outcome have been changed? Do we just drift through this fog of life until we reach the waiting waterfall? I became obsessed with these thoughts over the next few weeks, day and night. The rolling dark thoughts emerged from and sunk back into the density of grief over and over. The power of the coffee—of the Universe—frightened me for the first time. What other information was in there or out there, and how could we access it?

I didn't yet dive into actual reading and investigation into this topic. I was too busy with work and life. I wondered about it frequently, though. This life event did increase my confidence in my mom's coffee readings. They had always been good guidance, and I didn't think *too* deeply about how they represented the probability of future events. After this life-changing event, though, I would say I looked on the coffee readings with more respect. I also came to rely on them more because I viewed them as more accurate than I had before. This was a mistake.

EVENT #2: MY DARK NIGHT

A few years later, I was working for a research center at USC that focused on digital health (the use of digital technologies, such as mobile phones and wearables, to better track and understand health). The work combined my interest in neuroscience and health with technology. I appreciated the practical and forward-thinking conversations we had with health systems, start-ups, sports teams, medical device companies, pharmaceutical companies, the Big Tech companies, and the U.S. military. I worked with the California Governor's Office advisory panel on cybersecurity, helped draft guidelines around the ethics of digital health data collection with Stanford Libraries, spoke with U.S. senators about digital health data privacy, and designed and launched a multi-site research study with special operations forces in the U.S. Army and U.S. Marine Corps. All of it was great experience at first, but I became overworked and tired.

At times I felt fulfilled, but I was becoming restless. It is difficult to go from working toward a huge, clear goal, like getting an advanced degree, to showing up for work every day where your purpose is not always clear. I don't know how to describe it, but it's a very profound negative shift, in a way—or at least, that's how it was for me. I kept finding myself asking, "What is the point of all this?" We just wake up, go to work, come home exhausted, barely have time on the weekends to do anything, and then do it again over and over until we die? I guess this is what people mean when they question the meaning of life, or have an existential crisis, which, of course, I had never understood before.

I am sure that part of this is because I was so used to pursuing a goal, working toward it, and accomplishing things that when I didn't have that, I felt lost. As I think about it now, I realize that a very large part of my entire life had been constantly trying to achieve things. I probably thought that the point of life was to achieve and accomplish things. I bought into the whole idea of productivity for the sake of productivity. With condescension, but also envy, I used to look at people who were not like me, who did not have big goals or dreams, and who just showed up for work every day without much thought. I would wonder, "What does it feel like to wake up and not be planning and just . . . be?" I was so caught up in this accomplishment cycle that I even resented the daily things that ate up my time and took away from being productive, like eating, watching TV, reading literature for fun, and sometimes even celebrating with my social group. It makes sense, if you view those activities as taking away from your purpose in life. In any case, I did not have the next big goal in mind, and that left me adrift.

This feeling coupled with my new relationship with the coffee readings was a recipe for disaster. I showed up every Sunday hoping to hear about some victorious, glorious future that my mom saw in the cup, one that would descend on me miraculously from the heavens one day. In other words, I wanted to be saved. So when my mom did begin seeing something in the cup that signified change and that I wanted very much, I hung all my hope for meaning and purpose onto it. Since the coffee readings had been so accurate up to this point, I had little reason to believe that this thing, which was repeatedly showing up for months on end, would not happen the way she said it would.

Here's the thing: It did, and it did not happen. It was a romance, and it came together but then ultimately fell apart. But I had decided that it would be my life raft, the thing that would finally save me and make me happy. So when the life raft popped, I was lost at sea, drowning. I now realize that it could have been *anything* that caused my unraveling: a relationship falling apart, a job opportunity falling through, or a friendship that ran its course. It was a change onto which I had hung too much hope. My mom had seen the outcome as positive, repeatedly. The actual outcome was decidedly *not* positive (at least that's how I viewed it then, but I've since changed my mind).

I cannot explain my total and utter devastation. It completely broke me. Before I start the description of the darkest period of my life, I should explain that I have always been a very positive and optimistic person.

When I asked my friends for adjectives to describe me to include in this book, they said they view me as fun, full of energy, positive, optimistic, a go-getter, sociable, an extrovert, and a glass-half-full type of person. I tended to look at the bright side of things, woke up excited for each day, and considered myself resilient. I had always been a dreamer with my head in the clouds, imagining all the wonderful things that lay ahead for me in the future. When I did hit rough patches and would be knocked down, I would be caught by the net of my next goal or achievement and bounce right back up to fight another day. This time, though, there was no net to catch me, so I fell into the deep, dark cavern of despair.

WHAT'S THE POINT OF THIS?

I lost hope. I lost optimism. I lost the ability to imagine, which had been the secret to my prior resilience. I was heartbroken. I lost the ability to enjoy the brilliant Southern California sun on a perfect day. I lost the ability to reach out for support. There was just *nothing.* At this point, I didn't have enough insight to describe or explain the despair, so I isolated myself. What was the point in listening to someone tell you everything was going to be okay when you felt like it would never be okay again? It was so much easier to isolate. I didn't know what was wrong and why I was *so* sad. I was a zombie going through the motions of daily life, wishing I was anywhere but wherever I was. I was never mentally present. My essence had packed its bags and moved to the plane of melancholy.

Every single day felt like a million miserable lifetimes. Some days I would wake up and immediately start crying. I didn't even give the day a chance to impress me. I remember thinking that if I had a soul, it certainly decided to abandon this life and had ripped away from my body—and I couldn't blame it. I constantly wished that I could somehow disappear and just not exist anymore. I started crying into towels because tissues didn't cut it. How could I be so miserable? I read a bunch of stuff on positivity, gratitude, and happiness, but all I felt was resentment and pointlessness.

There was zero patience and an abundance of being irritable. Why didn't the stupid water filter work?! UGH!!! Why does the elevator at work take so damn long?! Why does my neighbor *always* slam her door when she gets home from work?! There was also oh, so much anger. Because I had never felt anything like this before, and I most certainly did not like it, my response was to be angry. There was a fire in the middle of my chest, just waiting for more kindling. It expressed itself in so many ways. I snapped at family and friends. I screamed into pillows. I dug my nails into my crossed arms at work during unbearable moments, trying to release the energy in some way.

The cherry on top of the misery sundae was the shock and disbelief of how I could feel so sad, because it had never happened before in this way. So on top of feeling sad, I felt sad about feeling sad! It was one big cat of sadness chasing its own tail.

You may be thinking, "There! That proves intuitive readings are baloney!" I began thinking that myself, too. That was actually the chocolate fudge on top of the misery sundae. The coffee readings had always given me a sense that I had a sneak preview of what was to come, which was very comforting. Now, the uncertainty of life hit me with full force. I began to wonder if it had all been coincidences all along, and my mind had woven a belief in the veracity of the coffee readings that just wasn't true. But as I looked over my years' worth of notes, it just couldn't be disputed. Plus, for this particular situation, the only thing that was incorrect was the outcome. The usual uncanny accuracy of all the other details of the situation were accurate, for months.

Since it was the outcome of the situation that didn't turn out as I had expected, I became obsessed with those questions about fate and destiny again. Was it meant to be this way and my mom just interpreted it incorrectly? Or did something change? How could she have seen it so many times and it not come true? In my despair, I just couldn't understand, and I needed answers. Looking back now, I can see that the true life lesson to be learned here was to be okay with the uncertainty of life, which is just a fact of it. However, at that time as a scientist—and as a human ignoring the obvious life lesson—I had a model in my mind about how the coffee readings worked, and this event questioned that model. It became imperative to me to find out how it actually worked and what was the truth. This became my new goal. My new purpose. Something that was a personal hobby that I casually used to guide my life suddenly became the all-encompassing question to which I needed to know the answer.

Around this time, one of my friends mentioned that she had recently gone to an intuitive who was pretty accurate. My friend said that she trusted this lady, because the intuitive had previously turned her away (twice!), explaining that she couldn't read my friend's energy and didn't want to take her money.

I had never considered going to an intuitive. Why would I when I had my mom's readings? However, my newfound desperation to understand the Universe, why things happened, and the meaning of life caused me to consider intuitives for the first time. Who knows, maybe they could provide some insight into my life and the nature of the Universe.

4

Chelsea Handler
Becomes My Guide

I was about to undergo a massive personal transformation that would rip the foundation of my reality out from beneath me and leave me unrecognizable to myself, but I (thankfully) didn't know it yet. Coincidentally, one of my favorite comedians, Chelsea Handler, had recently undergone a self-transformation of her own that would ultimately influence my journey. But before we turn to that, let me tell you about the intuitive readings.

I started going to intuitives with urgency to hear about my future and to get answers to my questions about existence and the Universe. I roped my friends into going to the intuitives with me, since a few of them were more experienced with this type of thing than I was, and also so that we could compare notes to investigate whether the intuitives had canned responses that they reused for clients—which is what most people believe—or whether any of the information they provided was true. Over the course of a year, my friends and I eagerly went to many intuitives—a feat not hard to accomplish in Los Angeles, arguably one of the epicenters of mysticism and spirituality. Most were intuitives that some of our friends had recommended as being accurate. Some of my friends were skeptics, and some were deeply spiritual. It was interesting to have a range of believers within our group, because we each had such different experiences and takeaways from our readings, even if we saw the same intuitive. We controlled for things as best as we could, such as not giving too much information away about ourselves in the reading, only giving our first names before the readings, and so on.

At first, we took handwritten notes during the readings, but we quickly noticed that it was hard to write fast enough to capture everything they were saying. Also, the readings would inevitably get emotional and, once emotional, it was difficult to remember to keep writing. Thus, we began recording the sessions with the intuitives' permission. Recording them was also useful because we could relisten at a later time and see if we were remembering things accurately. Recording the sessions had the added bonus of allowing us to play the recording of the reading at a later time for our other friends and to compare interpretations.

After the readings, we would go to a coffee shop to compare notes. Once it became clear that the intuitives were pretty good, since their readings were specific to each of us and they weren't using canned responses, we began brainstorming possible mechanisms. My friends were definitely less interested in the possible physics or neuroscience of the readings and more interested in either the spiritual aspect or in debunking the readings as a whole. I began just asking the intuitives themselves questions about free will versus destiny and the nature of the Universe, but I couldn't really make sense of their answers. They would talk to me about concepts such as *soul lessons, karma,* and *reincarnation*—things I did not believe in. The example at the beginning of the book was the first reading I had where I heard these concepts mentioned.

At the beginning of a reading, some intuitives would tell us that the information they were giving in the reading was true at that exact moment in time and would remain true *if nothing changed,* but that it's important to understand that things change all the time because people have free will. OK, they think there is free will! Good to know. But then they would also say things like, "This was fate" or "This was not meant to be in this life," which made no sense to me if there was free will. To make things more confusing, they would tell me to manifest things by visualizing and getting clear on what I want. So you could manifest, but there was also destiny? Why was this so confusing, and why couldn't I get a clear answer?!

While I couldn't get a clear answer to my questions about free will and destiny, I did notice that between all the intuitives I got a lot of overlap and *very* similar descriptions of: (a) their spiritual framework; and (b) the situation I was asking about—a description that differed from other things that I asked about and also from my friends' situations and readings. Sure, some of the things they said were generic, and I'm sure, for example, that everybody has change and transformation going on in their lives at all times. But I was uncomfortably surprised at the level of detail they would provide back to me about the people in my life and my thoughts and feelings regarding the situations I was inquiring about. It was reminiscent of the feeling of loss of privacy when my mom mentioned the long eyelashes in her reading. They were far too specific about the situation and my deepest personal thoughts. It was as though they could reach their arm into my mind, my tree of thoughts, and chose the deepest, most hidden, and inaccessible apples.

Overall, the intuitive readings were not 100% accurate, but I was surprised that the things they did predict accurately encompassed multiple variables such as specific people, places, time, and circumstances and were so specific to me at that particular time in my life that it threw me back. The readings were particularly noteworthy when they would include some kind of time metric, such as something happening "within five days, weeks, or months."

Intuitives, like all humans, can consciously or unconsciously make assumptions about you as a person based on many factors, such as what you're wearing, your race, your mannerisms, and so on. In a statistical model, these would be called *priors*. When you throw in timing, there is no prior for that because it is much harder to make general deductions about the timing of life's events, especially on shorter timescales. I know the skeptics are rolling their eyes, because that's what 'old me' would've done, too—and I respect that. There are some journeys you just have to take for yourself to fully understand and believe.

Although I did not get a very clear picture about the meaning of life or how intuitive predictions work, the readings gave me enormous comfort in a sea of darkness. Many of the things the intuitives told me carried me through my darkest nights, and that's not nothing. The readings also forced me to look at myself and situations in my life with more bluntness. Many of the intuitives gently brought my attention to the deeper issues behind my questions, and I was grateful for it. By now, I could probably write a best practices book on getting intuitive readings, with one big takeaway being: get it for insight and if you think it'll make you feel better, but don't plan your life around it.

FINDING SOME ANSWERS

During the darkest months when it hurt to exist, I listened to Chelsea Handler's latest book, *Life Will Be the Death of Me* (2019). The title was clearly speaking to me in that moment. I had been a fan of Chelsea's prior books, so I was eager for a laugh.

The book was unlike all the previous books she had written. It followed her while she attended therapy sessions with her neuro-psychiatrist, Dr. Dan Siegel (who coincidentally works with one of my dissertation advisors) and took an in-depth look at her life. I was floored by her honesty and vulnerability. I sobbed alongside her when she described how her brother had died when she was young and then happily soaked up the interwoven chapters of comedic adventures with her two pet chow chows. She talked about her reticence toward therapy and her skepticism about spirituality. By the end of the book, however, she had experienced major breakthroughs with Dr. Siegel, and therapy won her over. The book profoundly moved me, so when Handler released a podcast (Handler 2019) around the book's topics, I clicked "follow" immediately. I appreciated the discussions around the brain, psychology, and personality, but the magical episode was the one where she had a discussion with Laura Lynne Jackson, a psychic medium. I didn't know who Laura Lynne Jackson was, and I was surprised that Handler, a self-proclaimed skeptic, would have a psychic medium on

her show. I perked up to listen, since I used Handler as my own filter—
if she was interested in interviewing Jackson, then I was interested in
listening.

I listened as I was driving to see a friend who lived an hour away
and was completely mesmerized the entire time. I kept rewinding to
relisten to parts of the interview. Jackson described a model of spirituality that I had never heard before but that closely aligned with the
things the intuitives had talked about in my readings that I hadn't previously understood. The entire story started being pulled together for
me. Briefly, it can be summarized like this: Our purpose as souls on the
Earth is to learn lessons that evolve and advance our souls, and we do
this through many different lives (i.e., reincarnation). The thing that
ties us all together is love, which she described as a binding light energy.
Like all things in nature, there needs to be balance, so karma helps keep
that balance. She also described the concept of soul groups, the groups
of souls with whom we allegedly tend to continuously reincarnate.

I was so excited to hear someone finally explain this spiritual framework and couldn't wait to review my notes from the intuitives to see if
any of this would help make sense of what they had told me. I didn't
believe it, per se, I just wanted to understand it better so that I could
assess whether it was believable or not. At first listen, it seemed utterly
preposterous. I remember that the first time I heard these concepts from
an intuitive I brushed them off as her personal beliefs. Then, when
I realized that many intuitives seemed to believe in these concepts, I
didn't know what to think. Now I was hearing these spiritual ideas
again from yet another psychic medium, but one that was accepted by
Chelsea Handler, whom I respected so much. I began to wonder if all
intuitives went to the same school or got the same kind of training or
something. Where did they learn this spiritual framework that I had
never even heard of?

Jackson and Handler mentioned a book, entitled *Many Lives, Many
Masters* (1988), written by a psychiatrist named Brian Weiss, M.D.
Handler told a story of how she found the book in the seat pocket on
a plane ride from New York to Los Angeles the day after getting into

a fight with a friend over the ludicrous idea of reincarnation. I could relate to that condescending attitude toward others with ideas that I thought ridiculous. She read the short book on the flight to LA, and by the time she landed she thought to herself, "Everyone must read this book." On the podcast, she and Jackson did not go into detail about what the book was about and only mentioned it was a case study of one of Dr. Weiss's patients, but I was sold. I immediately ordered the book on Amazon without reading the description or looking it up further. I thought that if Handler liked it, I'd give it a read. A case study sounded legitimate.

Many Lives, Many Masters begins with Dr. Weiss's own background, which is impressive. He attended Columbia University, and then moved on to Yale University for medical school and residency. He had his own practice and was the chairman of psychiatry at Mount Sinai Medical Center in Miami. He was a complete skeptic and not at all interested in the "unscientific" concepts of parapsychology, past lives, or reincarnation. For a science snob like myself, his background was impeccable. I'm not proud to admit it, but the only reasons the book carried so much weight with me were Dr. Weiss's credentials and his logical, rational, scientific approach to the problem. I would not have given any merit to the same book if it had been written by someone less credentialed, less agnostic, and less scientific.

The story goes that Dr. Weiss was treating a patient named Catherine who was suffering from recurrent nightmares and anxiety attacks from an array of personal fears, including fears of water, choking, airplanes, the dark, and more. Essentially, it sounded like she was a walking anxiety-ridden, insomniac mess. After eighteen months of traditional psychotherapy with Dr. Weiss, Catherine was not getting better and still had anxiety and panic attacks. As a last resort, Dr. Weiss decided to try hypnotherapy. Although you may be conjuring the image of hypnotherapy that I also conjured when I read this—which was of a psychiatrist dangling a pocket watch in front of your eyes to place you in a hypnotized state—it turns out that hypnotherapy is a commonly used practice in therapy to help access repressed traumatic memories and basically just entails the patient being placed into an extremely relaxed, but conscious, state. Through this method, Catherine did uncover a long-forgotten trauma from when she was three years old, but her severe symptoms did not improve as Dr. Weiss expected. He was perplexed. He would normally see marked improvement and healing with other patients once a repressed or forgotten traumatic memory, and its accompanying emotions, were recalled (i.e., *catharsis*). He wondered if there was more trauma from before she was three years old. So in the next session, while she was in a relaxed hypnotic state, Dr. Weiss asked her to "go back to the time from which your symptoms arise." She began describing a very detailed life—her life—from 1863 BCE. Dr. Weiss wrote about his extreme confusion in the session and noted that no other patients had ever crafted such fantasies under hypnosis before, but he continued the session and jotted down all the details she provided of her name, age, appearance, topographical details of the surroundings, and more. She reported that she had died by drowning in this life. After this session, Catherine's choking symptoms and fears of water finally disappeared! Since the technique seemed to be working when nothing else had, they continued the hypnotic regression sessions, and Catherine continued to describe a series of seemingly past lives where she had died in ways that corresponded with her current-day fears. One by one the fears disappeared, and she was healed.

That's not all, although that's quite a lot already. In some of the sessions, after Catherine would describe how she had passed away in that past life, her tone of voice and manner of speaking would change and she would begin conversing with Dr. Weiss as one of the *Masters*, highly evolved spirits from the "space between lives." She channeled messages to Dr. Weiss about the purpose of life, reincarnation, karma, and soul lessons. Neither Dr. Weiss nor Catherine believed in reincarnation (Weiss was an agnostic, and Catherine was a Catholic). As validation, she channeled a message from these Masters about how Dr. Weiss's father and son were present in the session, and they gave specific details about the names and manner of deaths for each, including the fact that his son had died twenty-three days after being born just nine months earlier from an extremely rare (one in ten million) heart defect. As Dr. Weiss had not shared any personal details with Catherine, had kept a bare office mostly free of personal belongings, and there was no other way she could have known those details (this was the 1980s with no internet), he found himself starting to believe. He continued to receive messages from the Masters from the in-between space—messages that Catherine would never remember delivering. I was captivated and intrigued by the book and liked the way Dr. Weiss described his approach to reconciling the otherworldly experiences of the sessions with his scientific and rational approach to medicine and life.

I will admit that when I reached the section about the Masters, I got goose bumps, felt uneasy, and had to put the book down to digest what I had just read. On the one hand, it sounded absolutely ridiculous . . . like genuinely too insane to ever believe. I mean, come on, Master spirits? It was one thing to believe in karma, which could possibly be explained as a force or law of nature, but an entirely different thing to believe in spirits. But because Dr. Weiss's extreme scientific mind and skepticism resonated with me so much, I guess I took what he was saying under consideration rather than throwing the book in the trash, which is truthfully what part of me wanted to do. I thought to myself, "What if?" and kept reading. Plus, I wanted to finally understand this reincarnation theory, even if just to put the fragments from my own intuitive readings and Jackson's descriptions into a framework.

Here's my take at summarizing that framework based on what Dr. Weiss alleges the Masters conveyed to him through his patients: We have souls that incarnate on Earth to learn specific lessons through the events and relationships that make up a lifetime here. The point of learning the lessons is to evolve our souls and advance up through levels of spiritual being. With each advancing level we become more like the Source, or Godlike, which is apparently ideal and worth striving toward. At some point when you have become an advanced enough soul, like the Masters, you stop incarnating and help other souls. The lessons are things like learning to be kind, patient, and loving (I would have rolled my eyes at this in the past!). Souls typically choose just a few lessons to learn per lifetime, and if they don't complete the lesson (e.g., never learning that being an abusive alcoholic parent is a bad thing), then they have to incarnate again and again until they finally learn the lesson. Karma is real, and there are karmic debts to be paid that help you advance. The reason there are so many lives is that there are many karmic debts to be paid and many lessons to learn. Souls change race, sex, religion, and physical health or impairment throughout the different incarnations to learn everything by experience. For example, someone who was a violent racist in one life might reincarnate in the next life as a member of the race they discriminated against in the previous life. The answer to everything and the lessons is (predictably) love. This reminds me of Brian L. Weiss's words, "Since everything is energy, and love encompasses all energies, all is love." Also, souls tend to aggregate in soul groups, which are groups of souls at about the same level of development, and these soul groups tend to reincarnate together on Earth and switch off playing different characters in each other's lives. Souls in these groups can also be called soulmates, but these relationships are not necessarily romantic. For example, your mother in this life may have been a sister in a past life and a nephew in a previous life before that. Before birth, souls choose their parents, circumstances of life, and a plan for the upcoming life. So all the participant souls agree to the relationships. Souls are given a preview of the major events and key people they will encounter in a given lifetime, including soul group members. As for destiny and free will, they are allegedly complementary, and we have both. The idea is that you have "destiny points" in your life, such as meeting a soulmate, but how you behave and handle the situation is your free will, and ultimately what contributes to determining your karma. But according to this framework, *everything happens for a reason*—a saying that until this point in my life had been anathema to me.

According to the Masters, the purpose of life was to fully comprehend compassion, nonviolence, love, nonjudgment, non-prejudice, patience, generosity, charity, and hope. We are supposed to become aware that we are all interconnected, that energy connects us all, and that we never really die.

My first reaction still was that I felt like I wanted to throw up. Not in an "oh wow, I'm so overwhelmed by the beauty of the truth" kind of way, but rather a, "you have got to be fucking kidding me that the point of life is all that hippie-dippy bullshit" kind of way. I could not roll my eyes hard enough. Remember, at this point I was open to learning more, but I wasn't fully onboard with any of the ideas I was learning about. Cynicism was deeply ingrained in me. My second thought was that if this were true, humanity was failing miserably, given all the racism, self-ishness, and judgment that existed in abundance.

From a strictly scientific materialist viewpoint, the story is too incredible to believe. All the typical skeptical objections arose in my mind. Even as I read the book's incredibly fascinating description of events with Dr. Weiss's patient, my brain immediately started ripping it apart scientifically and logically. Although I respected his credentials and approach, I did recognize that he was still human and subject to all the same biases we all are. Perhaps this one case was unique, and this type of made-up story therapy worked for her for some reason. I should also highlight here that, despite being a neuroscientist, I knew shock-ingly little about psychology and therapy methods because neuroscience education focuses on the brain, not the mind. The one-and-done case study explanation didn't work because Dr. Weiss went on to incorporate the method of past life regression into his practice and treated *thousands* of patients successfully over his long career.

OK, fine, maybe there was something about Dr. Weiss and the setting of his office that elicited the sessions and their healing effect with his patients. In the book, he mentions that he found it hard to believe that he was the first to stumble across this finding, so he began searching the literature for others. He mostly found literature around reincarnation and near-death experiences, and while very similar to what he encountered in his practice, it was not quite the same. He real-ized that while he was surely not the first behavioral health practitioner to come across this healing technique, he might be the first one who had to write about it. He struggled with the decision for years, fearing ostracization from colleagues and loss of credibility, but finally decided to publish his findings. Instead of being met with hostility and skepticism, outreach from other behavioral health practitioners poured in with similar stories.

Now this really had my attention. One man is easy to brush off, but *multiple* practitioners with similar findings deserved a closer look. After doing some reading, I learned that Dr. Weiss was far from the only therapist or psychologist or psychiatrist who had inadvertently stumbled onto past lives in their clinical psychology or psychiatry practice and found it to be an effective therapeutic. I read all of Dr. Weiss's books, and those of many others in the same field, to better understand and scrutinize the methods and the spiritual framework. The revelation of wonders didn't stop here.

5

I Can't Live in These Conditions

There were thousands and thousands of stories of past life regression healing people both emotionally and physically. Some practitioners even began specializing in that special state between lives after a person had died in a past life and where patients could meet with spirit guides—other souls that have signed up to help guide your life and keep you on track for your soul's purpose—and obtain more information about spirituality and human life. All of the practitioners reported that their patients reported the *same* underlying story about reincarnation and soul lessons, irrespective of whether they believed in reincarnation or had been exposed to such material or beliefs beforehand. It was an incredible phenomenon! Just to give a sense of the profound healing this technique could provide I will give a couple of examples.

Diana was a forty-year-old woman who came in to see Dr. Weiss for depression (Weiss 1992). Dr. Weiss suspected that Diana's tumultuous relationship with one of her daughters was the root cause of this depression. Although having loving and healthy relationships with her other two children, Diana had felt an immediate dislike and revulsion for her daughter from the moment she was born. Mother and daughter had been archenemies for the entirety of the life of her daughter, who was eighteen years old at the time. A past life regression revealed that in a different life Diana and her daughter were not related to each other and were vying for the same man's affection! Astonishingly, the man from that lifetime was Diana's husband and her daughter's father in the current lifetime. After remembering this past life and understanding some of the conflict with her daughter, Diana's relationship with her daughter improved, but she never told her daughter about the past life because she thought it was an unusual experience and was not comfortable sharing it. However, unbeknownst to Diana, her daughter received a past life regression from a different therapist in a different state and regressed to the same past life with the exact same details! When she shared it with her mother, Diana was shocked and shared her own experience with her daughter. This shared understanding finally let them rise above the past and begin anew. There are many other examples similar to this one of two people independently remembering the *same past life* in completely different sessions or circumstances.

Past life regression can also heal physical ailments. Elaine, a respected psychologist and another of Dr. Weiss's patients, suffered from excruciating and incessant pain in her neck, shoulders, and upper back. She also had a lifelong terror of heights and drowning. In a past life regression, she recalled a life where she was a captured soldier on the losing side of a battle, standing on top of a castle tower blindfolded and with her hands tied behind her back. She was lanced in the back before being pushed off the tower into a moat and to her death. Days after the regression, she woke up with no pain in her back and her fear of heights gone. She came back for a second session and recalled a life in medieval France, where she was a male in his twenties who was dispirited and hopeless. This man lacked the courage to be different, speak out, and look for ways to change his circumstances and life. He was wrongly accused of a crime and hanged as a punishment. Elaine's chronic neck pain disappeared after the session. She also recognized how fear can hold one back from improving a life, and she carried this lesson forward into her current lifetime.

So it appeared that past life regression was an effective therapeutic as evidenced by improved outcomes in patients. What's really going on with these sessions, though? It doesn't necessarily prove that past lives are real. I thought that maybe the act of making up a story provided therapeutic relief, but Dr. Weiss and other practitioners wrote about how that is not the case, since the same emotional release, or *catharsis,* is not achieved with fictional accounts. Dr. Weiss considered whether patients were accessing what Carl Jung called the collective unconscious, a theorized collection of all human memory and experience that was represented by universal symbols and images, called archetypes, found across all cultures. Perhaps individuals were capable of tapping into the collective unconscious, and thus the things they described in the sessions were not memories from past lives but rather general archetypes from human experience. But Dr. Weiss and other practitioners decided that the memories were far too detailed about specific people and places to be explained by the collective unconscious. The concept of genetic memory—think of savants who know things they never learned—was considered as an explanation. But the concept applies to more procedural skill sets, abilities, and knowledge (e.g., how to play piano or how to sculpt) rather than specific explicit memories of places and events from an ancestor's life, which is the kind elicited in past life regression. Additionally, traditional neuroscience has not shown that explicit memories can be passed on by genetics in this way. Even if memories could be passed down in this way by some undiscovered mechanism, past life regression practitioners report that the array of past life accounts from a single patient come from too many different countries and lineages to reasonably conclude a direct ancestor as the source. Also, some of the remembered past lives would be of children who died young who had no opportunity to pass on their genetics to descendants.

The current scientific materialist paradigm assumes that your brain is a blank slate when you are born and that the knowledge you attain over your lifetime comes in through your five senses. So another possible explanation is that Catherine, and other patients like her, constructed the stories from knowledge of historic places and events that she or they had unconsciously picked up, something called *cryptomnesia*, or remembering something without realizing it is a memory. Dr. Weiss ruled this out, as have other practitioners, because the breadth of obscure knowledge of historic places, events, and practices was often far too wide to reasonably come from the patient's life experience. Imagine an Australian patient describing in detail an 1800s town from the southern United States that had subsequently been burned down before the year 1900, that ended up being verified. Also, keep in mind that Catherine's case, and those of many others, was in the 1980s and the internet did not yet exist, so easy access to information wasn't as available as it is in the current age. Additionally, there have been cases where patients report large amounts of factually correct historical information, and even cases of xenoglossy, where patients will spontaneously begin speaking a foreign language that the personality from the purported past life knows, but that that current person has never learned (Ducasse 1960; Ramster 1994; Stevenson 1977; Pasricha and Stevenson 1987; Tarazi 1990)! Dr. Weiss actually had a few cases like this. In one of his cases, a surgeon from China who could not speak English, had never left her country before, and who brought a translator with her to her appointment with Dr. Weiss began speaking very fluent English during a past life regression memory of a fight with her husband in California in the year 1850! Dr. Weiss hilariously described the confusion of the translator.

If past life regression patients are simply using imagination to construct vivid make-believe situations, rather than past lives being a real thing, then we would expect little to no past life reports outside this context. However, past life reports occur under an array of different contexts, such as in psychedelic therapy, deep experiential psychotherapy (e.g., primal therapy, rebirthing, and holotropic breathing), meditation, sensory isolation, bodywork, spontaneous episodes of non-ordinary consciousness (e.g., spiritual emergencies), in children (and even adults) in ordinary waking consciousness, in sleep during lucid dreaming, and of course, like we saw in the case of Dr. Weiss, in conventional psychotherapy sessions with therapists who neither work with past-life therapy nor believe in reincarnation (Pasricha and Stevenson 1987; Cranston and Williams 1984; Head and Cranston 1977). Reports of past lives have emerged from culturally diverse groups throughout history and across the globe in both ordinary and non-ordinary states of consciousness (Grof 1975; 1988). Past-life reports occur whether the participant believes in them or not (Fiore 1978). A truly widespread phenomenon!

I'm sure there are countless other explanations, but the one that Dr. Weiss and similar others came to was that reincarnation possibly exists. What other evidence was there? I dove into more texts. It turns out that using past life regression sessions to try to verify real past lives was not that simple, as it was hard to get enough details to verify, like full names (Mills and Tucker 2015). However, there did seem to be a very large amount of research work done on children between the ages of two and five who spontaneously and independently begin speaking, with emotion, about a past life. Dr. Ian Stevenson of the University of Virginia (UVA) pursued this unique and groundbreaking work and traveled the world collecting over twenty-seven hundred cases from six continents of children with past life memories. Dr. Jim Tucker continues this work today at the Division of Perceptual Studies at UVA.

YOU'LL NEVER WORK IN THIS TOWN AGAIN!

Although it may seem cliché, you know, being from LA and all, I'm going to tell you the story of the child who remembered a Hollywood life. Ryan, a four-year-old boy who lived in Oklahoma, began telling his mother that he wanted to be taken to the house where he'd "lived before." He once said, "I can't live in these conditions. My last home was much better." He would play at directing movies and said that he had danced on Broadway and knew tap dance routines. When Ryan would see images of the Hollywood Hills on TV, he would tell his parents that's where he used to live. He kept telling his mother that he was homesick, so she bought a book about old Hollywood that she thought might comfort him. Incredibly, while flipping through the pages of the book, Ryan shouted, "Mama! That guy's me! The 'old me'!" He had identified an extra in the 1932 movie *Night After Night* named Marty Martyn. At first, Ryan's parents, who are Baptist and do not believe in reincarnation, did not believe a past life was the explanation. Eventually, the family reached out to the research team at UVA to learn more. With Dr. Tucker's help, Ryan and his family contacted and met Martyn's daughter, and she was able to confirm over fifty details of Martyn's life that Ryan had reported! Ryan had said that he lived in a big house with a swimming pool that was on a street that had the word "rock" in the street name. Martyn turned out to have a home with a pool on Roxbury Drive. He had begged his mother to take him to Hollywood so he could visit his "other family," which included three adopted sons. Martyn had adopted his three stepsons. Ryan had said he had one biological child from his first marriage, and Martyn had one biological daughter from his first (of four) marriages. Ryan had said things like, "Do you know who I am? If you mess with me, you won't ever work in this town again." It turned out that Martyn had gone from being an extra to being a very powerful talent agent. There were many, many more specific details that lined up.

Then there's the case of Swarnlata Mishra from India who, while on a trip with her father to another village, suggested that they go have "good tea at her home." When she was finally taken to the home of the purported past life days later, she immediately recognized her past family, correctly told her former husband where he was hiding a box of twelve hundred rupees, and knew the fact that, in her former life, she had gold teeth. She even called her sons from the former life by their affectionate nicknames.

There is often an odd correspondence between birthmarks and birth defects and locations of mortal wounds from past lives. For example, a woman who remembered a past life where she was killed by three blows from an axe to her back had three separate linear hyper-pigmented scar-like birthmarks on her back. A boy from India named Ram recalled a past life where he was killed by a shotgun wound to the chest. He was able to give the name of the person from the past life, and Dr. Stevenson was able to locate the autopsy report of the deceased person. The location of the gunshot wound that was ascertained from the autopsy report matched that of the boy's birthmark.

Dr. Stevenson created a tool to assess the strength of evidence in each case and included these four items that provided quantifiable proof: (1) birthmarks and birth defects that corresponded to wounds of the previous personality, (2) verified statements about the previous life,

(3) behaviors in the child that appeared associated with the previous life, and (4) distance between the child's family and the previous family (Tucker 2000). The research showed that in 65% of spontaneous reincarnation cases, the identity of the purported past life personality could be verified. In the cases where birth defects or deformities correspond to the fatal wound of the purported past life personality, 35% of the cases could identify the individuals. Many of these cases contain descriptions from the children of a realm between lives that sounded extremely similar to the environment reported by individuals who have either had near-death experiences or had past life regression therapy. In many of the cases there were no biological connections between the family of the child reporting the past life and of the reported past life personality.

That's a lot to take in. Is it all legitimate research? An independent investigation and validation of Stevenson's work from three other researchers that included 123 cases of children reporting past lives concluded (Mills, Haraldsson, and Keil 1994):

> The investigations of three independent researchers into reported cases of reincarnation in five cultures in which such cases are reported suggested some children identify themselves with a person about whom they have no normal way of knowing. In these cases, the children apparently exhibit knowledge and behavior appropriate to that person.

These were incredible stories, and the research seemed solid, but it was still hard to wrap my mind around. The most common reaction from mainstream materialist scientists will always be that the research methods used were questionable or substandard. Yet in the course of reading the research I found praise from respected people and organizations for the reincarnation research at UVA. For example, the *Journal of the American Medical Association* in 1975 (King 1975) said that the research on reincarnation that Dr. Stevenson collected was done in a "painstaking and unemotional" manner and that "the evidence is difficult to explain on any other grounds." Based on Dr. Stevenson's work, Carl Sagan cited reincarnation as a topic that deserved further research.

The evidence for reincarnation from Dr. Stevenson's and others' work was even more compelling than the case studies from the past life regression therapy body of evidence. Each case was thoroughly investigated, photo evidence was included, and public records were verified. It was truly remarkable. What other lines of evidence were there that corroborated this reincarnation spiritual framework? Next up was *near-death experiences.*

According to the Near-Death Experience Research Foundation (Long and Long 1999), a near-death experience (NDE) is "a lucid experience associated with perceived consciousness apart from the body occurring at the time of actual or threatened imminent death." An estimated 13.5 million Americans have experienced an NDE. Reported elements of an NDE can include: (1) an out-of-body experience (OBE); in other words, separation of consciousness from body, sometimes with a point-of-view floating above the body, (2) a more clearly and rapidly functioning mind, (3) sensation of being drawn into a tunnel or darkness; (4) a brilliant light, (5) a sense of overwhelming peace, joy, bliss, unconditional love, and a feeling of oneness, (6) a "life review," or a review of important past events from the person's life, (7) a *preview* of future events of the person's life, (8) encounters with deceased loved ones, or other beings, such as religious figures, (9) an indescribable quality, and (10) a sense of being exposed to special and unlimited knowledge of universal order and life purpose. In some of the cases, narratives from past lives would emerge. A review of claims for and against NDEs is beyond the scope of this book, but I recommend *An End to Upside Down Thinking* by Mark Gober for an excellent and easy-to-understand overview.

By now I had learned that the narrative of reincarnation, karma, and soul lessons emerged from intuitives, mediums, patients undergoing past life regression therapy, children spontaneously remembering past lives, near-death experiences, and many other contexts. What?! This was nuts. My only association with reincarnation was Hinduism. Oh, but I was so woefully naive.

Apparently, the concept of reincarnation even used to be part of Christianity and Judaism (Head and Cranston 1977; Weiss 1988; Booth 2008) but had been deleted over the years for various political and religious reasons. There were references to reincarnation in the New Testament, and early christian church Fathers, such as Origen, Clement of Alexandria, and St. Jerome, believed in the concept. References to reincarnation were removed in the fourth century by Emperor Constantine when Christianity became the official religion of the Roman Empire. He desired that citizens believe their current life was their one and only life in order to encourage good behavior. In the sixth century, the Second Council of Constantinople officially declared reincarnation a heretical belief. Judaism also had a belief in reincarnation, called gilgul, that Dr. Weiss reported had been removed in an effort to better align the religion with modern day science. It is still, however, a part of the Orthodox and Hasidic communities of Judaism and has always been a fundamental aspect of the Kabbalah, a mystical teaching within Judaism.

Outside of the major religions, it has been widespread throughout the cultures of the world. The Gnostics and Cathars believed in the concept, as did many Greek schools of thought, such as the Platonists, Pythagoreans, and the Orphics. Many indigenous cultures still believe in the concept, and of course, reincarnation is a component of Hinduism, Buddhism, Jainism, Taoism, and many other religions and cultures.

It's not that learning that reincarnation was prevalent in many cultures and religions across the world and across time was proof to me that the concept was real. I was a subscriber to the school of thought that one origin story was likely passed down through human history. This reincarnation story is a common thread that runs through many of today's religions of the world. It was actually more a revelation to me that a concept that I thought was so fringe was actually quite widely accepted.

Spiritually, after all that analysis, I was very confused. I *finally* had a description that tied together the narratives I had heard from intuitives about souls reincarnating, soul missions, and karma. What was confusing is that it was coming from highly accomplished scientists, psychiatrists, and behavioral health practitioners. This wasn't woo-woo (an insult toward mystical or supernatural beliefs); this was evidence. I had never believed that we could prove spirituality with scientific evidence, which is why I was sort of an existentialist and definitely an agnostic. For weeks, I went over the books and cases in detail. I thought through every explanation I could think of. Some days I believed it, and some days I thought that I must be missing something that makes it false. The converging lines of evidence were compelling.

I don't think *Many Lives, Many Masters* would have had as profound an effect on me if I hadn't been recently primed to the idea of reincarnation and karma by the intuitives I had visited. At this point in time, I would say that my biggest wonder came from how a nearly identical spiritual narrative about reincarnation, karma, and soul lessons emerged from individuals of all faiths under various circumstances. What was so odd to me was that this isn't a wildly popular narrative in Western culture. In Los Angeles, sure, but definitely not more broadly. If we were to try to explain the stories that emerge from patients in relaxed states like hypnosis as subconsciously picked up cultural narratives that were subsequently woven into therapeutic fiction, we would probably expect the narrative to be that of a more prevalent and popular one, such as Christian thought. Or how about a scientific one?

What the books I was reading were suggesting is that if you entered a hypnotic state in therapy and were asked to visit past lives or the state between lives and describe the spiritual state of the world, regardless of your culture or faith, you would describe the narrative of soul lessons, reincarnation, and karma. How could that be? What did that mean? It made no sense from a neuroscience perspective. To know the story, you would have had to learn it in this life through your five senses, but many of these people were consciously naive to this spiritual framework. So they all somehow unconsciously picked up this detailed spiritual framework and then chose to describe *that one,* not the one they actually believed in, like Christianity, to a behavioral health therapist under hypnosis. What could the evolutionary explanation for that be? Is this some weird story that got coded into our genome and tucked away into our brain that just won't disappear? And then because of that deep-seated belief we make up stories about past lives that explain things in this life? What then of the validations? Could it really be that the narrative is true and remembered by everyone's "soul" (which was a concept I still didn't understand)?

To me, this was the closest thing that humans could investigate scientifically about spirituality. And it turned out that many had. By the sheer volume of work and the credentials of the researchers, I found it hard *not* to believe. In science, we follow the evidence. That was a lot of evidence. Was it hard to swallow? Absolutely, especially for someone like me who was not used to thinking of anything spiritual. But the flip side would be to believe that either all the researchers and their decades of work were fraud (unlikely) or fraught with errors. Those were pretty unreasonable assumptions to make. I began thinking, *Wouldn't it be really important—therapeutically and existentially—to understand why this story emerges from people in relaxed states?* I did still think it would be difficult to prove or disprove reincarnation, but we could certainly investigate a human behavior.

I decided that I needed a sanity check. I asked my close friends to read *Many Lives, Many Masters.* I reached out to other friends that I knew would enjoy it. I mailed copies to friends I knew would read it but would never buy it themselves. I chose that book of all the books I read because it was the shortest, easiest read, and because of Dr. Weiss's credentials. I honestly deserve royalties for how many people I made read this book. I had to know what other people thought. Did I believe it just because I wanted to believe it? Wait, did I even want to believe it? The idea of constantly reincarnating to learn life lessons seemed exhausting and wholly unappealing. I was barely making it through *this* life! Talking about soul lessons and soul evolution was all fun and games until you were deep in it. I felt enormous stigma and internal conflict around merely entertaining the belief. On the one hand, there was evidence, and you must follow the evidence as a scientist. On the other hand, this was at odds with scientific materialism, and thus, with my identity. I felt extremely uncomfortable at *all* times, but also compelled to continue exploring.

When I wanted someone to read the book, explaining the book went like this: "I read this really weird book. It's kind of crazy, but also a very interesting case study of a patient. It outlines an interesting spiritual framework about life. You need to read it and tell me what you think!" I felt way more comfortable framing it that way to everyone than saying the truth, which was, "I know this is absolutely insane, but I kind of believe it." (Quick note to say that "believe" is an interesting word here because it was more like I believed the evidence more than I fully believed in and embodied the theory of reincarnation and karma. You can't just flip a switch and start viewing your current life as one stop on a long train ride—or at least I couldn't!)

The responses from friends, family, and colleagues ranged greatly, from people who wouldn't even read it because it didn't align with their beliefs (to me, that is the equivalent of a scientist throwing away an outlying data point) to people who were completely transformed. I had one friend—one of my closest friends—who was *completely* turned off by even the *suggestion* that there could be spirits or that karma and reincarnation were true. As I began telling our friend group about the book and discussing it with them as they read it, she would roll her eyes and throw shade our way. Then one day she quietly read the book herself without telling any of us and came to the group chat "with many questions." Within a few months, she had devoured all the seasons of *The Haunting Of, Celebrity Ghost Stories,* and *Long Island Medium.* A subscription to Gaia network (a streaming service focused on "consciousness-expanding" content) soon followed! Never say never.

The simple answer to "What is the point of all this?" was "to learn lessons to evolve our souls." Although I didn't like the answer and didn't fully understand it, it was somehow comforting to have *an* answer. Oh, and one thing I forgot to mention earlier was that another reason souls incarnate is to experience earthly and bodily pleasures—like eating a delicious slice of pizza or having a nice warm bath—that they can't experience in soul form. I mention it because this simple idea changed my life so utterly profoundly that I had to share it. Instead of constantly focusing on goals and my next achievement or idea, I began to really enjoy my warm morning cup of coffee, the way the sunlight filtered through my windows in the late afternoon in my home, and those feelings of connection with friends. The point of being alive is to enjoy this exact moment with all its misery and bliss and beauty. That was already transformative.

I began to wonder: What if it were true? What if the Universe wasn't random and meaningless? What if we did have souls? What if our souls were constantly reincarnating to balance karmic laws and learn lessons for the purpose of evolution? And what if that hidden truth is inside all of us, available to be revealed through ultrarelaxed states? And what if some people, like intuitives, had easier access to this knowledge somehow?

Although I was still interested in the meaning of life questions, I also found myself thinking about the physical mechanisms by which intuitives could possibly obtain this otherworldly knowledge. As a neuroscientist, I wanted to know how they were perceiving the information. Also, what the hell was a soul made of? Essentially, I still had a lot more questions, and reading books wasn't getting me there fast enough. I decided to take a step through the looking glass and turn this into a real adventure.

6

The Project Begins

Can Science and Spirituality Coexist?

I had dipped my toe in the lake of spiritual knowledge, but I was eager to know more. I was curious whether intuitives had more answers to the universal truths plaguing my mind, and whether having this information made living life easier for them. I also began thinking about scientists and wondering what they believed. It dawned on me that in the decade or longer I had known many of my graduate school colleagues and other scientists, I had never discussed spirituality or religion with probably any of them. I could not tell you what any of them believed on these topics. Logically, that was partly because I was not previously interested in discussing these topics, but I probably also assumed that they, too, were not interested. I now wondered how they dealt with the difficulty of life and what they believed about the nature of the Universe.

I can tell you that suddenly having a narrative that made sense to me was definitely comforting; I now understood the appeal of spirituality. That in and of itself was such a profound transformation for me, but not one that I was comfortable with at all. I also knew that I could not have blindly believed any old narrative—I had tried and failed in my life. As I previously mentioned, I critically analyzed religion, and when I realized that it made no sense to me, I abandoned it. My brain really was my own worst enemy. Even if a belief had the potential to be comforting, my brain would reject it if it was not accompanied with at least *some* evidence. For me to believe in spirituality, I would need compelling evidence of some sort, which I believed did not exist, hence being agnostic for so long. Now though, I wondered if there was more evidence, be it circumstantial, of there being more meaning to the Universe.

There was an internal mental battle going on between 'old me' and 'new me,' and it wasn't getting me anywhere. I felt stalled. I needed to talk through the possibilities with other people, but with different types of people. Scientists were on that list, almost purely out of curiosity to learn more about their thoughts, but I was also craving peer review of my experiences and newfound knowledge. I also wanted to speak with individuals, such as intuitives, mediums, and mystics, who seemed to have unique insight and beliefs. Lastly, since I was amazed with how therapeutic past life regression therapy seemed to be for patients, I began to wonder about the overlap between psychology and spirituality. So I decided to start a project of interviewing intuitives, mediums, mystics, behavioral health practitioners, and scientists. The main reason for starting this project was to continue my exploration of universal truths, but it was also to help settle the battle between 'old me' and 'new me.' I imagined the scales of justice in my head, swaying back and forth between old and new beliefs. I would remind myself of the compelling reports from the fields of clinical psychology, psychiatry, and behavioral health, only to have 'old me' pop up and scoff at the possibilities of a soul existing and reincarnating and the Universe holding meaning. The back and forth was exhausting. I had done as much as I could on my own.

Over the following year, I performed in-depth interviews with an array of intuitives, mediums, mystics, behavioral health practitioners, scientists, researchers, engineers, and government officials. The conversations were wide ranging and took me down roads I never could have imagined. I was left with my mouth agape (not a good look on Zoom calls) during more than a few interviews at the things that were revealed to me, some of which I may never be able to repeat or reveal to others. I promised anonymity to some of the individuals I interviewed because people are much more willing to speak with you openly and frankly when done in confidentiality. Unfortunately, the identities of some of the individuals would give so much more credence to the things discussed in some cases, but such is life. I will just say that all the scientists, researchers, and behavioral health practitioners interviewed had obtained degrees and had careers in prestigious and accredited institutions such as Yale; University of Southern California; University of California, Los Angeles; Vanderbilt University; Department of Defense; U.S. military, and more—every single one of them was profoundly respected by 'old me.' As unfortunate as it is, you'll just have to take my word for it.

So let me take you on the crazy journey that followed and let you into my mind as it all unfolded.

I JUST NEED ALL THE ANSWERS TO THE UNIVERSE, PLEASE

In February 2020 I decided to start my interview project with an intuitive, because I was very interested to know how they were perceiving their information. I also wanted to ask point-blank about the meaning of life and how fate, destiny, and free will work.

The first person I interviewed was Rachel Lee, an intuitive and a medium I had been to once who had seriously impressed, or actually spooked, me with her accuracy. She would appear to be listening to some source, would say, "Spirit says . . . ," and then highly detailed true and specific facts from my life would pour out of her mouth. I had left her reading feeling that my mind had been read, which was simultaneously kind of cool, but also horrifyingly embarrassing, given the messy state of my brain at the time.

I reached out and told her about the project, and she said she would be happy to meet. We met one February night in 2020 at an Italian restaurant in the San Fernando Valley—little did I know that this would be the last interview I would conduct outside my home due to the looming Covid-19 pandemic. I was so nervous that I had nightmares the night before about not being able to finish the interview. I had never actually interviewed anyone before outside of a scientific experiment. I had a list of questions to help move things along. As I sat waiting for her in the host area, I thought to myself, "What the hell am I doing?" 'Old me' was not pleased that we were doing this. I looked around at the walls covered from floor to ceiling in framed photos of laughing Italian families and old Hollywood stars like Frank Sinatra and Isabella Rossellini. I wondered if any of them had struggled with spirituality and life and found themselves doing absolutely insane, out-of-character things from time to time, as I was doing now. It was too late to leave, so I tried to distract myself by analyzing the photos on the walls. Finally, she slipped through the front door, and I greeted her. Rachel doesn't have that stereotypical fortune-teller look! Rachel was dressed in a perfectly plain and forgettable manner, with her full, black hair in a messy bun.

Once we sat down, I began to calm a bit. I was excited to ask my questions, so my eagerness for the conversation overrode my anxiety and doubts. Rachel has an easygoing demeanor and was a pleasure to interview. For the record, and since I've been asked this before, I did not pay her for her time. Although I wanted to pay her because I value her time, she graciously declined payment. I did offer to pay for dinner, but she only ordered a decaf cup of coffee, while I devoured pizza. I brought a voice recorder that I borrowed from a friend, and although I had requested a quiet spot in the restaurant, we were comically seated in a room next to a loud birthday party.

I started off by telling Rachel that this interview was no big deal and I simply wanted all the answers to the Universe, and I would be so grateful if she would kindly oblige—to which she laughed and said, "Of course, honey." I detail Rachel's story here because I found a lot of hostility toward intuitives in my journey, coming from this cultural narrative that frames them as frauds, and I think it would do us good to remember that they, too, are human. I could write a separate book on how to get the most out of an intuitive reading, which would lay a practical foundation for the intuitive-client relationship. While I'm sure there are intuitives who are frauds, it is my opinion and experience that many are genuine, although some are far more talented than others. In fact, most of them report doing the work to help people heal. They are some of the kindest people I have ever met, and frankly, I would much rather spend an afternoon with them over some of the folks that haunt the halls of academia. If I can help society view them in a more friendly manner, then I would like to do so. They do, after all, provide a service (a $2.2 billion industry) that many people use in times of distress for comfort.

Rachel grew up in a family that was very skeptical and not in the least spiritual. Although she knew from a young age that she was different, her parents did not believe her. Luckily, she had a sister who did believe in her. When she was eight years old, she saw her first spirit guide, a Native American woman, sitting on the edge of her bed. Rachel said she did not feel any fear upon viewing her spirit guide, and that her guide explained everything about souls to her. She didn't have much formal training but started attending Friday night meditations when she was eighteen years old that opened her up intuitively, which led to her meeting more of her spirit and animal guides. The closest thing to formal training that she received was studying Native American spiritual ceremonies with a mentor.

On being intuitive, she said she always just knew things. She could hear Spirit (how many intuitives refer to a large powerful presence in the Universe), but she thought everyone else could, too. She never hid her gifts but didn't recognize them as psychic until her late teens and early twenties, when she was first exposed to metaphysical beliefs. In response to my question about how she perceives information, she said that she can hear, see, and sometimes feel information about others. For example, if she was visiting a murder site, she could sometimes feel the anger of the soul that passed, and Spirit showed her where the victim was killed on the body, such as the heart. She detailed numerous examples of Spirit interacting with her. Once, her grandmother's spirit came to tell her that her mother would be alright after her bypass surgery. When her father passed, his spirit visited her afterward, attended his own funeral, and made faces at his friends during the funeral, which provided her comfort. Despite these comforting messages from the other side, she confided that she battles anxiety—she mentioned this a few times.

I asked, "Do you ever wish you didn't have this gift?" She replied that yes, sometimes she does wish, as an empath, she didn't have to *feel* so deeply because it "hurts so much." In certain locations, such as Niagara Falls, she can't stay long because she can hear the voices and feel the pain of the individuals who took their lives there. She confessed that it is also hard to date because she attracts men who are afraid of her abilities of sensing what they're thinking and feeling.

She reiterated that we are here to learn lessons for our soul and that we have a preordained destiny when we come into our lifetimes. According to her, we already know the family we will be born into—something that aligned with Dr. Weiss's account and the other work I had read. She said that free will has a part in our lives but that if you are predestined for something, then nothing will stop it from happening. Using herself as an example, she said she knew she was destined to be an intuitive or healer, which is why her other career pursuits did not work out. She explained that if you don't live that destiny, life can be harder for you. Manifesting is real, but it is on God's or Spirit's time, not ours—so things will happen for you when they are meant to happen. With regard to reincarnation, she said that our souls have a choice to reincarnate or not but that when they choose to do so, it is usually to work on lessons. I asked her where she learned the spiritual framework, and she said she learned it from her spirit guide.

She told me there are eight or nine different realms or dimensions (Dr. Weiss reported seven in his books) and that sometimes spirits can walk through realms without noticing the change in realms because they only see their own. Up to this point, I had heard things that I was now newly familiar and comfortable with, such as spirit guides, other realms, and soul purpose.

Then the conversation steered into weird. She told me that there were (and that she had actually seen) such things as genies, fairies, and elves. I suddenly felt my stomach drop. I thought to myself, "Wait . . . is she actually nuts?" This was also the moment I decided to suspend disbelief. I thought to myself, "Well, if I'm assuming the other half of what we talked about (e.g., reincarnation, karma, soul lessons) is true, and I'm allowing for that assumption (for now) because it emerged from multiple independent sources, then shouldn't disbelief in this new data point be suspended for now?" So that's what I did. I just took notes, listened, and, for the first time since childhood, felt a sense of wonder at the world we live in. I looked around the restaurant and imagined fairies rolling over laughing as they floated through the air and harried elves surreptitiously watching us discuss their existence. I chuckled to myself and thought, "What if?"

Although I wasn't looking for a reading of any kind from her, she did say one thing that surprised me. Rachel was clearly an animal lover, as almost every answer to my questions tied back to animals somehow. As we were wrapping up, I offhandedly mentioned to her that I hadn't grown up with pets, so I wasn't that comfortable around animals.

> She said, "That's a past life thing."
> I was caught off guard and said, "Oh?"
> She said, "Yeah, you had your heart ripped out [emotionally] by one in a past life, and you never got over it."
> I stuttered, "It . . . it died?"
> "Yes . . . a horse," she replied.

Iciness came over me from head to toe, and goose bumps formed at every single damn pore. Anyone who knows me well knows that I *adore* horses. Despite not being comfortable with most animals, I used to take horseback riding lessons and dreamed of having a ranch with horses. My friends would always make fun of me, saying, "How can you love horses so much when you're scared of all other animals?" And when they'd tell me to get a pet, I would reply, "I wouldn't be able to bear it if it passed away." No, I wasn't wearing any horse jewelry or horseback riding apparel that night for Rachel to have deduced that I love horses. We had never discussed it before, and my horseback riding life was from childhood, so it wasn't plastered on social media. There's no way she could have known. Coincidence? Maybe, but that's a pretty specific guess to make from the entire animal kingdom. When I got home that night, I just shook my head in bewilderment when I saw my stuffed animal horse on my bed reminding me of the surreal moment.

All in all, it was an extraordinary night! I learned that Rachel really believed that she was receiving information from spirits. She wasn't taught this doctrine—I mean the belief in reincarnation, soul lessons, karma, and soul purpose—by her culture or her family, who actually seemed to doubt her gifts. Rather, she declared that it was taught to her by her spirit guide. That still sounded far-fetched to me, but it did match the past life regression literature, and I was trying to be open minded. She viewed her abilities as a gift and as part of her destiny but admitted that she still battled with anxiety herself. Rachel's struggle with anxiety surprised me because I had assumed that intuitives might be more at ease with life or have a higher level of comfort with life's suffering as they purportedly have access to more information than the typical person about the reasons that things occur, even if that is just their personal belief. In spite of that, it appeared that she, too, was still just a human trying to make it through each day.

I thought the mention of multiple dimensions was interesting. I feel like that would have bounced off 'old me' and her brain, but since I had heard it before from Dr. Weiss's books, the information actually stuck. Rachel said she had seen creatures of mythology, such as fairies and elves, which led me to believe that she may have been crazier than I thought. . . . But then again, if there are other dimensions, who is to say what exists there? Maybe that's where all the folklore comes from. It made me wonder what would be more unbelievable anyway: creatures existing on another plane of reality that differ from us (periodic sightings of which enter our folklore) or the brains of humans creating fictional creatures out of thin air—a feat no other known organism in the Universe can do—that are common across cultures and time?

THE STORIES ARE ALWAYS THERE

I next turned to interviewing a dear friend and a crazy impressive neuroscientist, Helder Araujo, Ph.D. He was one of the friends I had forced to read Dr. Weiss's book, and I wanted to discuss it with him, on the record. My experience with this friend is that he was open to looking at and thinking about atypical evidence of the Universe but looked for answers rooted in science.

In discussing Dr. Weiss's book, he thought it was interesting but leaned more on genetic memory explanations for the phenomena observed. He said that he just couldn't understand how a soul could exist, with personality, and come through cycled in the same form over and over again in different lives. To be honest, that was my initial struggle, and I can't say I had resolved that missing physical science piece at this point yet. I agreed that was fair.

Helder admitted that intuitive readings could be weirdly accurate, but shied away from using spirits as the explanatory mechanism, and rather cited as-yet-unknown physical mechanisms. He doubted intuitives' abilities to predict the future and surmised that it might be more likely that they are permeable in some way to others' thoughts (maybe telepathy?). That, in conjunction with making educated guesses based on physical visual cues, could allow them to piece together a prediction. However, he did say that he believed in the power of the unconscious mind and was especially interested in the collective power of multiple minds (e.g., three to four people thinking about you negatively could have power in some way to affect your life negatively). As for spirits, he said that he is too afraid to believe in them! He did think there was value in God, or some sort of spiritual narrative, because otherwise it would be too much for humans to bear the weight of existence.

I began to realize that while I was focused on the spiritual aspect, there could be, of course, mechanisms based in physical science to explain phenomena such as intuitive perception. That would not explain why the narrative of reincarnation, karma, and soul lessons emerges from individuals undergoing past life regression and from intuitives. After our serious scientific and philosophical discussion, my friend then began recounting personal unexplained phenomena from his own life. The stories are always there.

7

A Universal Pause in the
Fabric of Time

Now I have to interrupt this story, sort of in the way that Covid-19 interrupted our day-to-day life. Since early January 2020, there had been whispers of a worrying emergence of cases of pneumonia of unknown cause in Wuhan, China. By mid-February, scientists had isolated and named the virus that was causing the new cases of pneumonia as SARS-CoV-2, and the disease it caused as Coronavirus 2019 (which is where the shortened Covid-19 comes from). Not long after, my parents' home country of Iran was also reporting an abundance of cases. New York City would lead the news for weeks with images of overflowing emergency departments, exhausted health care workers, isolated sickly patients, and body bags being loaded into trucks. On March 11, 2020, the World Health Organization (WHO) declared a pandemic, and on March 13, my employer, USC, sent a memorandum to the university community moving classes online and instituting a work-from-home order from March 16 to April 13. In February, before all of this, I wasn't too worried about the coronavirus yet. I celebrated my birthday the third week of that month and flew up for a weekend getaway to Monterey, California, the following week. It wasn't until the first week of March when I read a *New York Times* article in which Covid-19 survivors described the disease that I began to realize it was a much more serious disease than the flu, which is what everyone kept comparing it to at the time. Once it was declared a pandemic and the images from Italy and New York started to flood in, the gravity of the situation—and the anxiety—began to take hold.

From a personal perspective, during this time I was feeling better, emotionally, but still not great. Going to work felt like stabbing my soul with a dagger for nine hours straight. Thus, my heart was filled with overflowing gratitude for the work-from-home situation. In fact, one realization that descended on me during this time was how our busy lives keep us away from ourselves and don't allow us to heal properly. Because I used to constantly be on the go, I frequently felt like I had no time, never enough time. If I did have a free moment, rather than sitting down to process my feelings or write in my journal, I would usually opt to do something more productive, or even something that needed to be done, like cleaning or going to the post office. During this pause in the fabric of time, I replaced my morning commute with a longer morning meditation and my evening commute with yoga (shout out to Ally Hamilton and her Yogis Anonymous) or an evening stroll. Despite the anxiety from the world news and the uncertainty of our collective future, I felt oddly calmer and more fulfilled than I had in a long, long time.

The majority of my relief came from having time to sit with myself, but one other factor may have contributed. I began playfully trying out the spiritual ideas about which I had recently learned. I allowed myself to wonder: What if the purpose of life's difficult moments is to learn certain life lessons? What should I be learning right now? What if the difficult relationships in my life are karmic debts that can teach me something? These simple questions provided a shockingly helpful mental reframing that made day-to-day living tolerable. Instead of feeling defeated by my circumstances and like an unlucky victim of a random and meaningless universe, a sense of *participation* seeped into me, and I rose to the challenge.

A GOOD SCIENTIST ASKS WHY

One month into the Covid-19 lockdown, after having adjusted to working from home and the daily barrage of apocalyptic news, I sat down to resume my project with my first Zoom interview. This was one of my favorite interviews: far-ranging, deeply insightful, boundless, but scientific. Dave Herman, Ph.D., is another neuroscience colleague but also a master of statistics. I wanted to talk about statistics and how scientists love to dismiss things as mere meaningless coincidences.

The conversation with Dave spanned religion, spirits, "paranormal" activity, the scientific method, limitations of the human brain, quantum physics, philosophy, and the limitations of language. (Quick note: I absolutely despise the words "paranormal" and "supernatural" because I believe everything in this Universe—or all the universes if there are more than one—is normal and natural.) It became clear pretty quickly in the conversation that Dave and I were on the same page in terms of admitting that humans do not know everything about the Universe and that things are being discovered daily. We also discussed—to the happiness of undergraduate me—that just because you label something, such as the "law of gravity," that doesn't explain how it works or why it exists. Dave launched our conversation, saying, "There are inexplicable things in the Universe. A bad scientist throws out or ignores an anomalous data point, but a good scientist asks why." He told me that he was personally always interested in things such as ghosts, the afterlife, and the great unknown—and this is exactly what I was looking for! I had known this person for years and did not know this about him! Dave told me that he thought what I was looking for was peer review of a phenomenon that I experienced myself. He completely nailed it, and I hadn't realized, until he said it, that that was what I was doing.

What I took away from this conversation is that I'm not alone as a scientist in acknowledging that we do not yet have many of the answers to the Universe and that many mysteries remain to be explored. It reminded me that the meaning of science is not to be skeptical but to be *open,* inquisitive, curious, and always striving for the best explanation of a phenomenon. Both Dave and I agreed that mainstream science is anything but that. A good scientist will always admit that data informs theories of the world, but that we should always be open to new evidence. I was delighted to learn that Dave was interested in mysterious phenomena such as the afterlife and ghosts, because, same! In hindsight, who isn't? He used neuroscience as a vehicle to explore his interest in philosophy, and that made me think about how scientists often turn to science to explore life's mysteries and find some sense of control in an unpredictable world. It amazed me how comfortable Dave was in admitting that there are some things in life that were inexplicable and mysterious. This was an aha moment when I realized that I was uncomfortable with this notion, although I was not sure why. Maybe it was my own need for control? I felt encouraged by this interview and happy to know that others shared some of my views.

As much fun as Dave and I had bashing the often closed-minded world of mainstream science, a few clarifications need to be made. What Dave and I were riffing on was the *dogmatic behavior* and *closed-mindedness* of certain institutions and practicing scientists who allege that scientific materialism is the only possible model of the Universe. The *scientific method*—which is simply a method of using measurements and theories to understand our Universe—is a very valuable and reliable tool that provides quantifiable, empirical evidence. The scientific method is *not* inextricably linked to scientific materialism, and we can use it to explore other models of the Universe. I believe that the scientific method is the best method (although definitely not the *only* method) we have for understanding the world that surrounds us and our experience within it. So to clarify, I am for the scientific method and against closed-minded allegiance to any one model. In relation to my personal journey, I'm grateful that I was forced to think through these distinctions, as I sometimes began to feel like my dismay with the scientific establishment was traitorous, or even dangerous. But then again, a good scientist should ask why!

WHY DON'T THEY TEACH US ABOUT THE MIND?

I next interviewed another longtime neuroscientist colleague and friend. She preferred to not be named, so let's call her Daphne. I had a vague memory that this colleague was into Buddhism, but I wasn't sure. We certainly had not discussed it together before.

I told her my story, and she listened kindly. We started off by discussing the limitations of science and the multiple assumptions that go into any scientific experiment. She said that society's assumptions that intuitive predictions are impossible are based on our assumptions about how time works, but that our assumptions could easily be wrong. We also turned to a discussion of language and how words and concepts, although helpful with many things, can be a hindrance when words do not exist that accurately capture ineffable concepts, such as spiritual experiences.

Turning to the field we know best, neuroscience, we delved into what we do and do not learn in graduate school, taking a particularly long pause to appreciate the fact that not much is taught or known about the mind. People are often surprised to learn that we are not experts in psychology. In fact, the focus is much more on how the brain integrates incoming sensory information into a representation of the external world, makes predictions, and coordinates behavior. Even in cognitive neuroscience, where we try to investigate the neural correlates of higher-level complex human behaviors, including social behaviors such as group membership, jealousy, and ethical decision making, it is up to the individual scientist to identify and read all relevant literature. Let me give an example: As I mentioned previously, my dissertation's focus was on the neural correlates of psychopathic traits, such as being coldhearted, deceptive, charming, and a pathological liar. More simply, I was interested in whether we could observe differences in the structure of the brain and how it functioned between people with low and high psychopathic traits. As I began delving into the research, I naturally started with other neuroscience studies investigating brain structure and function. I quickly realized, however, that human behavior is complex, and that includes psychopathic traits, and since there are so many nuances, you need to *really* understand the behavior you are studying—and you do not get that from neuroscience research articles since they are more focused on describing the methods and results of a particular experiment. This required me to fill my personal library with academic and historical books on psychopathic and antisocial people, research, and behaviors. In the long history of research on psychopathic traits, as I'm sure you can imagine, many theories have been proposed about the root cause of the emergence of such negative traits. Sometimes the scientific studies would mention a particular psychological theory that I would then have to look up to familiarize myself, but since I needed to learn the technical methods of my own experiments, I never had time to deeply understand the psychological theories and how they could relate to the neural correlates. What a shame. Even as I'm writing this, I am again amazed at the gulf between psychology and neuroscience. It seems common sense that we would integrate these fields, but in fact, neuroscience tries to keep an arm's length from psychology. Finally, in the last couple of decades we have had pioneering neuroscience researchers begin to tie together these fields, and cognitive neuroscience is where we can see this marriage. More generally, it really is wondrous how little regard and respect the field of science has bestowed upon the inner life of humans. Daphne and I were just amazed at how little progress humankind had made on understanding the mind.

About halfway through our conversation, she began telling me about her own mother, who claimed that she would receive premonitions and visions of upcoming events—such as correctly predicting a heart attack in her own boss!—and how she was typically, eerily correct about the predictions and had very few misses. Once that memory doorway was opened, a flood of other memories and stories began pouring out of my friend about her mother's spiritual practices and beliefs, and even her own experiences. I got really, really excited at this point in the conversation and probably could not hide my glee. First of all, I was excited to hear that I was not the only one who had this in their family, but I also enjoyed watching my friend recollect these memories with sheer joy, memories to which she clearly had not previously paid much heed.

At the end of the conversation, I asked her what she believed with regard to spirituality. She said that she used to be an atheist, but that she would not label herself in that way now. While she wasn't sure what she believed in, she did say that she believes in trusting your gut or intuition because when she did not do that, things did not go well for her. She also said that, in terms of spiritual practices, she has found Buddhism to perfectly nail the nature of the human mind and what causes suffering in life. Beyond that, she said, she did not believe that anybody knows the answers to these mysteries, but there was awe in wondering about where life comes from.

She too, like Dave, was fascinated by the mysteries of existence, albeit through a Buddhist lens, while I was more frustrated. She gifted me with a list of recommended spiritual texts.

This was the third conversation with a neuroscientist that left me feeling like I was not alone and that perhaps scientists were more open minded than we gave them credit for. Then again, I reminded myself, these conversations were in private, and I could not be sure any of us would be comfortable taking them public. The consensus so far was that we do not know everything about the Universe, and it is arrogant to presume that we could know everything. I felt justified, or at least not completely insane, to entertain the idea that there could be a spiritual nature to the Universe that we haven't yet been able to measure.

SOME THINGS ARE JUST A MYSTERY

As I was debating whom to interview next, one of my former dissertation committee chairs and neuroscience mentor, Laura Baker, Ph.D., emailed me out of the blue. Right when I saw her email in my inbox, I decided to briefly describe to her the project I was doing and ask if she would be interested in having a discussion around it. She agreed, and we set up a meeting. I was rather uneasy about this interview because this was different from the ones I had done so far. This person is someone older than me who had mentored me in my career and for whom I have great respect. She is one of the most brilliant scientists I know. I was worried that once I disclosed my story and began asking questions, she would be upset that I was wasting her time. Worries plagued me that she would think that all my graduate training was for nothing since now I appeared to believe in intuitives. She was definitely going to think I had lost my mind. But I genuinely wanted to know how scientists thought about these topics, and that included well-established, serious scientists—so I told myself to be brave and just do it.

We had a two-hour-long, warm discussion during which I was blown away. I was so glad that I asked her to discuss these topics with me! She started off by reading me a quote: "Sometimes it's okay to accept that something is just a mystery."* Gah! Yet another person who was comfortable accepting mysteries! Was I the only person who was uncomfortable with this?

She told me her personal story of how her relationship with religion and spirituality had evolved over the years, and she now considered herself more spiritual than not. Spirituality provides her comfort. Like my colleague Daphne, she viewed spiritual education to be studying how the mind works, by going inside yourself and finding new ways of thinking or seeing yourself or the world. To her, the mind is a machine, and the ego is directing it, but it does not have to be that way. You could turn the mind around and watch the ego, instead. It occurred to me in that moment that I was coming to understand that many scientists are comfortable discussing their spirituality as it relates to viewing the mind and its operations, rather than, say, spirits. This could be because it best matches our understanding of the world. It is also, for some reason, the most acceptable form of spirituality to admit to in mainstream culture.

Laura was amused that I had such a difficult time wrapping my head around the fact that spirituality could exist alongside science. She pointed out that, while many empirical scientists are atheists, many others have spiritual practices and are interested in questions such as, "What is the soul?" and "What is consciousness?"

This conversation really brought together all the previous ones. The

---

*Laura attributed this quote to Evan Thompson's *Waking, Dreaming, Being: Self and Consciousness in Neuroscience, Meditation, and Philosophy*, but I was not able to confirm this.

thing that stuck with me the most was the point Laura made about its being okay to just accept things as mysteries. This notion had never occurred to me, so I just kind of sat with it for a week or so. Looking back over my notes, I realized that all the scientist colleagues I had interviewed had said variations of the same thing, but I hadn't really heard it until Laura said it.

I was looking for permission to believe in phenomena that science hadn't *yet* come to understand the mechanisms behind. But what if there are phenomena in the Universe that we *cannot* understand? Those are the mysteries. Why did I feel uncomfortable with this idea, though? I believed there *must* be some underlying truth to reality and that if we could find a scientific basis for it, we could bring society up to speed, and we would all finally understand. Suddenly, there was this option of *not* doing that. Maybe sometimes all we need is the experience, not the mechanism.

8

Wait . . . People Have Studied This?

Can't say I've ever thought much about mediums. In fact, in the past, I was one of those people who would have dismissed them as frauds. After my friend Stephanie read *Many Lives, Many Masters,* she recommended that I watch a couple of TV shows about mediums that were some of her regular favorites, because she realized the mediums repeated many of the spiritual narratives we learned from the book. Since I was already, if a bit ironically, a fan of anything spooky, macabre, grim, and ghostly (hey, I'm a scientist, but I'm also a human who likes to suspend disbelief for entertainment as much as the next person), I eagerly watched these new series, *The Haunting of* and *The Long Island Medium.* They did, in fact, repeat many of the same philosophies, which made me even more intrigued and curious. I read Kim Russo's and Laura Lynne Jackson's books and noticed that both of them mentioned being scientifically tested and certified as accurate mediums by the Windbridge Research Center. I looked up the center and found that their mission is dedicated to "conducting world-class research on phenomena currently unexplained within traditional scientific frameworks" and one of the cofounders had a Ph.D. in pharmacology and toxicology. What?! I also found that they had a program where they had implemented a strict scientific protocol through which they tested and certified sixteen psychic mediums and published their findings in peer-reviewed journals.

Then I remembered that in the interview between Chelsea Handler and Laura Lynne Jackson, Jackson had mentioned that she is happy to have scientists study her brain to understand what is different about her, to understand what allows her to perceive psychic information. This definitely piqued my interest, and I went into research mode to find everything I could. What studies were being done? What kinds of methods had they used? Had they already proved mediumship's reality? Of course, I immediately tracked down the publications and dug into them.

Here's what I found. Research into mediumship has come a long way since the infamous seances of the nineteenth and early twentieth centuries. Researchers have leveraged modern scientific methods to evaluate the accuracy of information that mediums report having anomalously received from deceased individuals. As an example, the Windbridge Research Center had implemented a *quintuple* masking protocol in their studies to rule out effects of information unconsciously picked up from sensory cues, either from the individuals getting the readings or from experimenters. Typically, studies are double-blind, meaning that both the researchers and the participants are blind to the study conditions—the gold standard for clinical scientific studies. This quintuple masking exhibited a Herculean level of blinding that went above and beyond the level used in traditional clinical trials.

The studies went something like this. A *sitter* is a person volunteering to have a mediumship reading about a deceased person they knew, called a *discarnate*. The medium is asked to give two separate readings (i.e., describe the discarnate's appearance, personality, activities, and cause of death) over the phone, one reading for the discarnate that the sitter personally knew (*target*) and one reading as a decoy. Rather than hearing the two readings directly from the medium, the sitters receive two blinded transcripts that they then score for accuracy.

The level of blinding in their studies is what most impressed me, and this was accomplished as follows (Cardeña, Palmer, and Marcusson-Clavertz 2015):

- Mediums were masked to the identities of their discarnates and sitters.
- Sitters did not know which of the two readings they were receiving (i.e., target or decoy).

- Research assistants who collected the descriptions of the discarnates were unaware of which discarnate was being read by which medium or for whom the resulting reading was intended.
- The experimenter did not know the details about the discarnate.
- When the sitters came into the laboratory to rate the readings, the experimenter did not know which of the readings was that sitter's target.

I read their studies and a few others from different groups doing similar research into mediumship. The research is really interesting because not only did it try to quantify the accuracy of the information that mediums claimed they were receiving, but it also investigated and reported on the experience of the psychic mediums themselves (i.e., their phenomenological experience), which is something in which I was interested in my own interview project. It appeared that there had been research into the descriptions of the psychic mediums' experiences from themselves. Serendipitously, I found a scientific paper published just that year (2020) reviewing all the multiple previously published studies of mediums perceiving accurate information about deceased individuals. The review found that, together, these studies showed that participants were able to accurately convey information about a deceased individual that they could not possibly have known (Sarraf, Woodley of Menie, and Tressoldi 2020).

As for what the psychic mediums experience physically while doing readings, it varies a lot, but another paper describes the commonalities across psychic mediums, especially how they describe the "energy" of readings (Beischel, Mosher, and Boccuzzi 2017). Interestingly, they describe psychic/intuitive readings differently from mediumship readings. People who are more numbers minded might object to subjective experience descriptions like these, but I personally think the best scientific insights come from listening to the people you're researching. This is especially true in a field like neuroscience where a map of brain activity would be meaningless without knowing what the participant was thinking or doing.

To share some of the more powerful insights from these mediums,

I included the following excerpts from those who were certified by the Windbridge Research Center in their research I discussed earlier in this chapter (Beischel, Mosher, and Boccuzzi 2017).

Psychics' Descriptions of Readings:

"The information generally comes to me in either quick bursts of visual and/or verbal communication."

"Getting psychic information is more like picking pieces of information off a person. If we all walked around wearing sticky notes that describe us, such as tall, smart, funny, mother, teacher, drives blue car, etc., then doing the psychic reading is like picking the sticky notes off one-by-one and reading them."

"I see very clearly all things pertaining to their life. I am shown a very slow, old, black and white movie . . . my senses are heightened and it's during this process that I am seeing with my non-physical eyes very quickly past, present, and future events the sitter has gone through, or is going through, or will be going through."

"The Masters and teachers of the Universe then show me where they need to be healed or their blocks for living the best life they can. What is holding them back?"

"Psychic information comes from someplace different than the energy of the dead. It is all around us, less focused, less of a high vibration than the dead. . . . It is the potential energy."

Descriptions of Mediumship Readings:

"The only thing is where I place my awareness. I shift my awareness to the Spirit World and when a spirit blends with me, I sense them coming into my essence from behind on my right. The Spirit is in control of the information given to me. I don't seek it out."

"The information contains things that are in a way that relates information that is personal to the person receiving the information. Names of people, streets, personal experiences. Once I said the word pearls relating to a male and pearl beads were strung into a garland and placed over the gravestone."

I needed to speak with the founders of the institute, so I reached out. This was the first time I was contacting someone outside of my circle of contacts, and I did not have high hopes that they would respond. To my luck, they replied and were happy to speak with me!

When I began telling my story to Mark Boccuzzi (one of the founders) over Zoom, on a lovely afternoon in April, he listened patiently. He told me about their mission, how they got into the work, and how difficult it had been to do this type of research. It was not only difficult to do the research because there were no mainstream funding sources for parapsychology (or "psi," as it is now known) research, but they also suffered attacks from religious individuals who did not believe in such things as reincarnation or communicating with spirits that have passed on. The stories of harassment they had to endure in doing this work—work that was their lives' passion—moved me.

I began telling Boccuzzi that I could not believe that more research hadn't been done in this field, given the implications. I figured that their group was one of the few, if not the only, looking into the topic of psychic mediums. At this point, Boccuzzi became visibly frustrated, and he seemed tired. He told me that people come to this field of study all the time thinking that they are the first to arrive at these insights, but really these questions have been looked at for hundreds of years by serious scientists and have been repeatedly validated through many different types of research. Descriptions he shared of these psi experiments floored me. He said that there were many published papers and books outlining all the research that had been done that is ignored by mainstream science and that is sometimes physically difficult to locate, as it can be left out of internet indexing. I wanted to read more, and he agreed to send me more information.

After speaking with Boccuzzi, I felt a bit deflated and, honestly, ignorant. First of all, I was actually naive enough to think that I may have been the first person to come across these realizations and to look into psychic research and related universal phenomena. I also naively believed that no one else had actually scientifically researched these topics. Both bubbles were promptly burst by my conversation with Boccuzzi, and I'm grateful for it. In my inbox the next day, I had a huge list from Boccuzzi of books, articles, and websites to read to catch up on research in this field, and I placed them into my ever-growing queue.

Around the same time I spoke to Boccuzzi, I began reading the book *Phenomena: The Secret History of the U.S. Government's Investigations into Extrasensory Perception and Psychokinesis* (2017) by Annie Jacobsen, which confirmed everything Boccuzzi had alluded to with regard to research having been done on unexplained phenomena. The book is a deep dive into the secret research programs implemented by the U.S. government into "anomalous mental phenomena" (e.g., extrasensory perception [ESP] and psychokinesis [affecting matter with mind]). Ms. Jacobsen sifted through a remarkable amount of research for this exceptional book. It was a complete information overload for me, and I had to listen to the book slowly and relisten to different parts multiple times while constantly jotting down names and events to research at a later time. It spurred me to start a spreadsheet to keep track of all the things I needed to research further, and the spreadsheet, along with all its tabs, was incredibly long by the time I finished the book. In fact, I don't think there were many things, if any at all, in the book that I had known before I had read it.

The book detailed how multiple divisions of the U.S. government, including NASA, the CIA, and the U.S. Army, had been interested and involved in research examining unexplained mental phenomena. Briefly, they worked with extraordinarily gifted psychics to better understand the nature of possible unexplored capabilities of the human mind, including the ability to remotely view other places and other times, as well as the ability to move and affect physical matter with thought alone. The government funded this work for about twenty-five years, and much of the work is still classified.

I suddenly was extremely interested in this research. Up to this point, I wouldn't have bothered to look up research into any of these unusual phenomena, and I most definitely would not have tried to defend it or explain it to others. This journey had been a personal quest to better understand my own observations of phenomena that should not exist based on our current understanding and acceptance of physics. I was more interested in the phenomenological experience of intuitives and my experience of using psychic predictions. This book changed a lot for me.

It's not that I believe that everything the U.S. government investigates is valid and necessarily true—I'm sure they have some wacky things in those classified files. However, in my role as a research scientist at a respected academic institution I have worked with the U.S. Department of Defense and other federal government agencies, and I know firsthand how difficult it is to: (a) get any type of funding for research and (b) get renewed funding. The fact that this research had been funded for over two decades and by multiple different divisions of the government made me curious if there was something really there, scientifically. I found it hard to believe that the program could have gotten funding for so long without there being some kind of evidence that warranted further investigation. I wanted to read the work and was dismayed that much of it was still classified. I did find that the scientists (Hal Puthoff, Ph.D.; Russell Targ, Ph.D.; and Edwin May, Ph.D.) who worked on the program had published some work and a few books. One of those books was on Boccuzzi's recommended reading list, so I ordered it but wouldn't read it until two months later.

I realized I was changing direction. I had started the project thinking that no serious scientists had in earnest examined spiritual or metaphysical topics, thinking that it was not possible to do so. That's how far outside the field of view the research into the "paranormal" is for mainstream scientists. The project was more about sharing my experience with other scientists to ascertain if I was crazy and to discuss the nature of the Universe to get a sense of their beliefs. I also thought that better understanding intuitives' phenomenological experience of their readings would give me hints about the possible mechanism of action of psychic predictions. Lastly, it would be a bonus to find some universal truths and a better understanding of life as we know it. After speaking with Boccuzzi and reading Annie Jacobsen's book, though, I realized that in fact a *lot* of research had been done in this field and on these topics, and I was way behind.

Before moving forward, I needed to learn more. On the one hand, it was exciting to realize that some of the answers I was seeking might already exist in the scientific literature, if off the beaten path. On the other hand, it did appear that the amount of reading I had to do was, to put it lightly, enormous. I felt overwhelmed and discouraged. I wanted the answers *now*, but it would take me so long to read everything. But so it is. I dove into the many books on Boccuzzi's list and particularly the ones that went into detail regarding scientific research that had been performed in the field of psi.

MY SPIRITUAL FRIEND

Not wanting to stop the interviews and lose momentum, I thought a low stakes interview would be to have a conversation with one of my best friends, Stephanie, whom I had dragged along on this journey. Stephanie and I have known each other for many, many years. We went to the same middle school but did not become close friends until our twenties when a mutual friend brought us together.

For as long as I can remember, Stephanie has been offhandedly telling our group of friends that she can see and sense spirits. Of course, I feel like I have to qualify that by saying that she is a very intelligent and rational person with two degrees, in business and industrial design. I don't mean to make it sound like she was always trying to convince us, but more like she would mention it in passing or after she would have an experience. As a ghost story aficionado, I loved hearing her stories. Did I know if spirits were real? No, but I trusted my friend's experiences. It is an interesting exercise to think back now to the time when I had not yet undergone this transformation and how I reacted to her stories. The skeptic mind would always first try to find a rational explanation. And as it goes with these things, it is difficult to prove or disprove someone else's experience when you aren't present for it.

Then there was the time when I actually was, unhappily, present for one of her experiences. I had just moved into a new place, and Stephanie was over for dinner. The setup of my new home was such that the dining room intersected both the kitchen and the living room, so that half of it faced the kitchen and half faced the living room. I was in the kitchen finishing up cooking dinner, and Stephanie was sitting at the far end of the dining table, the half that faced the living room. I was telling her a story, but she seemed distracted and kept glancing off to the side in the living room. Feeling unheard, I accused her of not paying attention to me. She quickly apologized and said, "I'm sorry, I'm listening. I'm just distracted because something keeps walking back and forth in the corner of my vision over in the hallway." I got chills and demanded to know what she saw. She said that it was the figure of a man. My blood ran cold, and I got very upset. I walked over but of course didn't see or sense anything myself. You bet that I didn't sleep well that night, imagining a shadowy manly figure looming over me as I drifted off to dreamland. Over the months and years that I lived in the space, she would periodically tell me when she would see him. We even affectionately named him Bob. I never sensed anything myself and eventually came to peace with having Bob as an invisible roommate.

She had other weird things happen to her. When out and about, she has been approached multiple times by strangers telling her that they are an intuitive, psychic, or a medium and that they can tell she has a connection to "the other side." They also would give her accurate, specific information about her life that they could not possibly have known. These types of people flew to her like moths to a flame. She was one of the friends I asked to join me on the visits to the intuitives to assess their abilities. Even though she believed some people could come to know things about other people intuitively, she was skeptical about whether anyone could actually sense the future. She was willing to go with me to the intuitives, determined to find out the truth. We noticed that she tended to have a deeper connection with the intuitives in some weird way, getting more detailed readings and information than the rest of us. Almost all the intuitives informed her that they could sense she was a "feeler" or an "empath." I forgot to mention that Stephanie most absolutely did not want anything to do with any of these "gifts" or "powers." She was terrified of the spirit world and was not interested in conversing with it in any possible way. Can't say I blamed her.

Although she didn't want to engage with the spirit world, Stephanie was interested in everything esoteric and paranormal. I was aware of some of the more fringe shows on television because of her, such as *Ancient Aliens*. I now remember thinking back to times when she would send me articles about strange stories of people who seemed to have knowledge from a past life expressing itself in the person's current life. I'm sure all of us have heard examples of at least one of these kinds of stories. I remember one in particular that Stephanie sent me that was about a British woman, Dorothy Louise Eady, who had an incredible story. She claimed to be able to recollect her past life as an Egyptian high priestess named Bentreshyt. She was obsessed with ancient Egypt since being a little girl, kept asking her parents to take her home (to Egypt), learned hieroglyphics, and eventually moved to Egypt and worked with the best Egyptologists of the day. Allegedly, one of the Egyptologists even took her advice to look in the Valley of the Kings for Nefertiti's tomb! I remember reading this article and thinking it was an incredible story. I remember being intrigued but also confounded, not knowing how to react. Even though it was a compelling story, it didn't change my mind, at the time, about reincarnation. This is an excellent example of how humans tend to mentally bypass things that don't fit into their framework of reality or understanding, which is exactly what I did in most of the cases when I was presented with evidence for something that I did not believe in.

While on this journey, when I was trying to excitedly show my friends and family evidence for something like reincarnation and I wouldn't get the response I wanted from them, I would become confused. Wouldn't you want to know this? It's so interesting! Doesn't it change *everything* for you? Alas, I tried to remind myself of all the articles Stephanie had shared with me that bounced right off my brain. Like a boomerang, the information went in, my consciousness noticed it, my interest engaged with it for a fleeting moment, and then it was off into the ether, never to be thought of again. I came to think of it in this way: We all have a hand of cards, and some people just don't have the card you are referring to in their hand yet. You can't force them to see a card they don't have, so just let it be. They may be dealt the card later in life, or not at all.

We had been on this path together. As I was digging into the psi research, I would punt a book to her as soon as I had finished. So naturally, I wanted to pause and have a conversation with her to inquire about her experience thus far, and to see if her thinking had changed at all based on the things we were learning.

I started off by asking her to describe her sensory experience during the times she is having an otherworldly encounter. She said that, visually, she has always seen things out of the corner of her eye, but when she turns to look it will be gone. She can usually make out a general shape, such as being able to make out a male figure. Occasionally, she can smell certain things that are not present, such as the scent of the perfume her grandmother always used to wear when she was living, or a lit match in a room where no one lit a match. She said she has also "felt energy and presences," but did not know how to further describe these experiences. She explained that the experiences scare her, and she doesn't enjoy them. Her examples were numerous, and she confided that her mother shares the experiences.

Because of her experiences, she has always been open to spirituality. The new philosophies and frameworks we had been reading, including *Many Lives, Many Masters,* had changed her in some ways and had also changed her viewpoint about life and the people in our lives, giving deeper meaning to the reasons events unfold the way they do for each of us. Since she has always been open to spirituality, she has always wondered about why certain stories and extraordinary beliefs—such as Jesus being resurrected or Moses parting the sea—are easily accepted by Christians, while others, such as reincarnation, seeing spirits, or knowing the future, are questioned. For her, the fact that many historic texts, novels, and even films have very similar stories about tapping into and utilizing a universal force—think *Star Wars*—suggests there is probably some underlying truth to the stories. 'Old me' would not have agreed with that because she would have thought that it was one fictional story that wove its way through history to continuously reappear in different forms. 'New me' was beginning to wonder, though. What if . . . ?

Stephanie said that what she found the most interesting in our journey thus far was the difference between her and me. She said that it had been amusing to watch me approach these questions from a science-first perspective, and then to eventually allow for spirituality after I found evidence. In contrast, she begins from a spiritual viewpoint and will look to see if science has any evidence to back it up—but she could take or leave the science.

I envied the way she was able to easily express her belief and conviction in spirituality. Once again, it seemed to be pretty easy for others to do it, but much harder for me. Why?!

9

Bridging the Worlds

Science Meets Spirit

While I was reading the books on scientific research into psi phenomena, I wondered how it related back to spirituality. There were two different issues for me: The first was that some people were able to perceive information about other people and the future by an unknown mechanism, and the second was the meaning of life that the spiritual philosophy of reincarnation, karma, and soul purposes provided.

In June, I was listening to *The Paranormal Podcast,* which Boccuzzi had included on his list and which I had started keeping on regular rotation, when a guest of the show caught my attention. Royce Christyn, a former Disney star, producer, director, and self-empowerment coach, came on to discuss his recently released book, *Scripting the Life You Want*. Royce discussed how he grew up in a spiritual household and learned from his mother and grandmother the power of positive, affirmative thinking in manifesting the life you want. Over the years he tried different methods to perfect the technique and understand how it worked scientifically. While I'm all for self-help books, I would not say I am an avid reader or particularly well versed in the field. However, as I previously mentioned, back at the beginning of graduate school I was interested in learning more about the possible mechanisms of synchronicities and manifestation. In graduate school I realized that it didn't matter if an exercise, such as writing your intentions down, actually worked magically or worked through fine-tuning your brain's attention on your goals—all that mattered was that it worked and could help you direct your life in an effective way.

On the podcast Royce explained that he wanted to bridge the two worlds of science and spirituality with his book, so along with describing his technique for manifestation, he outlined possible neuroscientific and quantum mechanisms that could be contributing to the manifestation of a person's goals. I perked up when I heard him describe it in this way: "science and spirituality." Although that was definitely the quest that I found myself on, I hadn't really thought of the two words together in that way, as an acceptable pairing.

I wondered about his book. I ordered it and then went to his website to see if I could get any more information and found that he was offering three online workshops through an independent bookstore to discuss his book and methods. The first workshop was the following day, so I figured I would purchase it and attend while I waited for the book to arrive. Then I noticed there was a package deal for the three workshops, so I purchased all of them, even though I was feeling skeptical and wasn't sure I would attend all of them.

The first workshop was fun and intimate, and he seemed very friendly and nice. I was worried that the workshop would be espousing the same old tenets of New Age thought that did not resonate with me and were not based in science, in my opinion, but he was very different. He emphasized that he believed manifestation worked through adjusting your brain's filter to be more laser focused on your immediate goals and to look for things in your environment that support attaining those goals. I loved that, and it definitely was true. He expressed his love for science and declared more than once his support for not depending solely on spiritual practices to address medical issues—which is an important point to raise and was one of the reasons New Age spirituality never resonated with me. I will always support modern-day science and medicine, which for all its flaws, works pretty well most of the time. Overall, it was time well spent. I decided that I would attend the second workshop, because why not. The Covid-19 lockdown had me quarantined, anyway.

Since Royce kept mentioning neuroscience during the workshop, and since the workshops were intimate, with under twenty people attending, I felt obligated to let him know that I was a neuroscientist. It felt weirdly disingenuous not to tell him. I emailed him to let him know that I was attending the workshops and that I was a neuroscientist and that I'd love to discuss the topic of "science and spirituality" with him sometime, if he was interested. I did not expect him to reply, but at least I felt like I had done my duty. He wrote back immediately in an effusive email, telling me about how he had been manifesting for months to meet a neuroscientist that he could bounce ideas off! How funny, I thought. He said he'd love to chat and gave dates and times for a meeting a few weeks away.

At the next workshop, even though we had exchanged a total of two emails, it was like we were immediately best friends. We had an instantly warm connection and at certain points during the workshop, we were speaking to each other like no one else was on the Zoom meeting. He emailed me maybe ten minutes after the workshop ended and said that he felt like we had known each other forever. He also said that we "have to 'catch up' (I know you know what I mean)"—and I did know what he meant! 'Old me' never would have understood that, but 'new me' believed that he meant we had a soul connection. He said that he could make time to speak that upcoming week since he so strongly felt we needed to connect.

We did connect and a great friendship was born, our phone calls never lasting less than two hours. Over the next few months, we shared our experiences and our theories about how science and spirituality interconnect. I had indeed found a kindred spirit, and I consider him and his husband dear friends to this day.

We discussed the problem with both fields, science and spirituality. He was far more familiar with the spirituality world than I was, and vice versa. I learned from him the surprising fact that some in the world of spirituality have contempt for science! I had no idea. I knew that they were not always keen on modern-day medicine, but I did not know there was actual contempt. Sadly, I had to inform him that the same was true for science's view of spirituality, for some people. We constantly brainstormed about why it was this way and how we could help bridge the worlds. I was so excited to meet someone who felt the same way.

PSYCHIC SPIES

In June, I had another turning point when I read *The Reality of ESP: A Physicist's Proof of Psychic Abilities* by Russell Targ (2012)—another book on Boccuzzi's list. Now, writing this in the future, I chuckle to myself at all the "turning points" I thought I had because I had no idea of what was yet to come. Every time I thought, "Okay, I definitely believe this," or "Ah, it's all in our minds," I would inevitably round another corner of information and have to start my analysis all over. Having said that, I did round a corner forever on believing that there is solid evidence for psychic or intuitive functioning in humans after reading this book and some of the original published scientific papers.

Russell Targ was one of the researchers, along with fellow laser physicists Dr. Hal Puthoff and Dr. Edwin May, from the remote viewing program called "Stargate" that was funded by the U.S. government and performed at Stanford Research Institute (SRI) that was outlined by Annie Jacobson in her book *Phenomena. Remote viewing* is a perception technique that allows a person to quiet his or her mind and describe mental images with regard to some person or event that is distant in space or time.

The program was funded by the CIA, NASA, the Defense Intelligence Agency, Army and Air Force Intelligence, and many other government agencies. Why would the U.S. government be interested in such a capability? The program was initiated in the 1970s when the United States was engaged in the Cold War with the Soviet Union. You can likely imagine how useful it would be to the U.S. government to have their personnel capable of reporting on activities in the Soviet Union from the comfort of Virginia. Also, the Soviet Union had an active research program on psychic phenomena for spying purposes, and the United States did not want to be left behind.

In his book, which is geared toward scientists, Targ systematically lays out the experiments conducted, and the evidence accumulated by the team over the twenty-five years of the program, or at least the amount that is unclassified. Much of it remains classified to this day. Targ described experiments in which they tested remote viewing participants' abilities to draw randomly selected target locations that were distant in space, meaning not colocated with the participant. All told, the total body of research work contained 26,074 trials from 154 experiments involving 227 different subjects (May et al. 1989). Since I found the work so interesting, I will describe some of it here, but I do highly recommend Dr. Targ's engaging and easy-to-read book to anyone interested in learning more.

Keep in mind that this research was conducted from the 1970s to the 1990s. The first experiments were conducted with psychically gifted individuals who were already skilled in remote viewing. The researchers would receive the latitude and longitude coordinates of a location about which the funding organization, for example the CIA, was interested in acquiring information. Then the researchers would sit with the participant and ask them about their impressions of the location. Participants would verbally describe what they "sensed" about the location and would also sometimes draw their impressions by hand. Through this method, the participants described and sketched a Soviet weapons factory, a failed Chinese atomic-bomb test *three days in advance,* and other military targets.

In one case, the participant drew and described a secret National Security Agency (NSA) listening post on the East Coast, even going so far as to accurately write the code words that were written on the file cabinets! What was interesting about this particular case was that the coordinates provided to the viewer were actually for the vacation cabin of the CIA agent monitoring the study, which was located a quarter mile over the hill.

When asked why the NSA listening post was described rather than the cabin, the participant said, "The more intent you are on hiding something, the more it shines like a beacon in psychic space."

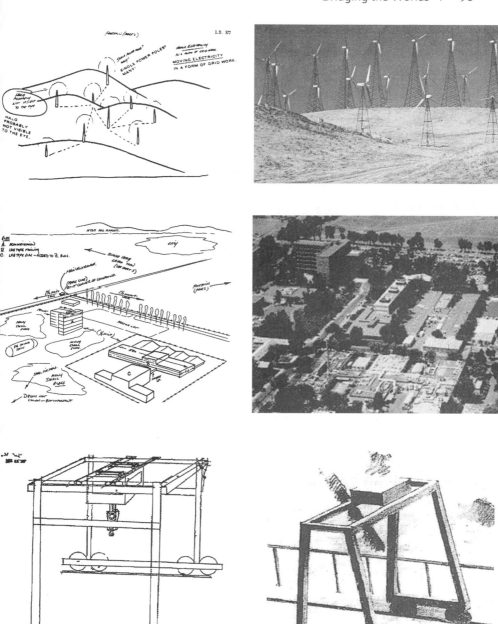

Figure 9.1–9.6. Drawings from the SRI remote viewers (left)
alongside photographs of the targets (right) by the
U.S. Air Force Threat Analysis Center (AFTAC)

The SRI team also performed studies more locally to test these abilities. In their very '70s-era experimental protocol, the SRI researchers had a box of sixty file cards, each containing a target location somewhere in the San Francisco Bay Area and within a half hour's drive from the SRI research lab (located in Palo Alto, CA). These cards resided in a secure office safe of the vice president of the research institute to reduce the suspicion of foul play. The remote viewing participants stayed on-site at the research institute with one of the researchers in a Faraday cage—a room sealed off from electromagnetic signals—while another researcher would use a calculator with a random number feature to choose one of the target locations from the file cards. Then two of the researchers would drive out to the target location while the researcher with the remote viewing subject would guide the subject to draw and describe his impression of the target location of the other two researchers by asking questions about what they were perceiving. The participants described these distant and unknown locations with amazing accuracy.

One thing I found particularly interesting about the studies was what they discovered about time and how it relates to space in remote viewing. Sometimes the participants would describe or draw items from the target locations that did not exist at the time of the experiment. The researchers would initially believe these were mistakes or misconceptions, but in some cases, it would turn out that the item that was drawn was either previously located at the target location in the *past* and had since been removed or would be built in the *future*! Through this, the researchers learned that they must not only specify location to the participants, but also a *specific time frame*. Another seemingly impossible, yet reliably replicable, feat the researchers observed was the participants' abilities to know and describe the randomly selected target location that the second researcher would drive out to *before* the second researcher had selected the card listing the location.

This team of psychics and scientists even assisted the Berkeley police department in the kidnapping case of heiress Patricia Hearst by having a remote viewer identify and *name* the kidnapper from a book of mugshots and describe where he saw the kidnapper's current location, which led to the capture of the kidnapper and the release of Patricia Hearst. Then President Jimmy Carter admitted to the media that the coordinates provided by one of the program's remote viewers was used to accurately locate a missing plane (Stilwell 2018; Targ 2012)! I am not kidding and highly recommend Targ's book for the firsthand account of these incredibly unbelievable, yet true experiences.

Some of the participants that were recruited as controls turned out to be psychically adept themselves, so the researchers discovered that this remote viewing/psychic ability is latent in many humans and can be enhanced with training. Once the researchers had a protocol down for teaching naive participants how to do remote viewing, the Army Intelligence and Security Command (INSCOM) asked them to organize a remote viewing training center under army command on the East Coast where they trained army officers in remote viewing with great success. The chain of education continued, as these army officers that were trained with this unique skill set went on to teach remote viewing across the United States and the world to anyone interested. They organized a professional society called the International Remote Viewing Association that still holds an annual conference where the latest applications of remote viewing are discussed, such as investing in the stock market!

Due to the nature of the research topic, extraordinary precautions were taken with the SRI research to ensure results were genuine, including the use of double-blind experimental protocols. Additionally, research monitors were dispatched from the funding agencies (e.g., CIA, Army Intelligence) to overlook the scientific methods and execution, and SRI had a special committee, the Scientific Oversight Committee, composed of top-level SRI scientists and managers. For a full rundown of all the precautions, of which there were many, I recommend the original published work.

Many of the results from experiments conducted on remote viewing at SRI were remarkable (Targ 2019). Results that could be made public were published in top scientific peer-reviewed publications, such as *Nature* and *Proceedings of the Institute of Electrical and Electronics*

Engineers (Puthoff and Targ 1976; Targ and Puthoff 1974). All in all, the evidence was solid by current scientific standards. Further, an independent review of the evidence was even commissioned by the CIA that included analysis by Jessica Utts, Ph.D. (1996), a renowned statistics professor from UC Davis and former president of the American Statistical Association (ASA), who found that "psychic functioning had been well established." She said the following of the evidence in her report to the CIA concerning the remote viewing work done at SRI:

> Using the standard applied to any other area of science, it is concluded that psychic functioning has been well established. The statistical results of studies examined are far beyond what is expected by chance. Arguments that these results could be due to methodological flaws in the experiments are soundly refuted. Effects of similar magnitude have been replicated in a number of laboratories across the world. Such consistency cannot be explained by claims of flaws or fraud. The magnitude of psychic functioning exhibited appears to be in the range between what social scientists called a small and medium effect. This means that it is reliable enough to be replicated with properly conducted experiments with sufficient trials to achieve the long-run statistical result needed for replicability.

Now that I've laid out the important experimental and statistical facts about the program, I turn to the actual phenomenological experience of the remote viewers and how they describe it. One of their most gifted viewers, an artist named Ingo Swann, described the process as cutting through the "mental noise." He highlighted the tendency that our brains have to name things, invoke memories, analyze, and imagine while trying to perform a remote viewing exercise, and he called this "analytical overlay." He explained that analytical overlay prevented him from going further into the remote viewing experience and getting the information he wanted to get. He had to quiet his mind to increase the odds of perceiving the intended information over all the other noise.

After reading Targ's book, it occurred to me that none of these results were aligned with the current scientific materialist paradigm, but the methods used to get the results were scientifically sound. So either our methods are wrong or the paradigm is wrong. Of course, my scientist brain began to emerge and question whether the results were unique to this particular group and could have been attributable to an experimental flaw. Many of the great book recommendations from Boccuzzi were summaries of over a century of research, so I began voraciously reading much of the work in this field to see what else had been done. I also began locating and reading the original scientific literature myself to discern the details of the studies, as well as to explore what research had been done recently. If this was like any other scientific field, there were surely discoveries happening daily.

I want to take a minute here to discuss the stigma around research into the paranormal, which is highly stigmatized in both the scientific realm and larger society as a whole. When I started this project, I wanted nothing to do with any paranormal research. My idea of paranormal research was untrained individuals going to various haunted locations trying to record ghost activity. Don't get me wrong—I love a good ghost hunting show (shout out to *Ghost Adventures*)—but only as entertainment. I would not have wanted to look at their data or read their reports. I know that this is also how mainstream scientists view *any* research that smells of paranormal, because that's how I viewed it. However, reading the work of Targ, Puthoff, and May changed this for me. It made me want to throw labels such as "paranormal" or "parapsychological" out the window because who cares what it's called; it's interesting research!

While I was deliberating on whether I should just accept that some things in life are mysteries and leave it at that, in came these scientific findings showing the validity of mediumship and psychic phenomena.

I was aware that the research topic, subjects, and methods were unusual and taboo for mainstream science. I was sharply reminded of this every time that I went to excitedly discuss these bizarre findings with a scientific colleague and found myself saying qualifying statements such as, "I know this is weird and kind of crazy, but . . . " I would then immediately start rattling off the multitude of scientific safeguards taken by the researchers in their work and the statistical robustness of the research as justification for what I was going to say next. Yet numbers are numbers, and the work was convincing. It made me wonder what other research might be scientifically sound, important, and groundbreaking but ignored because of unusual topics. Might there be other well-credentialed, brilliant scientists who happened to focus their talents and interests on fringe areas of science that others ignored? I found the answer to be a resounding yes.

10

The Upside Down
(Research)

I am not sure exactly what I was expecting to find in the literature, but I probably thought there might be just a few studies or anecdotal reports at most. I definitely was not expecting research at the scale that I discovered it to be. As a quick summary, psi research has been conducted for over a century, by hundreds of scientists, from multiple labs across the entire world, in *hundreds of thousands* of participants and in many prestigious institutions, such as Princeton, Cornell, Duke, UC Berkeley, and UCLA. Despite having almost no funding at all from the main source of science funding—which is the United States federal government—the field has managed to produce a substantial amount of research. Since it was such a well-established field, there had been many reviews and meta-analyses conducted.

Spoiler alert: There is substantial evidence for the reality of psi that cannot be discounted by the common criticisms of faulty study design, selective reporting, or fraud. In fact, due to the heightened scrutiny that psi research has received over the years and the vetting of study designs by critics, the study designs can be more rigorous than those found in typical social science research (Watt and Nagtegaal 2004). The evidence for the reality of psi is on par with that for other established psychological phenomena, although there is no current understanding of the mechanisms behind the phenomena. I know that almost no mainstream scientist will read those sentences and believe it—or if they're trained well, they won't—so I invite them to do the reading themselves, like many others have.

Because I was so unaware of the field and research methods, and of course the mind-blowing findings, I found all of it so engaging. Some of the protocols were very paranormal, and even reading them made me uncomfortable, and I almost discounted them immediately based on my emotions alone. In spite of that, I kept reading and found just *so much* evidence and learned that the study designs had been through layers and layers of scrutiny, criticisms, and corrections. The researchers used the same statistical methods we use in "normal" science, and sometimes they used even more conservative statistical analyses than we use. It genuinely seemed like good research, even though my bodily reaction of disbelief just goes to show how deeply embedded our beliefs become and how difficult it can be to overcome them. I was even more surprised to learn that many of the studies used basic protocols from psychology and neuroscience with only slight tweaks! For all these reasons, I will share the protocols and findings with you since it is likely that you, too, had been unaware of this invisible world of psi research. I came to think of the psi research world like the Upside Down from the TV show *Stranger Things,* because it seemed like an alternate dimension, out of sight but actually occurring in parallel right on top of us.

BUT FIRST, SCIENCE BASICS

Before I dive into the summary of findings from the review, let me back up and explain a few key science concepts. Let's start with correlation. A correlation is when two variables have an established relationship, such as always increasing or decreasing together. Just because two variables are correlated to each other does not necessarily mean that one *causes* the other. For example, if a correlation exists between the consumption of ice cream and sunburns such that sunburns increase as ice cream consumption increases, it doesn't mean that ice creams cause sunburns. In this example, both variables are probably related to a third variable, such as spending time outdoors during a hot summer day.

Now, I'm sure you've heard of probability before, but let's examine it further. Probability is how likely an event is to occur. For example, if I took a coin and tossed it, I would expect the probability of the coin's landing on heads and tails to be equal, or 50%. If I tossed the coin one hundred times, I would expect the distribution of results to be approximately fifty heads and fifty tails over a series of rounds. In science we use statistics to calculate probability in experiments. A metric known as the *probability value,* or *p-value,* is used to tell us how likely it is that a correlation between variables or a difference between groups would have occurred by random chance. For many technical reasons I won't explain here, science typically uses p-values that are less than 0.05 to indicate that an effect is *statistically significant,* or less likely to be caused by random chance alone; in other words, a meaningful correlation is shown to exist between two variables, or a meaningful difference between two groups.

Let's now introduce reviews and meta-analyses for those who are unfamiliar with these research methods. In science when a particular research topic has been investigated for a while, the scientific community likes to take a step back and look at the cumulative evidence to see what the general findings are. Because biological systems have so much variability, we can see dramatically different results across studies, even when the studies are seemingly identical or nearly identical in methods. Due to this issue, we never rely on just one study to be the final word on proving or disproving something. Rather, we look at all the studies together to see if the hypothesized effect can be repeatedly measured by different labs, as well as get a sense of the strength of the effect. A *review* gives a summary of the current state of knowledge on a particular topic. For example, a review of all the studies investigating the neural correlates of psychopathic traits might report that particular brain regions, such as the medial prefrontal cortex and the anterior cingulate cortex, show consistent dysfunction across all psychopathic trait studies, suggesting that they play a key role in the expression of these personality traits. The review may go on to report that other brain regions, such as the mirror neuron system and cerebellum, also show dysfunction, but that which brain areas are found to be dysfunctional depends on the tasks of the study and potentially other factors. Then an analysis of the experimental designs and how they differ from each other may be conducted to find reasons for the discrepancies, such as finding, in this example, that the mirror neuron system and cerebellum seem to be associated with the emotional detachment aspect of psychopathic traits, in particular (Johanson et al. 2020).

Similar to a review, a meta-analysis examines the relevant research studies on a particular topic for similarities and differences but also examines the *effect sizes* of the findings. While p-values can indicate whether an effect exists and is likely not due to random chance, an effect size can indicate how large or small the effect is. Due to the variability of biological systems that I just mentioned, the weaker an effect is, the easier it can get lost in the noise. But if a claimed effect can be repeatedly observed by independent researchers, even if it is a weak effect, we can reasonably surmise that it is likely to exist. Effect sizes (ES) can be classified as small (ES = 0.10), medium (ES = 0.30), or large (ES = 0.50) (Cohen 1992; 2013). Another way of thinking about the effect size is to say, the larger the number, the stronger the relationship between two variables or the stronger the difference between groups.

Large effect sizes are typically observable by anyone, whereas small and medium effect sizes are evident to careful observers. Here's an example to tie p-values and effect sizes together: Imagine we want to know whether having a bunny as a pet makes a person more likely to think baby bunnies are the cutest baby animals in the animal kingdom. A survey is conducted to gather the opinions of 900 individuals on which baby animal is the cutest: 300 individuals who do not own pets, 300 individuals who own pets other than bunnies, and 300 individuals who own bunnies. From the results, a relationship appears to exist between thinking baby bunnies are the cutest baby animals and having a bunny as a pet, as opposed to having any other animal as a pet or having no pet. The p-value will tell us how likely it is that this observation is a true effect and did not occur due to random chance. The effect size will tell us whether the difference in thinking baby bunnies are the cutest baby animals is small (such as twice as likely) or large (such as one hundred times as likely). As a frame of reference, social psychology experiments typically report effect sizes of 0.21 (Richard, Bond, and Stokes-Zoota 2003). Meta-analyses can also report additional analyses that examine publication bias (the field of science encourages the publication of positive results more strongly than negative results, so there is a bias for that in the literature), and the relationship between effect size and the quality of study design (sometimes, effects that are seen in studies with low-quality design disappear in better designed studies). Anyway, with all of this to consider, reviews and meta-analyses are a great way to get the most recent overall picture of the current research on a particular topic.

Conveniently for me, a review of the major meta-analyses of psi research was published in 2018 in the journal *American Psychologist*, which is a journal of the American Psychological Association (Cardeña 2018). This recent review well encapsulates the decades of psi research and highlights the diversity of the types of experiments, the length of time they have been investigated, and the number of investigators and participants that have been involved. In short, I was blown away by the scale and robustness of the research. Under the psi umbrella, there are a few different types of phenomena, and the meta-analyses in the review were divided by these types, so I will discuss them each in turn below. However, before I do that, I want to take a minute to discuss how scientific materialism posits that reality is a thing that exists independently of our observing or measuring it. And it assumes the human body perceives information about reality via its senses. I will briefly describe some of the ways that researchers measure human perception and behavior. It will be necessary in order to understand the experiments in the research I'm about to describe.

The assumption in scientific materialism is that time is linear and that your body perceives sensory information about objects or events that are in reach of your senses. Information coming in from the senses can be perceived consciously or unconsciously and can influence behavior and physiology. Let me give some examples using emotional pictures.

Emotional content is processed faster than other content in the brain, and it is theorized that the reason is that the brain cannot process all of the incoming information and needs to prioritize. Since emotional content is usually related to evolutionary processes, like survival and mating, these get priority (Dijksterhuis and Aarts 2003; Eimer and Holmes 2002; Eastwood, Smilek, and Merikle 2001). Emotional pictures (e.g., erotic pictures) in comparison to neutral pictures (e.g., a lamp) cause changes in physiology, such as increased heart rate and skin conductance (i.e., sweating). This effect occurs even if the picture is processed by the person unconsciously, meaning that the picture was flashed on the screen too quickly for the participant to consciously report that they saw it. In a task where participants are asked to choose which picture they prefer from a set of two equally neutral pictures, and if an erotic picture is subliminally paired with one of the pictures, participants will choose the erotically paired image more frequently, thus demonstrating the effect on behavior.

As for data collection methods of science, when you come in for an experiment, there are a few things that scientists might measure. One research method is to measure behavioral responses such as having the participant consciously give a response to a task, which may be writing responses (e.g., surveys) or making selections and choices on a computerized task. Another method is to measure cognitive responses, such as measuring the speed at which a participant responds to a task. A third research method is to measure automatic, unconscious, autonomic responses, such as heart rate and skin conductance.

With that, let's get started with looking at the scientific evidence of unexplained, or psi, phenomena.

REVIEW OF META-ANALYSES OF PSI RESEARCH

Anomalous Cognition

One of the categories of psi is called *anomalous cognition,* when a person has seemingly perceived information when there is no obvious means of normal perception. There are subcategories to this called clairvoyance, telepathy, and precognition. *Clairvoyance* is the ability to gain information about objects or events that are distant in space and out of sight, without the use of the ordinary senses. *Telepathy* is mind-to-mind communication. *Precognition* is a form of clairvoyance when the perceived object or event is distant in time, usually in the future.

Forced Choice

One type of experiment to evaluate anomalous cognition is called a *forced choice experiment*. In a forced choice experiment, over a series of *trials* you might be presented (by a randomized computer program) with five types of cards, each with a different symbol (e.g., a circle, square, triangle, squiggly line, or cross), and asked to choose, ahead of the trial, which symbol the computer will randomly choose in the next trial. In some studies, participants are randomly selected from the general population, but in other studies, participants are preselected for having known or claimed psi abilities. In these experiments the participants know the possibilities of the outcomes—meaning, they are aware of the five different types of cards. Statistically, we would expect the participant to choose the correct card 20% of the time, just by random chance and not due to any particular psi ability. But one large meta-analysis showed a strong ability for participants to correctly choose the right card before it was shown, far more than chance alone would predict. This analysis was conducted on 309 forced choice experiments carried out by sixty-two investigators from 1935 to 1989 with more than fifty thousand participants and two million trials (Honorton and Ferrari 1989). The finding was extremely unlikely to have occurred by random chance, as evidenced by the p-value $(p = 6.3 \times 10^{-25})$. The effect size, which, again, is a measure of the magnitude of the phenomenon, was very small (ES = 0.020), but the overall significance was greater than 10^{20} (more than a billion billion). They also reported that the effect size had remained constant through the decades and that the quality of study design was not related to the study outcome. An analysis for determining whether it was possible that the study outcome was biased due to the use of solely positive results being published also could not reasonably explain away the results. In forced choice studies, it has been reported that results improve if participants are selected based on having performed well (above chance) on prior experiments. Basically, some individuals are better at psi than others. However, it has also been shown that performance can be improved when participants were given trial-by-trial feedback, letting them know when they got something correct. Based on those experimental methods, another meta-analysis using the 17 best studies that had selective samples and trial-by-trial feedback were examined and revealed that preselected participants knew the symbol on the hidden card more than would be expected by chance on the forced choice experiments, and the overall effect from this group of studies (ES = 0.12) was higher than the previous analysis that combined preselected participants and the general population, suggesting that the general population waters down the effect.

A second meta-analysis using 91 studies of forced choice experiments conducted between 1987 and 2010 (Storm, Tressoldi, and Di Risio 2012) supported the results of the first meta-analysis. The effect sizes are small across the studies, but we would expect that. Remember, larger effect sizes are typically observed by everyone and are more readily accepted as evident. The fact that anomalous cognition is not widely accepted as fact because not every person experiences it or is aware of the phenomenon would already hint at the phenomenon's having a small effect size. If the effect sizes were very large, we would expect to see something akin to what is portrayed in the *X-Men* movies where the differences in superhuman abilities between mutants and humans are very pronounced.

In summary, some individuals can correctly select, with higher than chance accuracy, which of five cards will be next presented during an experiment. For example, if you and I were conducting a non-computerized version of this task, it would be like if I held up a card that was printed with one of five symbols, just like Bill Murray does in the first *Ghostbusters* movie, and you were able to know the symbol on multiple rounds more frequently than could be due to random chance alone.

Free Response

Another type of experimental protocol used to evaluate anomalous cognition is called a *free response protocol*, in which participants freely report, without restrictions, the impressions they get about a future target, such as a location or a picture. In these types of experiments, the target is part of a large pool of targets that is unknown to the participants, such as a randomly selected photo from a large pool of photos. There are multiple different possible protocols of this nature, including remote viewing, ganzfeld, implicit anomalous cognition, and presentiment, and I will discuss each briefly below.

Remote Viewing

Let's say one of your friends drove out to a location that is unknown to you, and you were asked to describe what you sense about your friend's location. If your friend randomly chose the Golden Gate bridge, you might report sensing "red, tall, steel, water, traffic," or you might even draw something resembling a bridge.

As I discussed in earlier sections of this book, many remote viewing experiments were conducted at SRI. Similar to the forced-choice experiments from above, a given number of targets is preselected for a remote viewing experiment, such as having five preselected photos. Before the experiment even begins, it is ensured that each target is as likely to be selected as any other of the targets. After the remote viewer records their impressions during the experiment, the impressions are given to a blinded judge, or a judge who is blinded to the actual target. The judge is provided the five preselected targets (the actual target and four decoys) and asked to rank each of the possible targets, where a rank of one indicates that the target matches the impressions from the remote viewer most closely and five means it matches least. By chance, the true target would receive each rank with equal likelihood, and the average rank would be three. Anomalous cognition is thought to have occurred when the average rank is lower than three over a series of trials (see Utts, 1996 for more details). An analysis of 770 free-response remote viewing tests conducted at SRI resulted in the true target's being ranked as the one most closely matching the remote viewer's impressions over a series of trials with odds against chance of over 300 million to one (Utts 1996; Milton 1997) suggesting that the remote viewer's impressions are due to anomalous cognition and not random chance. After the remote viewing program at SRI was discontinued, one of the SRI research team members moved to Science Applications International Corporation (SAIC), a research and development consulting firm, to continue the research. An analysis of 445 remote viewing tests from SAIC's data resulted in the true target's being ranked as the one most closely matching the remote viewer's impressions over a series of trials with odds against chance of 1.6 million to one. These analyses also showed that preselected participants were more likely to provide impressions of a target that could be correctly matched to the target by a blinded judge (ES = 0.38) than were novices (ES = 0.16). Even the well-known psi skeptic Hyman (1995) couldn't refute the strength of these findings, saying that the SAIC experiments were "well-designed and the investigators have taken pains to eliminate the known weaknesses in previous parapsychological research. . . . I cannot provide suitable candidates for what flaws, if any, might be present."

Remote viewing experiments were also conducted at Princeton University's Princeton Engineering Anomalies Research (PEAR) Lab. A meta-analysis of a total of 653 sessions was conducted, resulting in the true target being ranked as the one most closely matching the remote viewer's impressions over a series of trials with odds against chance of 33 million to one (ES = 0.20) (Dunne and Jahn 2003), again suggesting that anomalous cognition is occurring rather than random chance driving the results.

In summary, scientific research, with sound experimental design and methods, has repeatedly shown that some individuals are able to sense a remote target, such as another person's location. They can give accurate descriptions of a randomly selected, unknown, distant location, and this is not just good guesswork, because the statistical analysis of these findings showed, again, that they were happening at a rate far greater than random chance alone.

Ganzfeld

One of the most common free-response protocols is the ganzfeld experiment. *Ganzfeld* is a German word meaning "whole field." In this type of experiment, a relaxed state is induced in the participant by placing them in a comfortable chair, having them listen to physical relaxation instructions and white or pink noise, and covering their eyes. The task for the participant is to become aware of an unknown image or clip chosen randomly, which might be shown simultaneously on a distant computer with nobody watching it (clairvoyance) or someone watching it (telepathy) or is chosen after the participant makes a selection (precognition).

I'm going to describe a telepathy ganzfeld experiment as an example. I realize that of the research I have presented thus far, this example will seem the most far-fetched, but stick with me. In this type of experiment, there are two participants who are separated into two rooms. One of the participants is placed into a relaxed state with the methods I mentioned above, and the other participant is given the task of sending thoughts about the experimental target (e.g., a randomly selected photo from four photos) to the other person for thirty minutes. Yes, that's right. Sending thoughts. The person in the relaxed state then gives verbal impressions of what they perceive, and at the end of the experiment they are shown the four possible target images and asked to choose the one that most closely matches what they perceived. In these studies it is assumed that 25% of the time, the perceiving participant will select correctly, simply by chance.

There have been more meta-analyses conducted on ganzfeld experimental protocols than any other type of experimental protocol in the field of psi. Since the first ganzfeld experiments started being conducted in 1974 to the present, there have been at least ten meta-analyses conducted (Storm, Tressoldi, and Di Risio 2010; Honorton and Ferrari 1989; Milton and Wiseman 1999; Bem and Honorton 1994; Storm and Ertel 2001; Hyman 1985; Williams 2011; Tressoldi 2011; Rouder, Morey, and Province 2013; Baptista, Derakhshani, and Tressoldi 2015). A majority of the analyses found that the receiving participant was able to correctly identify the image chosen by the other participant and that this was happening at a rate far greater than chance alone, with the odds against chance ranging from twenty to one to over one trillion to one. Some of the studies included in this analysis used preselected participants, and these had larger effect sizes (ES = 0.26), compared to the studies that used nonselected participants (ES = 0.05). In other words, these findings confirm that the ability to receive another person's thoughts is present in some people, but not necessarily in the general public.

In summary, some individuals appear to have the ability to correctly select an image chosen by another person, simply by apparently receiving thoughts from that person. Time and again, this was shown to be accomplished at rates far beyond what would be considered random, or chance, accuracy. So it might not be so far-fetched to try to send thoughts to your best friend from across the room.

Implicit Anomalous Cognition

In *implicit anomalous cognition* protocols, the psi component is hidden from participants, and that's why it's called "implicit." Participants will respond to a seemingly normal psychological task. In actuality, however, an aspect of scientific materialism is flipped surreptitiously in the protocol. For example, Cornell professor Daryl Bem executed a series of experiments flipping the assumption that time is linear.

Bem used a well-known social psychology experiment that leverages the "mere exposure" effect. The way the experiment usually works is that the participant will look at a pair of images that have been matched for similarity and will be asked to select the one they prefer. It's a pretty simple task for the participant. What they don't know is that the computer has randomly selected one of the two images to be repeatedly paired with a subliminally presented different image, such as an erotic, neutral, or negative image. In a typical experiment, the subliminal image would be presented before the participant chooses which image they prefer, and participants tend to prefer images subliminally associated with erotic images more frequently than other images; conversely, they avoid selecting images subliminally associated with negative images.

In Bem's studies, he presented the subliminal images (i.e., an erotic, neutral, or negative photo) *after* the participant's response. Counterintuitively to what would be expected by scientific materialism, he observed the expected effect of participants' preferentially choosing images associated with subliminal erotic images at odds greater than chance of one hundred to one, even when the subliminal image was presented *after* the participant made their selection.

He performed nine different studies with over a combined one thousand participants and found that, in all but one, experimental manipulations that occurred *after* the participants already gave their responses somehow affected the responses (Bem 2011). I'll tell you about one more of the experiments he did, because this could be a useful one that you could use in your life, if you feel so inclined. In this experiment, Bem tested whether memory could work both ways. We know if you study a list of words before a recall test, the number of words you can recall from the list improves. Bem had students rehearse the list *after* the recall test but still found a significant difference between the groups. Studying the words *after* the test affected performance on the test!

A meta-analysis of all replication attempts up to 2015 that included 90 experiments from 33 laboratories found that content from the future can influence a person's behavior in the present, at a rate of eight billion to one or, in other words, far greater than chance alone would predict (Bem et al. 2016). A deeper analysis allowed the researchers to divide the replications into two groups: "fast-thinking" unconscious processing and "slow-thinking" deliberative processing (Kahneman 2011; Kahneman, Lovallo, and Sibony 2011). The most remarkable results came from the experiments using fast-thinking/unconscious protocols and erotic stimuli.

In summary, this body of research shows that a person's decision making in the present can be influenced by information from before or *after* the decision is made, raising many questions about our models of time, and about the *independence* of events in the present from events in the future. Think of how this could play out in your own life! Practically, before you take a test, it might not be the worst idea to plan to carefully review your test performance after you take it, hoping that what you learn posttest will travel back to improve your performance on the test. You might even consider pairing the review with erotic content. I realize that sounds ridiculous, but that's what the research suggests. In summary, randomly selected priming stimuli could significantly affect a participant's response even if presented *after* the participant's response was already recorded. This effect was more likely to occur when erotic photos were used as priming stimuli and for fast-thinking and nonconscious responses.

Presentiment

Presentiment experiments rely on automatic physiological responses, rather than conscious choices or reporting. Our bodies' physiological responses, such as heart rate, skin conductance, and breathing, change in response to emotional, evocative, or startling stimuli. For example, if someone jumps out to spook me unexpectedly, my heart rate will increase, and I will start to sweat. The hypothesis behind presentiment is that the information perceived about a target *before* the event happens (anomalous cognition) will also cause a physiological response in the participant before the event, and the physiological response will be in line with the emotional value of the target.

An example of a presentiment experiment would be a typical psychology experiment where photos are randomly selected from a set of photos that range from neutral to emotional, such as the International Affective Picture System, which is a database of standardized images for studying emotion. They are presented to the participant in a random order, and one or a few physiological responses are recorded from the participant. The experiment becomes a psi experiment when the researcher analyzes the physiological data in the time frame *before* the stimulus is presented to test for physiological changes during emotional trials.

A meta-analysis was done on twenty-six relevant presentiment experiments from between 1978 and 2010 (Mossbridge, Tressoldi, and

Utts 2012; Mossbridge et al. 2014). The studies reviewed showed that participants displayed a physiological response *preceding* the randomly presented stimulus far more frequently than chance alone would suggest, ranging from 17 million to 370 billion to 1 (ES = 0.21). Further, the authors split the studies based on quality of study design into one group with 13 higher-quality studies and another group of 13 lower-quality studies. While the result was still statistically significant in both groups, the higher-quality studies had a higher effect size.

The experimental design used in presentiment studies is widely used in psychology and neuroscience, leading cognitive neuroscientist Julia Mossbridge, Ph.D., to surmise that data in studies that were *not* specifically looking for psi effects (i.e., traditional research studies) would contain the presentiment effect if the time frame before the stimulus was analyzed in the data. Mossbridge looked at studies that were not looking for presentiment, identified twenty-four studies, requested the data from the authors, and received data from two of the studies. In the studies, there were four categories of photos: neutral, pleasant relaxing, pleasant arousing, and unpleasant arousing. She found evidence for presentiment in skin conductance, heart rate, and skin temperature, as well as differences in brain activity.

Another analysis was done on 37 presentiment studies and showed evidence of presentiment at a rate of 1.5 billion to 1, compared to chance alone (Tressoldi 2011). A more recent update to Mossbridge's meta-analysis from 2018 included 27 new experiments and also found evidence of presentiment (Duggan and Tressoldi 2018).

In summary, physiological responses can increase *before* emotional stimulation, again raising the possibility that our models of time are incomplete. In practical terms, might there be a way to monitor, track, and use physiological responses when weighing the future outcomes of decisions? This could look like checking in with how your body feels before making decisions. Is your heart racing? Are you sweating? This might help you come to a decision.

That's a lot of experiments! Let's stop for a moment to take a breath. The studies showed that (at least some) humans, at levels above random chance, can accurately (1) choose which card will be randomly selected, (2) receive mental impressions of items or distant locations, (3) perceive thoughts about specific items or locations sent from another person, and (4) receive content from the future, both in their behavior and physiology. What?! Seeing such strong results from so many different labs (some Ivy League!) and in scientific protocols with which I was familiar was a game changer. It turns out that you don't even need to test intuitives specifically because some people from the general population also exhibit anomalous cognition, or intuitive, skills. While these experiments did not test for *spiritual* phenomena (such as reincarnation or the existence of spirits), they did provide evidence for the fundamental basis of intuitive readings, while also calling into question our models of space and time. *Our minds can access information from other locations and times.* Confidence in the intuitive readings I had received were not a huge problem for me since many were extremely accurate, but I liked having the scientific evidence. It was bringing spirituality *and* science together in my personal experience, something I did not think was possible. But does the information only flow one way? If we can receive information, do we also emit it?

Anomalous Perturbation

The second class of psi phenomena, after anomalous cognition, is called *anomalous perturbation*. This category requires a little more explanation than anomalous cognition. The idea behind anomalous perturbation is that focused attention and intention from a human can influence the physical environment. This phenomenon, even more so than anomalous cognition, can be very counterintuitive. Although it is prevalent in self-help, self-actualization, and New Age or New Thought philosophies, the concept of our thoughts affecting our physical environment can be difficult to swallow because this cause and effect is not seen as readily in our daily lives. However, as you will see from the results below, there is evidence to suggest the phenomenon is real, although small effect sizes were reported in the literature.

Noncontact Healing

A *noncontact healing* experiment, which is one way to evaluate anomalous perturbation, typically has a participant intentionally send healing thoughts or energy to a second participant. Other names for this type of healing that may be more familiar are Reiki, energy healing, intercessory prayer, and distance healing. Noncontact healing experiments have been conducted on humans, animals, plants, and in vitro cell cultures. An example of this kind of study would be comparing the reduction of fibromyalgia pain in a patient group receiving Reiki healing versus patient groups receiving sham Reiki healing (a person not trained in Reiki pretending to do a healing) and standard care. For nonhuman studies, a sample study might be comparing heart rate variability in rats during or after Reiki healing or sham Reiki healing.

A meta-analysis by Roe, Sonnex, and Roxburgh (2015) divided studies into two groups, one that contained plants, animals, and in vitro cell cultures and another that included humans. (They separated the studies in this way due to a known placebo effect on humans, which can be difficult to rule out in the human findings.) After adjusting the number of studies in each group to account for other differences, the meta-analysis researchers found evidence of effective noncontact healing among study participants in both groups of studies (ES = 0.115 and 0.22, respectively). Although these effect sizes are small, they are almost comparable to the average effect size reported by psychological studies (ES = 0.2) (Richard, Bond, and Stokes-Zoota 2003). Also, the studies used in this meta-analysis varied *widely*, probably because there is not an overabundance of studies in this particular area, so it will be necessary to do more targeted analyses in the future to determine effect sizes for each type of noncontact healing.

In summary, there seems to be some evidence for a valid effect of noncontact healing (although much more good quality research is needed)—so don't feel bad sending those healing thoughts to others! It might be working. Currently, scientific materialism disregards the idea that sending healing thoughts to another person could physically help them heal. But again, there are many phenomena in nature for which we do not yet have explanatory models, and this is not a reason to dismiss evidence. Rather, we should view the lack of explanation as an invitation to explore. These findings seriously question our current scientific materialist understanding of mind-matter interactions.

Random Number Generators and the Global Consciousness Project

Since living systems are so variable, anomalous perturbation experiments over time have turned to using devices called random number generators (RNGs) as targets. An RNG is a small box that can be hooked up to a computer with circuitry that drives them to randomly produce zeros and ones from quantum processes. The Princeton Engineering Anomalies Research (PEAR) Laboratory, run by Princeton's former dean of engineering, Dr. Robert Jahn, produced one of the largest data sets using an RNG and found that participants' directed attention and focus could significantly influence the output of an RNG in the intended direction; for example, producing more ones than zeros (Bösch, Steinkamp, and Boller 2006).

In 1997, based on the findings from the RNG experiments that suggested mental intention could cause RNGs to behave nonrandomly, the Global Consciousness Project was started by Princeton University psychology professor Roger Nelson, Ph.D. The idea behind the project was to examine whether the coherence of human consciousness around larger world events, such as 9/11, could affect the performance of RNGs. The project set up a global network of RNGs at sixty-five different sites around the world to continuously generate data (random 0's and 1's). Data from the time frame around specific world events, such as the three hours following the 9/11 attacks, was collected from all the spatially separated RNGs and analyzed. The team looked for structured data in the normally random output and for correlations across the disparate RNGs; this data was then compared to other time frames when no such events occurred. In an analysis of 461 world events, the data from the RNGs were found to be more structured (less random) than you would expect by chance (ES = 0.33) in the time frames closely surrounding the world events.

In summary, mass consciousness of the planet can influence the output of an RNG to behave nonrandomly when there is a common point of directed attention and focus. This may be the ultimate discovery resulting from all of the psi findings listed in this chapter. Synchronizing our attention in a positive way has the most potential for the planet, demonstrating that we are more powerful if we come together on the issues we focus on. Damn. This implication dropped a sense of responsibility into my lap. How can we focus on important common issues when we are so distracted by surviving our busy lives and chasing material goods and success? Asking people to focus on the collective good while they are struggling with mental health issues and unresolved trauma seems unfair. During my own existential crisis, it had been too difficult to get out of my own head. But maybe that's why we should prioritize healing ourselves, so that we can show up centered, focused, and ready to get to work on issues for the collective that require our immediate attention and effort, like climate change and social justice. If our collective energies or subconscious are intermingled, we should be invested in the welfare of all, including ourselves.

WHAT IMPROVES PSI PERFORMANCE IN RESEARCH?

One thing that became clear from all the psi results is that some people do in fact have heightened psi abilities, such as being able to correctly receive and describe mental impressions of a remote location or correctly guess the next randomly selected card. This is not unexpected. But whether it is due simply to some people being born with these abilities or whether these are skills that can be practiced and strengthened, just like cooking or basketball, is that classic nature/nurture debate. What I believe is that humans range in skill on various traits, including psi abilities. Yes, we can always improve skill by practicing, but it is likely that we are born with certain predispositions and advantages. For example, I know I could never play basketball like Kobe Bryant, no matter how many hours I put into practice.

What are the traits that distinguish individuals who exhibit psi abilities in these experiments from those who do not? The research shows that the individuals who *believe* that they have this ability have openness to experience, have a mental practice such as meditation, and have previous experience in a psi experiment (Cardeña, Palmer, and Marcusson-Clavertz 2015; Zdrenka and Wilson 2017). Interestingly, artists, in particular, tended to show more psychic abilities than other groups (Holt, Delanoy, and Roe 2004).

There is also evidence that experimental protocols that induced altered states of consciousness, such as meditation, induced relaxation, hypnosis, and ganzfeld, produced above-chance results in some of these psi studies (Baptista, Derakhshani, and Tressoldi 2015). This is in line with the personal report from Ingo Swann from the SRI remote viewing studies, in which he described his remote viewing process as cutting through the analytical overlay of his mind to retrieve the target information. Quieting the mind gets you access to more info.

IS THE DATA FOR UNEXPLAINED AND ANOMALOUS PHENOMENA STRONG?

Because of the variability of natural systems that I mentioned earlier, science operates on a preponderance of evidence. In the case of psi, as is being discussed here, there is more than enough evidence to support the claim that these phenomena exist. There is at least as much evidence as is used to validate other psychological phenomena. In fact, psi studies have shown reasonably good replication, while the replicability of psychology studies has recently come into question. In the "Many Labs" project, 36 independent laboratories attempted to replicate 16 psychology studies that were published in top journals. Alarmingly, only 34% of the replications reasonably statistically matched the original studies (Open Science Project 2015; Open Science Collaboration 2015). This is what we in the sciences call the "replication crisis."

For comparison, I looked up a recent meta-analysis of a number of studies that investigated the neural correlates of empathy for pain

(Fallon, Roberts, and Stancak 2020), a very popular topic of study in cognitive neuroscience. The meta-analysis found 123 studies possibly appropriate for review but dwindled that number down to 39 studies after the review deemed a majority of them inappropriate for inclusion for various reasons. These 39 studies made up just 31% of the body of research, and combined, these replicable studies had a total of 1,112 participants. This is the *entire* literature for the neural correlates of empathy for pain. For comparison, Daryl Bem's *studies—not* meta-analyses—on precognition, which I discussed earlier, had over 1,000 participants—and then subsequently had over 90 replications from 33 different labs, meaning that there is substantially more replicated evidence for precognition than exists for the entire literature on neural correlates for empathy for pain! Someone might argue that my first example, which uses brain imaging technology that is a newer and more expensive experimental method, might be hard to replicate for that reason alone, so that could be an unfair comparison to make. I'll concede to that point, but I'll add another point of comparison: I also looked up a second recent meta-analysis on another popular research topic, fear conditioning, with studies that examined physiological responses, such as skin conductance, to stimuli (Mertens and Engelhard 2020). This meta-analysis started with 110 studies, but after reviewing and removing inappropriate or poorly conducted studies, they were left with 41 studies, but meaningful results could only be found for 30 of those 41 studies; so about 27% of these studies were replicable. The 30 studies had a combined total of around 1,000 participants, so right in line with the other examples I gave here. It's clear to me when I compare these examples: The amount of evidence in support of psi is much higher than other common topics of research in neuroscience and psychology.

The effect sizes from the psi meta-analyses ranged from 0.012 to 0.39, with many being comparable to the average effect sizes of social psychology experiments (ES=0.21) (Richard, Bond, and Stokes-Zoota 2003). In fact, the effect sizes of some psi protocols are much larger than those for the clinically recommended uses of some common medications, such as aspirin for the prevention of heart disease (0.12), metformin for type 2 diabetes (0.03), statins for cholesterol lowering (0.15), antidepressants for depression (0.38), and angiotensin-converting enzyme inhibitors for hypertension (0.16) (Leucht et al. 2015) and would be classified as "evidence-based" applying the criteria of clinical practice (Haidich 2010).

This is not a comprehensive review. There is so much data and so many interesting experiments that I could never do them justice, and other people have eloquently described them elsewhere. The point of this book is not to go over the scientific evidence in great detail, but I touch on it here to show its importance in my own journey. And it's kind of cool, right?

Even at the beginning of reading all of this material, I was still skeptical. After having finished Russell Targ's book, I thought that I was convinced, and the case was closed. Despite all that, and as it goes with these things, as soon as I started reading new material, I began questioning everything. It is *exceedingly* difficult to overcome years of training, *even if you've had personal experiences*. After a certain amount of time digging in, however, it was just not debatable any longer. This is especially true given that I work in and understand social cognitive neuroscience so well. I know that many of these findings are very hard to replicate; that makes it hard to find consistent evidence. The fact that there had been so much work done across the field—work that had been vetted by professional statisticians—made it undeniable for me. It is as Jessica Utts (1996), former president of the American Statistical Association (ASA), said: "If we use the same standards applied to all other scientific research, then there is no reason why the results of this kind of research are debatable except for the fact that no theoretical explanation exists—but this has never stopped science before."

There have been countless observations in scientific research that have no explanation from modern scientific findings and theory. In modern medicine, the placebo effect is accepted as a real effect and considered such a serious confound that it is controlled for in clinical studies, but we still have no current explanation for the mechanism behind the effect. We are not even sure of the true purpose of laughing, sleeping, or yawning! Lest I forget, the biggest mystery of all in humans is how and why we have consciousness. How does our experience of the world and our lives arise from firing neurons? Do I experience the sunset the same way that you do? How does the sensation of feeling arise from neurotransmitters crossing synaptic clefts? I have a secret: Neuroscientists have absolutely no idea whatsoever.

Actually, the more I thought about it, the more I realized that we have many missing explanations or theories for many of the observations we make in human biology, psychology, medicine, and cognition. In that context, these results were not that odd. What was odd was the animosity the psi field received—but I get it. Scientific materialism has made us trust only what we can perceive with our five senses, and this theory is so well perpetuated in society that to tug at it with something like supernatural theories is to pull the metaphorical rug out from under our feet—and humans don't like that.

LET'S TAKE A PAUSE

This was an incredibly important inflection point in the journey, so I want to stop for a moment.

Whether or not the findings in these psi studies are believable also relates to our own experiences. We saw in the discussion above that, often, the research showed rather large differences between people who were adept with or practiced at their psi abilities and those who were not. So if you've genuinely never experienced any of these unexplained phenomena for yourself, then I can understand how it's hard to believe it exists for anyone else. Even for those of us who have experienced cosmically good intuitive readings (or any other unexplained phenomena), it can be challenging to come up against prevailing paradigms and worldviews.

However, the effects also seemed ubiquitous to me. I wondered, as I read these studies, if these same practices would work for me, and in fact, I have seen a notable difference in my own life brought about by developing a meditation practice. Unfortunately (or fortunately?), I have a mind that practically never shuts off; I feel like it runs at the speed of light. My thoughts come so fast that I have a hard time keeping up with myself. But adding a meditation practice has been astronomically helpful in quieting my mind and allowing space between the thoughts to emerge and hold. Meditation has helped me cut through the analytical overlay. I have been trying to become aware of what and how I am thinking, *generally*. But if I pay attention to the images that come to my mind during meditation, maybe then I would see more spiritual phenomena for myself.

One day during meditation after I had reviewed this research, I decided to set an intention to allow any information about the next few days to enter my consciousness. I watched myriad images flash across my mind, but I had trouble making sense of them. The strongest image that arose was of an elongated half dome shape, like an oval cut down the middle, with a concave surface, and the thought that the shape looked like the Disney Concert Hall in downtown Los Angeles. When I came out of the meditation, I shrugged off the experiment as a failure and went about my day.

A few days later, a friend and I decided to take a spontaneous road trip to Joshua Tree, California, a nearby desert town, where neither of us had been before. She convinced me to drive out to Giant Rock, a large freestanding boulder in the Mojave Desert. After parking the car, we stepped out into the staggering heat and dead silence of the desert. While I was pulling my hat down to shade my eyes from the blazing sun, we walked toward the huge boulder. I looked up to take in the majestic view. Just as I took in the sun-illuminated shape of the rock—a half dome with a convex surface—a feeling of familiarity washed over me, and at the exact same moment (I swear it happened all at once), my friend said, "Wow, cool. It reminds me of the Disney Concert Hall." Goose bumps ran down my entire spine in the 115° Joshua Tree heat as the realization hit that this exact moment—the shape of the rock, the angle from which I viewed it, my friend mentioning the Disney Concert Hall—was what I perceived during my meditation days before. I turned to my friend, wide-eyed and in disbelief. No freaking way! Had I just perceived the future? As my newly favorite spiritual teacher Ram Dass would say, "Far out!"

11

Back to the Intuitives

Armed with all this new scientific literature and phenomenological descriptions of how clairvoyance, precognition, and remote viewing work, I thought back to the intuitive readings that I received. I reread my notes and viewed the readings through a new lens and with a better understanding of the intuitives' perceptions. Alongside all the scientific research, I was also reading work from skeptics to balance it out. In regard to common criticisms about "faulty study design" (scientists can always find something wrong with any experimental design), psi research has been so intensely scrutinized there actually existed solid experimental designs—better than in some other lines of research—that have been vetted and approved by skeptics. There are serious people doing serious research in this field, with other serious people examining and scrutinizing the work. My deep dive into the science made that clear to me.

Then there are the anecdotal stories you hear about people trying to debunk intuitives. You will hear criticisms such as, "The description they gave me was vague," or "They didn't see me getting fired," or "They could not correctly give all the details of the clothes I was wearing accurately," so "Ha! They're a fraud!" I now had a better understanding of the nature of intuitive perceptions from the scientific literature, and from personal experience: It comes in flashes of images and colors, parts of the whole are seen, a general overall sense or impression of something is received. With this, I realized that the real problem is one of—assumptions: Some people who go for intuitive readings often have expectations that do not match the reality of the situation. They're asking for a play-by-play of their life for the upcoming year; expecting names, dates, and details is an unreasonable request. As we saw in the SRI studies, intuitive impressions can be vague, can require interpretation, and can be subject to the intuitive's own personal bias (they are human). There is a range of abilities in the level of detail an intuitive can provide (and maybe intuitives could be more upfront about what's possible). It's like going to your doctor, telling them you need a diagnosis that same exact day, with a course for treatment that includes insurance-covered prescription medicine that you can pick up from your pharmacy, a list of the exact side effects that you will have from the prescription medicine, and a date by which you will be fully healed. Ambiguity from medicine is acceptable, but not from a "fuzzy phenomenon" like intuitive reading? Absurd. Maybe if more people understood the nature of this phenomenon, expectations for readings would match what's possible.

Just like anything else that has to do with humans, we should also expect that the ability to use psi—one expression of which is an intuitive reading—might be highly variable. Some human behavioral or physiological responses—like reflexes—are relatively constant. But other human behavioral responses—like mood—are highly variable, as pretty much any human on Earth can tell you. The point being that if you receive what you consider to be an intuitive reading that is off, there could be a myriad of unknown factors affecting the reading.

The motivation behind debunking intuitive readings is a different story. Some people simply like the idea that they are in complete control of their lives too much to allow for the possibility that their future can be known in advance. As a Type A control freak, I get that. But one thing the science shows is that just because aspects of the future can be predicted does not mean they cannot be changed. Even the extremely talented psychics from the SRI experiments reported that the future was malleable, not concrete. From a personal and spiritual perspective, I can share one more thing. The greatest (and by far hardest) lesson I was learning on this journey was that the more tightly I grasped and gripped for control, the more I suffered. The life lesson that I had been ignoring, that life is unpredictable and you can't plan and control everything (even if you get one hundred intuitive readings), pummeled me until I finally caved in. The fastest path to peace was to just *let go* and surrender to what is. Everything is as it should be.

In any case, these amazing scientific findings started to reveal the conditions under which psi talent could be elicited and leveraged, but the mechanism still remained elusive. I had already validated through personal experience that certain intuitives could know or perceive specific and accurate things about my past, present, and future that they would have no other way of knowing, such as the private details of a family accident from my childhood, my real name in Farsi that only my extremely close family members use, and the timing of specific job changes. One of the most impressive intuitives accurately described my current situation by explaining (without my having said anything much on the phone call) that she could see that I felt like my world had been "shattered, like a broken mirror" and that I was on a bridge between science and spirituality. She also used the metaphor of a fully formed butterfly still in the chrysalis to ensure me that the transformation would eventually end. My research review simply amplified and extended the validation I had witnessed with statistics. If intuitives are providing verifiable information, then is the spiritual framework they described more likely to be true?

Thinking very deeply about these findings, I just did not see how you could accept the scientific method and not accept these results. Some people argue the phenomenon goes against our understanding of physics and thus cannot be true. Well, something's gotta give here! Luckily, recent findings in physics are beginning to pave a path toward understanding how we could live in a world where our minds can access other places, times, or even other minds.

DO THESE RESULTS VIOLATE
THE LAWS OF PHYSICS?

I knew that looking further into the psi studies wasn't likely to get me answers to the spiritual questions, such as how these observable psi abilities were related to spirituality and what they meant for my own life and humanity. I was deep into the research by now, though, and too curious to not read further about possible mechanisms. We know that observed psi effects are not due to traditional electromagnetic forces, for example, because when Faraday cages are used in experiments to block out all traditional known electromagnetic signals, like they were in the remote sensing work at SRI, psi effects are still observed. Many people are uncomfortable with the results of psi research because they appear to violate the laws of physics—I mean the Newtonian laws of physics. But if we threw out evidence for which we had no existing theories in science, we would not have discovered most things. People who are very greatly bothered by the fact that no explanatory mechanism exists to explain unexplained phenomena may take comfort in the current conversations going on between classical physicists, quantum physicists, philosophers, neuroscientists, and others in an effort to produce a unifying theory.

Now we're about to get pretty far out there, but hang with me. This chapter is about physics and quantum physics, and the main point of this section is not for me to pretend that I am an expert in quantum physics—because I most definitely am not—but rather to highlight that there are precedents for some of the observations seen in psi research. Many of these discussions surrounding mechanisms for psi include quantum physics.

There are multiple assumptions that we use in the construction of the scientific materialist concept of reality that appear to be broken by the evidence from psi research. The assumptions are about *realism* (the assumption that there is an external reality with physical properties that exists independently of observation), *locality* (objects are completely separate), and *causality* (time moves forward like an arrow—the past affects the future). However, experiments from the field of quantum physics have already brought these assumptions into question and upended the traditional view of what we consider the physical world.

Take, for example, *the quantum observer effect,* or *the quantum measurement problem,* one of the most mind-bending findings of quantum physics. The basic finding is that an observer of the experiment can change the outcome of the experiment simply by observing or measuring it. It can be a difficult concept to wrap your mind around if you've never heard of it before. This is how it works: Quantum physicists use the famous double-slit experimental protocol (Davisson and Germer 1927) in which they send particles of light (or any other elementary particle) to a barrier that has two slits and then measure the pattern or behavior of light on the other side. When we think about reality, we think matter is solid and is made of particles, and that those particles exist no matter what. That's realism. If that were true, then the light would behave as particles, go through one or the other of the two slits, and be measured as particles on the other side, independently of whether the particles are being observed or measured. But what actually happens is that the light only behaves as particles (and you can thus tell which slit the particle went through) if the experiment is measured by a detector or observed by the experimenter. If they do not observe the experiment and it is not measured, then the light behaves like waves of probability, and you get an "interference pattern." That's what I meant earlier by "collapse of the wave function." It's like an array of possibilities exists (also called waves of probabilities) before an observation is made. Once an observer interacts with the light by observing it, the probabilities collapse into a particle. *The act of observing changes physical matter.* So the #1 assumption of realism doesn't hold under all conditions. What classical physics would define as a solid piece of matter became dependent on the state of observation. About the results, John Wheeler (1973), an eminent American theoretical physicist, claimed that "in some strange sense the universe is a participatory universe." Niels Bohr, renowned quantum physicist, said, "When we measure something, we are forcing an undetermined, undefined world to assume an experimental value. We are not measuring the world; we are creating it."

The second strange finding from quantum physics is called *entanglement.* The basic idea behind this principle is that two particles are entangled in some way such that when they're separated, even by a great distance up to one hundred kilometers, the particles' states mirror each other instantaneously. So if you shook one particle, the other would also shake at the same exact moment. "Instantaneously," in this case, means faster than the speed of light, which Einstein had predicted would not be possible. Einstein called this "spooky action at a distance." This breaks the locality assumption—which assumes that all objects are separate—and is known as nonlocality. *Nonlocality* is a property of both time and space. Based on these findings, it has been suggested that, in principle, any objects that have interacted are forever entangled and that there exists quantum interconnectedness of the whole Universe. Erwin Schrödinger (1935), Nobel Prize winner and one of the pioneers of quantum physics, said that entanglement was "the characteristic trait of quantum mechanics." John Stewart Bell (1964), physicist and creator of Bell's theorem, said, "No theory of reality compatible with quantum theory can require spatially separate events to be independent."

The third principle has to do with time. The classic understanding of time is that it moves along an arrow from past to present to future. We do know from Einstein's theory of relativity, though, that space and time are, in actuality, both relative and dependent on the position and speed of the observer and the gravitational field. Again, recent findings from quantum physics suggest that future events may affect past events, something that is called *retrocausality*. In *delayed-choice double-slit experiments,* the decision by the experimenter to turn on measurement detectors occurs *after* the photon has passed through the two slits. The results of the experiment (i.e., whether waves of probability are observed) again depend on whether the detectors are turned on, even though they had been turned on *after* the event (Kim et al. 2000; Manning et al. 2015)! Daryl Bem, the professor from Cornell University, modeled his precognition experiments that I discussed earlier on these findings from quantum physics.

These are classic findings from quantum physics, but new findings are emerging every single day that question the standard model of physics. In 2021 the Fermi National Accelerator Laboratory discovered that a tiny subatomic particle called a muon did not behave as predicted in an experiment, suggesting that it was sensitive to something that we could not yet measure with standard physics. The *New York Times* reported on this important finding's implications, saying, "The result, physicists say, suggests that there are forms of matter and energy vital to the nature and evolution of the cosmos that are not yet known to science" (Overbye 2021).

In sum, these findings from the field of quantum physics show how the assumptions we make about reality are not necessarily true and that examples of these principles are found elsewhere in nature. However, I also want to highlight that the theories of physics and quantum physics, for now, do not fit nicely together, and there is no unifying theory, so I do not want to suggest that these quantum processes would necessarily extrapolate to systems at a larger scale. However, there is reason to believe, from recent evidence in the field of quantum biology, that this may be the case.

Quantum physics was independent of other fields for a long time, and it was unthinkable to suggest that the observable quantum effects could be extended to, say, animal or human behavior. However, more recently it has been discovered that it's not that quantum effects do not exist in larger systems, but that they are easily drowned out by environmental noise, and thus harder to detect (Barreiro 2011; Kominis 2015). Quantum phenomena have now been linked to photosynthesis (G. Engel et al. 2007), the human sense of smell (Turin 1996), and the ability of birds to migrate (Ritz 2011; Ritz et al. 2009; Solov'Yov et al. 2010). For the human sense of smell, based on the finding that two molecules with different chemical compositions smell the same, it has been proposed that rather than the *shape* of the molecule being what is translated into a smell, it is the *energy* contained within the bonds of the molecules that are signaled to the receptors via quantum tunneling. For birds a photon of light that hits the bird's retina causes two molecules, each with an unpaired electron, to become entangled with each other and coherent with the Earth's magnetic field. The coupling between the molecules and the Earth's magnetic field is translated into vision so that the bird can actually *see* differences in the Earth's magnetic field as it tries to navigate to its destination! More research is needed to examine quantum effects in larger systems and to bridge the two fields of physics.

These findings from quantum physics go against the common sense perception of reality. Nonetheless, they are facts. I'll leave here this quote from Richard Feynman (1967), one of the most distinguished physicists of the twentieth century and winner of the Nobel Prize for his work on quantum electrodynamics, in case it comforts you:

> The difficulty really is psychological and exists in the perpetual torment that results from your saying to yourself, "But how can it be like that?" which is a reflection of uncontrolled but utterly vain desire to see it in terms of something familiar. . . . Do not keep saying to yourself . . . "But how can it be like that?" because you will get . . . into a blind alley from which nobody has yet escaped. Nobody knows how it can be like that.

I did have a difficult time reconciling the psi research with my evolving idea of spirituality. I thought I was on a spiritual journey, and suddenly I was reading "paranormal" research. I was aware that a more comprehensive theory of everything was needed to tie it all together, but somehow knowing that there was a precedent in quantum physics for psi effects was comforting. I needed to pause because I had gone far adrift from where I started, trying to understand the novel spiritual framework that I had learned about that involved soul lessons, karma, and reincarnation. Most of the peer-reviewed psi research was very scientific in that it focused on methods and mechanistic explanations but lacked any discussion of the connection of how these findings related to spirituality, so there was no help there.

In my mind, spirituality and psi were very different. But after doing some more reading I found that many authors outlined the way the two concepts are intertwined. Targ, for example, explained how psi phenomena allow firsthand experience of the transcendence of space and time and the awareness that we are more than our physical bodies. When unbound from our minds, our fundamental essence, divine nature, or consciousness is one with all of existence. There is no time, space, or separation. These concepts have been discussed since ancient times in spiritual schools such as Buddhism, Hinduism, and many more. In texts like *The Yoga Sutras of Patanjali* (Satchidananda 1984) (written twenty-five hundred years ago), psychic abilities were understood, accepted, studied, and considered by society, rather than shunned. Psi phenomena were viewed as nothing more than discovering your divine nature of nonseparation, or that your consciousness/soul was connected to a greater, wider reality. The Buddhist text *The Flower Ornament Scripture* (Cleary 1993), written in 100 CE, also describes precognition, telepathy, and communication with the dead as part of our nonlocal and timeless awareness, where the past, present, and future are all infinite. Many of these traditions believe the essence, soul, or consciousness evolves and is reborn into different lives and that these rebirths are dictated by karma. They also believe that spirits exist, which can be understood simply as unembodied consciousness. It was all there, and it was all conceptually related.

Consuming books and podcasts from various spiritual schools had a slow but marked effect on my day-to-day thinking and feeling. Over time, the seriousness of everything dissolved. A levity began to emerge in me, which was a totally foreign feeling, and it wasn't unwelcome. I welcomed back joy. That's not to say that I wasn't still a total emotional mess, because I was, especially since I was flipping personal long-held beliefs left and right, and my identity was slipping through my fingers. My ego was throwing a tantrum to be rivaled by no one. But I started amusedly *observing* my reactions instead of *identifying* with them. Actively practicing compassion for myself and others became a habit, and that drastically changed my approach to most things. Whenever a desire for something arose, I would immediately think about how it would be okay if it didn't happen the way I wanted because there might be a better thing that could happen. Maybe the Universe did have my back. My existential suffering—my lifelong companion—was quieting down, and I thought to myself, "Is this . . . could this maybe be what everyone calls . . . peace?" The road to here was to let go and stop struggling against myself so much. That was it? Simple, but excruciating! I wondered how long it would be before I started wearing kaftans and speaking in soft, hushed tones. All jokes aside, I was beginning to realize that I could either be right and pretentious or I could be content. My ego furiously thrashed around when it realized I was leaning toward choosing contentment; but I had *never* felt this good with my old identity. Not even close. Happiness is one sunny day, but existential contentment is a seventy-two-degree sunny yearlong climate.

But I was still curious how it all tied together, how spirituality and science could blend. Why would they be separate anyway? If the Universe has a spiritual nature to it, why wouldn't science be able to describe or measure it? Or could spirituality also somehow explain the scientific nature of the Universe? There wasn't a very good model for how psi phenomena could occur, and I definitely did not know of any model for disembodied consciousness. For some reason, I felt like I needed some sort of foundation in science to solidly believe, still. That was my ego. I did not feel comfortable and secure in solely trusting spirituality, because . . . well, how would I explain that to others? My go-to style of communicating ideas was to provide theories or data as evidence. Even though my intuition was telling me that I had enough experience to trust what I knew, my ego wanted proof of a spiritual nature to the Universe. Otherwise, the baby dandelion seeds of belief would float away. To be fair, phrases like "science-backed," "evidence-based," and "data-driven" increasingly permeate our society, so they seep into our modes of thinking and are difficult to discard. And nowadays, any belief not backed by science can cause others to label the believer as crazy, stupid, or delusional. So I still wanted more proof. Who might be able to help me get to these deeper answers? Enough reading—I needed to speak to some experts.

12

The People Who Know

In the period between July and December 2020, I was able to have discussions around spirituality and psi phenomena with a variety of current and former scientists, engineers, researchers, physicians, and U.S. government personnel from various sectors and agencies, such as the Department of Defense, the U.S. military, and the "three-lettered agencies" (CIA, FBI, etc.). I dubbed this group "the people who know" (a.k.a., the experts). One introduced me to the next, and that one to the next person, and that to the next person, and so on. Since I'm sure the introduction email I sent them was an unusual one, I would bet it was my credentials that got me callbacks. I chose them because they were familiar with the catalog of psi research and unexplained phenomena.

They were more than happy to discuss with me the nature of the Universe, how much we don't know, possible models of reality, and possible explanations for these unexplained phenomena, which are actually, as it turns out, not really that uncommon since they are widely experienced and reported all over the world, across all countries and time. Just to be crystal clear, *no classified information was shared with me at any point*. All the people I spoke with were very clear about what they could discuss with me, what they had personally witnessed, what they personally believed, and what they were conjecturing.

Each one suggested various books, and based on their recommendations, I found myself diving into literature on physics and quantum physics, ancient spiritual texts, transpersonal psychology, altered states

of consciousness, magic, philosophy, theories of the Universe, unidenti-
fied aerial phenomena (UAP), and the secret societies of the world. To
say it was a rabbit hole would be a massive understatement. I genuinely
felt like Alice, excitedly bumbling my way through Wonderland! Since
I had to wake up at four or five in the morning to fit this new learning
adventure into my normally busy schedule (I did still have a demanding
day job), I was more like a disheveled, sleep-deprived version of Alice
who started thinking it might not be the worst idea to burn some sage
once in a while—you know, just in case. Looking back, I still cannot
believe I woke up so early for, basically, independent study—but *that's*
how compelling and intriguing it all was!

Isn't it so like life to give you the most life-altering conversations
and then prohibit you from sharing? I wish I could share the conversations because the details were so incredible, but instead I will share
my reactions to them and hope that conveys how profound a shift they
initiated within me.

For millennia and across every human civilization there have been
whispers of a source that runs through everything and that connects us
all. *Star Wars* fans will recognize this as "The Force." It is possible this
source actually exists, although we cannot directly measure it yet.

It is also very possible that there are other dimensions of *reality* in
addition to our own. It may be possible that something about certain
individuals, such as intuitives, and certain locations on Earth make it
easier to access the source or other dimensions. For example, there are
certain locations on Earth where there seem to be higher than normal
reports of sightings and experiences of unexplained activity that seem to
belong more to folklore than reality. As to what could be found in these
other dimensions, I leave it to you to imagine.

Although I can't provide the creepy, unnerving details of *everything*
I learned from my new friends, the important point is that their version of reality was far different from mine. Their version only raised
many more questions about spirituality and the nature of our Universe
for me. I didn't really know what to think. One of my contacts asked
me at one point whether I thought, as a scientist, all the evidence he

outlined for me was legitimate, true, and possible, or whether I thought he was nuts. I told him that I wished I could show him my brain over the course of a month so he could see the ups and downs of belief. One day I would wake up believing everything I had heard and read, and then the next day I would wake up thinking that I had fooled myself, only to then run again through all the evidence that initially convinced me. This was a difficult time for me, and I relied heavily on my new-found spiritual practices to ground me, having compassion for myself during this transformation, and letting go of whatever I could. I also told my contact, and this was very true, that I find it more unlikely that such accomplished, intelligent, capable individuals of diverse back-grounds and experience (ages, ranks, professions, etc.) would come to the same or similar conclusions about the nature of reality (based on evidence they had seen) without there being some truth to it. To this point, these individuals also knew much more than they were ever able to tell me. At the end of the day, although we revere science so much in our modern-day society, sometimes it just comes down to whether you trust and believe in someone or something, because evidence is not always available for you to analyze yourself.

On the one hand, I was more inspired than I had been in many years. I woke up each morning excited to read and learn more about these new topics that could help me piece together a theory about the nature of the Universe—you know, a really casual hobby. I felt like I had been living in a box and the top of the box had just been blown open and I was stepping out. The flip side of that is the identity issue. While I was intellectually enjoying the new knowledge, part of me, the part who was a trained scientist, 'old me' was flipping out. She was los-ing her grip, and she didn't like it. Did all this new information mean that I couldn't look down on people with fringe beliefs anymore? Who would I even be then? (Answer: a much better person!) Looking at the new material I was reading, I would periodically think to myself, "Ugh, I can't believe I'm the kind of person to be reading this stuff now." I would have to step back and ask myself, "And what kind of person *is* that? Someone who follows evidence where it goes?" Because that is what I was doing. Just because the evidence led me somewhere that 'old me' thought was fictional and ridiculous simply because it did not fit within my former worldview did not make it any less real. In science you cannot just erase data with which you are uncomfortable.

I trusted and believed these individuals, but more importantly, I started trusting myself and believing in my own experiences. I began questioning why I would have to explain, justify, or provide proof for my newfound beliefs to anyone. They were *my* experiences and *my* truths. What constitutes "proof," anyway? For one person, proof might only be considered definitive when they see it with their own eyes. Another person may not trust their own perceptions, and for them, proof can only be obtained through multiple eyewitnesses. For yet another person, the only acceptable type of proof may be the kind that can be measured on electromagnetic instruments, or through the scientific method. My entire journey was about searching for proof of spiritual phenomena, and it began with the last type of proof I just mentioned. I needed scientific proof. But eventually, I realized that my definition of proof was changing.

I will take this moment to say that I hope more of the fundamental and foundational research that has been done on the nature of reality, but that has been kept classified, eventually becomes more readily available. It could be the innovative spark that is missing from science today.

Lest you think I used this project to distract me from myself—which I admittedly most definitely did do—I swear that I also did work on myself in other ways. I was too curious about the past life regression literature and the reportedly profound healing effects to not explore that further. In case you're wondering, yes, I did try past life regression. I have a wonderful therapist, Susan Fisher, Ph.D., who was trained by Brian Weiss, M.D., Michael Newton, Ph.D., and Roger Woolger, Ph.D., the heavyweights in past life regression, who practices both typical psychotherapy and past life regression. Since I had been practicing meditation, I found it easy to relax and watch the images that floated into my mind. The regression took me to a past life in the 1860s in Ireland, and the life lesson of the lifetime was to keep my heart open after heartbreak and not shut people out because I had closed my heart after my parents in that lifetime had died when I was fourteen years old. My therapist had told me before the session that I might feel like I was making up the entire thing, but to ignore that and just keep going. When I reached the end of the life in the regression, I did indeed feel as though I had made the story up, although I don't consider myself a very creative or imaginative person, and there were tons of details. I felt that way until my therapist directed my soul to meet with the souls of the people from that life in the "space between lives."

For each relationship my therapist asked, "What are you saying to them, and what are they saying to you?" To my utter surprise, I began telling her about the exchanges and immediately started weeping from the deepest depths of *my soul*. I was so entirely caught off guard that I can hardly describe it. It was the kind of fast and deep emotion that feels like it comes from your belly and hits you so hard that your brain doesn't even have time to process the feeling. It's the kind of emotion that your body feels first, to which your mind then reacts. I have only felt that way a few times before in my life when hearing extremely emotional news. I honestly could not believe how much emotion was pouring out of me. If it had stopped with the first conversation between souls, then maybe I would have thought it was just a reaction to the whole experience, but the waterworks kept flowing for each one, and I just could not stop myself. I swear I felt *true relief* being able to say things with regard to these relationships like, "I'm sorry" and "Thank you." It was very weird. There weren't any details from the life that I could try to validate because it was just a quiet Irish farm life. At the end of the session my therapist pointed out that in the regression I kept mentioning how cold I felt. She asked if that was significant to me at all. I laughed and said, "Well, I do hate being cold, which is why I could never live anywhere with extreme winters."

My therapist said that's how you know it's real, the emotion. The session actually did have a very profound effect on me in that it automatically extended my view of the relationships in my life. For example, since my parents had died early in that life, I came to view every minute in this current life with my parents as extremely precious. I had always felt that way, but it was now amplified. I also got an extended view of some of the current relationships in my life that helped me reframe and better understand them. It was, as I have come to learn, what people call "healing."

13
Neuroscience and Consciousness

In many of the conversations that I was having, I found that the people who were not neuroscientists began asking me about what the field of neuroscience has discovered about consciousness. Because I had been reading the spiritual texts, I understood what they meant by the question and by their implicit definition of consciousness, which was very different from the definition of consciousness in the scientific field of neuroscience. It had been a while since I thought about how neuroscience investigates consciousness, and my memory was that we didn't know much about it and did not have great methods or protocols to investigate it.

Of course, like every other human I have been amazed at the way we experience the world through our senses. That astonishment only blossomed as I learned over the years how the brain operates, because it really is a very big leap to go from neurotransmitters to the feeling of joy in watching *Schitt's Creek* or the way a movie score lifts you up or the transcendence you can feel in viewing a piece of art you love. I had never personally given too much analysis to the mechanism of consciousness. Since I was being asked this question, though, and reading all this novel evidence about reincarnation and anomalous perception, I had finally become interested in consciousness and wondered what progress neuroscience had made recently. So I began reading again.

Whenever consciousness was raised in these conversations, the various definitions of the word would come to mind. In fact, there were so

137

many different definitions of consciousness that I wasn't even sure what it really was. Eventually, I realized that it was one word being used to describe multiple things. No wonder it was so confusing. I'll explain how I ultimately came to think of it at the end of this section.

In neuroscience, consciousness is assumed to arise from the physical brain. That means that if you do not have a brain, you cannot have consciousness. It is assumed that consciousness is an emergent property that somehow arises from the combination and integration of all the individual processes of the brain. To demonstrate, let's do a quick consciousness awareness practice. Take the present moment that you're in right now. Take a deep breath in, hold it for a beat, and let it out. Bring your awareness to your body first, and then next to your surrounding environment. Your eyes might be taking in the words on the page of this book, while your ears are listening to sounds inside or outside your home, and your body is tracking its position in space, so you are aware of whether you are lying down or sitting up. Take a moment to become aware of how you feel. You might feel joyful and grateful to have the time to read a book. Notice how your attention moves from one object to the next as you take everything in. All this information comes together somehow to give you the conscious awareness of your present moment. The individuals I was speaking with for my project, though, were thinking more along the lines of a more nuanced question: What is consciousness such that it contains our true essence and moves from body to body and life to life? Or more along the lines of, if our brains are transmitters and receivers capable of accessing other space-time dimensions, how? Or is consciousness the foundation of everything so there is no distinction between mind and matter? I was *pretty* sure neuroscience had not even bothered to tackle these questions yet—and to be fair, how would we?

Regardless, let's look at this question: How does neuroscience study and define consciousness? Well, it depends on what you mean. First, there is the classic juxtaposition of conscious and unconscious processing (think subliminal messages presented too quickly for the conscious brain to process, but that are ultimately processed by the unconscious brain)—let's set this one aside. Second, there is the study of the moment-to-moment construction of reality that is altered in various states, such as waking, sleeping, dreaming, meditation, psychedelic use, and under anesthesia—I think of this as the "spectrum of consciousness." Third, there is the study of the "inner subjective experience of being" (the simple consciousness awareness exercise we did earlier is an example of this), which is the most difficult to study and is the most commonly used definition across disciplines. The third is related to the second in that we use studies of the spectrum of consciousness to understand the subjective experience. This last definition, the "inner subjective experience of being," is the one neuroscience knows the least about. What I mean by that is that we know how the receptors in the body can detect a painful stimulus, carry the signal from the body to the somatosensory cortex in the brain, and translate it into the sensation of pain, but we have absolutely no explanation for how this sequence of electrochemical events causes the subjective experience of pain. We have no idea how firing neurons give rise to the sensation and experience of falling in love, being moved by a piece of art or music, or the beauty of a shared meal.

Identifying and describing the neural correlates of these experiences is called the "easy problem" of consciousness, and understanding the mechanism of how the experience emerges from the neural correlates is known as the "hard problem" (Chalmers 2003; 1995). Over the years, neuroscientists have mostly tackled the easy problem, while philosophers have tackled the hard problem. It has been argued recently that we need both science and philosophy to understand consciousness because, while science focuses on the objective third-person perspective, philosophy takes on the subjective first-person perspective—and of course, a key feature of consciousness is the subjective component, so both are needed (Keppler and Shani 2020).

For our discussion, to tackle this very complicated picture, we have to bring in philosophy (sorry!). We also have to bring back scientific materialism. Since I want to keep this discussion fairly approachable, I refer the superinterested reader to the Recommended Reads to find a list of some very good references that go into greater detail about the philosophy of consciousness and the Universe.

A CONSCIOUS UNIVERSE?

Because of the three key assumptions of the scientific materialist paradigm—realism, locality, and causality—that I briefly mentioned earlier in the book, the conventional scientific paradigm assumes that everything is made of matter and energy, contained within ordinary space and time, and can be measured experimentally and proved by logic or mathematics. In this scientific materialist paradigm, anything spiritual or that could be considered psi phenomena cannot exist, which is why you see quick dismissal by the scientific establishment of such ideas. (Oh hi, 'old me'!)

However, with quantum physics we have seen these assumptions broken, spilling open a world of possibilities and questions. The findings about the observer effect, in particular, have caused a ripple in scientific and philosophical thinking because it threatens the scientific material-ist idea that the physical world would exist even if no one was around to observe it. Scientific materialism was already on shaky ground from a philosophical point of view because no one could ever experience reality outside consciousness. Think about it. At first, you might find yourself thinking, *Of course the Earth would still exist if humans did not exist.* But how can we know? We cannot verify it. It is an unprovable theory. Everything comes through our minds and our consciousness—it is the beginning, the limit, and the end. Even Max Planck, one of the brilliant physicists that laid the foundation for quantum physics, said:

> I regard consciousness as fundamental. I regard matter as deriva-tive from consciousness. We cannot get behind consciousness. Everything we talk about, everything that we regard as existing, postulates consciousness.

Physicist Carlo Rovelli expands on this idea in his relational quan-tum mechanics theory, suggesting that the physical universe is relative to the observer, meaning there is no objective physical world, only our sub-jective perception of it (Rovelli 1996). University of California, Irvine neuroscientist Don Hoffman also believes that consciousness precedes the brain. In his book *The Case Against Reality: Why Evolution Hid the Truth from Our Eyes* (2019), he describes research from his lab demonstrating that, from an evolutionary perspective, it is not favorable for humans to perceive reality as it truly is. Instead, reality is represented in terms of evolutionary fitness like a graphical user interface. According to this theory, a tree may actually be a collection of vibrating atoms, but it appears as one solid object to humans because it is evolutionarily beneficial to human survival to perceive the tree in this way. Hoffman argues that his interface theory of perception is needed to reconcile the hard problem of consciousness.

As it turns out—and of course I had no idea about any of this until I did some exploration—the idea that consciousness is fundamental and ubiquitous in the Universe is actually a very ancient idea, but one that is gaining ground again recently in some philosophy circles. A few different schools of philosophical thought exemplify this. Idealism states that consciousness is fundamental because it is the only thing that exists; in other words, everything is derived from a cosmic mind. Descartes put forth dualism, suggesting that consciousness and physical reality are separate and distinct entities, but that both are fundamental. Panpsychism suggests that every physical particle has an inherent property of phenomenal experience, and thus, consciousness is fundamental (Note: This wouldn't mean that every particle experiences the full range of emotions that you might when, say, you suddenly inherit millions of dollars out of the blue, but rather that there is some level of awareness). Many schools of thought, mystery schools, secret societies, and religions subscribe to ideas such as these that consciousness is primary.

In recent times, we've been seeing this re-emergence of the idea of consciousness being the true building block of the Universe (rather than matter) because it seems to better fit the data from contemporary physics, including quantum field theory. I want to put a pin in this deeper discussion of consciousness, however, because I will come back to it after I review the neuroscientific evidence. For now, I just wanted to give you a taste of some of the models of the Universe out there and how the disciplines are trying to reconcile the differences in their data.

Bernardo Kastrup (2014), a computer scientist, gives us a useful metaphor for how humans might emerge from a field of consciousness that will help frame the discussion. He suggests imagining that our reality is a stream of water, a stream of consciousness. We can think of ourselves as whirlpools that form within the stream. The whirlpool is its own little separate unit, but it is still made from the same water and connected to the larger stream of water.

In his metaphor the stream is the field of consciousness, and humans are the whirlpools. Kastrup gives another analogy that might be helpful in understanding the concept. He uses individuals with dissociative identity disorder as an example. These individuals display multiple personalities, with each personality having its own set of private inner experiences, even though they are all contained within one physical body. He suggests that "we may all be alters—dissociated personalities—of universal consciousness" (Kastrup 2018; Kastrup, Crabtree, and Kelly 2018).

From the neuroscience perspective, the most typically pursued question around consciousness is how our brains create subjective experience. To bring it back to the whirlpool and stream metaphor, materialist neuroscience is only looking at the whirlpool. From a spiritual perspective; there is a universal field of consciousness (the stream) that is connected to your core essence/soul/consciousness (whirlpool). There's one more layer here, though: your core essence/soul/consciousness is separate from your human mind, and using tools like meditation, you can separate the two to observe your true (quiet) nature that is connected to everyone and everything else. Remember how we talked about how the brain uses our expectations, beliefs, and conditioning to form our perception of the world? That's your human mind. Slipping into altered states of consciousness, like meditation, can pull us back from those workings of the mind into the inviting awareness of existence. This is what I had been practicing in my day-to-day and from where my thoughts, emotions, and behaviors could be objectively observed by my broader awareness. I cannot recommend this practice enough.

Thinking of the new spiritual framework (i.e., soul lessons, karma, reincarnation) I had learned about, I realized that you could just extend the Buddhist framework past the current life and see consciousness coming into a body for this earthly and human experience, using the chatter in our heads, all our brains' mechanisms and quirks (our human mind) to work things out and learn lessons that evolve the soul. These spiritual perspectives are looking at how the whirlpool is connected to the stream. That's the best I could come up with to help me think about the research.

NEUROSCIENCE'S TAKE ON CONSCIOUSNESS

Consciousness is a massive research field in neuroscience, and a full review is beyond the scope of this book. I thought the best way to bridge the classic concept of consciousness from neuroscience with the spiritual version would be to look up studies that investigated the neural correlates and subjective experiences of spiritual or mystical experiences. These can be considered altered states of consciousness where experiencers report sensing a meaningful connection to something greater than themselves. Classic neuroscience had definitely tackled this one.

The words "spiritual" and "mystical" were meaningless to 'old me.' Did they mean you believed in spirits? In a higher power? In the Universe having order and meaning? In magic? What I mean by that is that if you had asked me to describe what a spiritual or mystical experience was, I genuinely would not have been able to tell you one adjective to describe such an experience. I really had no model in my mind of what these words meant. So if you are like 'old me,' it will be beneficial to start with a simple definition of these kinds of experiences. 'New me' can bring us up to speed. A spiritual or mystical experience can be described as an experience that stirs a sense of unity or interconnectedness, transcendence of time and space, positive mood, a feeling of sacredness, and ineffability—or at least that's one definition from the literature that allows an empirical investigation. From the spiritual perspective, I think it can be viewed as stepping back from the mind to see the true nature of consciousness as interconnected with everything else—or, in other words, looking past the whirlpool to see the stream. So what's going on in the brain during one of these states?

Lesions

My favorite kind of neuroscience experiments is brain lesion studies because they are so revealing. These usually entail examining what human behaviors are altered after a certain region of the brain is damaged. For example, if Broca's region in the left hemisphere is damaged, the ability to produce language is impaired. When a motor region is knocked off-line, we see deficits in motor movement, or your ability to move.

In thinking about brain lesions and a spiritual or mystical type of experience, the first thing that came to mind was the book *My Stroke of Insight: A Brain Scientist's Personal Journey* (2006) by neuroscientist Jill Bolte Taylor. Dr. Taylor experienced a left hemisphere stroke and beautifully depicted the experience of having her left hemisphere off-line. Her poetic narration of feeling nirvana, being one with the Universe, a loss of ego, and boundless compassion can leave you envious. Reliance on her right hemisphere seemed to make her more sensitive to subtle energies, and she explained that she could feel the energy of the people who walked in her hospital room. The loss of her inner dialogue caused the negative traits of such inner dialogue, such as self-criticism and embarrassment, to disappear. Quotes from Dr. Bolte Taylor's book capture the experience well:

> I no longer perceived myself as a whole object separate from everything.

> My right hemisphere relished in its attachment to the eternal flow. I was no longer isolated and alone. My soul was as big as the Universe and frolicked with glee in a boundless sea.

> My consciousness soared into an omniscient, a "being at one" with the Universe . . .

She had reached that feeling of oneness and simple existence that so many seek to find!

Case studies of patients with lesions to the area of the brain near where the parietal and temporal cortices intersect (temporoparietal junction)—the same brain location where Dr. Bolte Taylor had her stroke—demonstrated that damage to this brain region could cause experiences that seemed spiritual in nature, such as the sudden feeling of spiritual awareness and a connection to the transcendent (Urgesi et al. 2010), as well as out of body experiences (OBEs) (Blanke et al. 2004; Brugger 2006; Ionta, Gassert, and Blanke 2011; Ionta et al. 2011), which are the sensation of a person's being detached from their body and the sense that they can view their own body from an external viewpoint, such as looking down on one's own body from the ceiling. This made sense, since the temporoparietal junction is one of the places where sensory information, emotions, and memory are brought together to construct a body schema (Decety and Lamm 2007). This brain area tracks your body in physical space to give you an idea of where your body is and what it's doing. Really weird things can happen to perception when there is damage to this region, such as disownership of a body part, i.e., not recognizing one's arm as belonging to oneself (Aglioti et al. 1996), and not being able to locate a body part on oneself (autotopagnosia) (Berlucchi and Aglioti 1997). From lesion studies, the temporoparietal junction seemed like a solid initial target for a neural correlate of spiritual or mystical experiences.

Neurostimulation

Another experimental technique used in neuroscience is neural stimulation. In these studies the researcher can apply electrical or magnetic signals to the brain to alter neural activity and behavior. Neurosurgeon Wilder Penfield found that patients reported spiritual experiences, such as seeing God, leaving their bodies, and seeing the dead when the temporal cortex was stimulated. Stimulation to the temporal cortex (either experimentally or through natural causes like epilepsy) can elicit the "sensed presence effect," which is a feeling of presence of an entity, being, or individual (Thompson 1982; Cheyne 2001; Blom 2010; Luhrmann 2012; Alderson-Day 2016; Arzy and Schurr 2016; Cook and Persinger 1997; Pierre and Persinger 2006). These sensed presences can be accompanied by the feeling that something cosmic, meaningful, and significant has occurred, as well as sensations of communion with universal forces (angels, entities, God, other dimensional creatures), hearing-knowing from "internal sources," vestibular sensations (such as internal vibrations or spinning), and complex visual perceptions (Persinger 1989; Bear and Fedio 1977; Geschwind 1983). Other researchers have also found that brain stimulation at or near the temporoparietal junction can elicit out-of-body experiences (Blanke et al. 2002; Blanke et al. 2005; De Ridder et al. 2007; Daltrozzo et al. 2016).

These regions are not only associated with spiritual experiences, of course. Similar to the lesion studies, we can see other pretty wild effects when neural activity is altered here, and we can actually get a sense of how fragile our construction of reality is. In one experiment when neurostimulation was applied near the temporoparietal junction, the participant reported that she was "falling from a height" or "sinking into the bed." When the stimulus was increased the patient reported an OBE but said, "I see myself lying in bed, from above, but I only see my legs and lower trunk." An even higher stimulation induced a feeling of "lightness" and "floating" about two meters above the bed, close to the ceiling.

Other brain regions have also been implicated in the sensation of spirituality by neurostimulation, such as the posterior cingulate/precuneus (Herbet et al. 2014; Balestrini et al. 2015) and the inferior parietal lobule (IPL) (Crescentini et al. 2015; 2014), both of which have also been theorized to have a role in consciousness (Vogt and Laureys 2005; Cavanna and Trimble 2006), which I will discuss in more detail below.

The scientific protocols that are most frequently used to study the feeling of spirituality or mysticism, as well as consciousness, are those using meditation or psychedelic drugs. These studies typically use functional magnetic resonance imaging (fMRI; recording of blood flow presumed to be associated with brain activity) or electroencephalography

(EEG; recording of electrical signals from the brain) to record brain function. I will discuss these in the next sections.

Meditation

Since the 1970s there has been exploration of the neural correlates of meditation to better understand the feeling of oneness and interconnectedness that can arise from the practice. Meditation is interesting because there is both the aspect of feeling unity (one part of a spiritual experience) and allowing the person to step back from the mind's typical chatter into pure existence and awareness. It's a favorite tool of neuroscientists to examine consciousness. There are different kinds of meditation, and each kind has different effects on the brain and body (Nash and Newberg 2013), but discussion of these different types is beyond the scope of this book. For a deep dive into the effect of meditation on the brain, I recommend *Altered Traits* (2017) by Daniel Goleman and Richard J. Davidson. Neuroscience studies have mostly focused on a few specific types of meditation, and they include focused awareness, open awareness or open monitoring, and nondual awareness (Lutz et al. 2008; Josipovic 2010).

It appears that meditation has an effect on a few parts of the brain and decreases activity in one particular network called the default mode network (DMN). The DMN is active when a person is *not* engaged in a task and is simply at rest, sitting quietly (Raichle et al. 2001; Raichle and Snyder 2007; M. D. Fox et al. 2005). The best way to understand what the DMN does is to close your eyes for ten minutes, try to relax, and observe what you are thinking about. Go ahead and try it! If you're like most people, you are thinking about what you said to someone yesterday, what you have to do later in the day, how annoyed you were by that email from your coworker, wondering why she is the way she is, and then checking yourself for getting annoyed in the first place. It is basically a mix of thinking about yourself and others, and the future and the past (Northoff et al. 2006; Denny et al. 2012; Svoboda, McKinnon, and Levine 2006).

The three main brain regions of the default mode network

are the medial prefrontal cortex (MPFC), the posterior cingulate cortex/precuneus (PCC), and the parahippocampal complex (PHC). The MPFC and PCC are involved in self-recognition, self-awareness, and self-referential tasks (van Veluw and Chance 2014; Kelley et al. 2002; Renes et al. 2015), while the PHC encodes certain types of memories, especially self-relevant ones, and is thought to play a role in consciousness since it stitches together moment-to-moment information in a useful representation for the brain (Behrendt 2013).

One additional brain region involved in the default mode network, and the only one that is in the lateral side of the brain, is the IPL (Buckner, Andrews-Hanna, and Schacter 2008)—which we touched on earlier in the neurostimulation studies that elicited experiences of spirituality. This brain region is very complex and is involved in many tasks, such as spatial cognition, semantics and memory, empathy, attentional processing, and processing of time and temporal relationships (Humphreys and Lambon Ralph 2015; Kubit and Jack 2013; Scholz et al. 2009; Battelli, Pascual-Leone, and Cavanagh 2007; Bueti and Walsh 2009).

It is thought that meditation practices alter activity and connectivity in these DMN brain regions, causing there to be less of a focus of perception on the self (quieting the mind), which decreases the contrast (and increases the blending) between internal and external objects (sense of unity); in other words, what is me or about me and what is not me or not about me (Berkovich-Ohana et al. 2016; K. Fox et al. 2016; Josipovic et al. 2012). Additionally, it is thought that the altered activity in the IPL is what causes the sensation of timelessness and spacelessness (Newberg et al. 2001; Newberg and D'aquili 2000).

Psychedelics

The next area of brain research that I turned to for neural correlates of mystical or spiritual experiences was psychedelic drug research. Psychedelics are a class of psychoactive substances that can illicit intense sensory and consciousness-altering experiences and can include drugs such as psilocybin, ayahuasca, mescaline, lysergic acid (LSD), and N, N-Dimethyltryptamine (DMT).

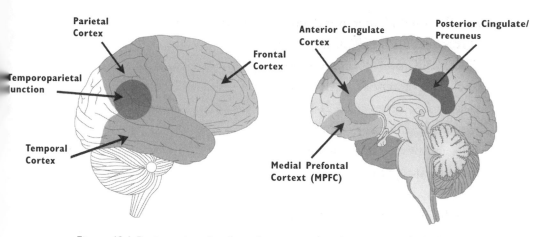

Figure 13.1 Brain regions implicated in spiritual and mystical experiences
© 2022 Mona Sobhani

Since many people who have taken psychedelic drugs have reported spiritual or mystical experiences, changes in consciousness, and positive behavior change, there has been a recent surge in research looking into the neural correlates of these experiences. Similar to the studies on meditation (see figure 13.1), it appears that the DMN in the brain is affected by the use of psychedelic drugs, causing reduced activity and reduced connectivity between the brain regions. Reduction in activity in these regions correlates with a self-reported reduced sense of self from participants. Other self-reported effects included "reduced time travel to the past," "ego dissolution," and "disintegration of self."

Looking at the evidence together, it appears that psychedelic use, like meditation, preserves perceptual processing and local functioning within brain regions but causes a breakdown in the long-scale coordination between brain regions, preventing an integration of signals that create the sense of self in space and time that one is used to experiencing (Carhart-Harris et al. 2012; Tagliazucchi et al. 2014; 2016; Riba et al. 2002; Muthukumaraswamy et al. 2013; Kometer et al. 2015; Carhart-Harris, Leech, and Tagliazucchi 2014; Hermle et al. 1992; Vollenweider et al. 1997; Riba et al. 2004; Kometer et al. 2013). It has also been proposed that the gating function of the cortico-striato-thalamo-cortical loop might be disrupted by psychedelic drugs causing the brain to be flooded with sensory information that would usually get filtered out, causing massive shifts in perception, which aligns with reports from users and conjures that stereotypical psychedelic imagery (Vollenweider and Geyer 2001). However, I should highlight here that there was a *decrease* in brain activity in psychedelic studies rather than the expected increase.

Connectome Harmonic Decomposition

I also came across some recent research proposing and exploring a new metric for measuring the power and energy of different brain states that may provide a useful tool in examining the relationship between the brain and various states of consciousness. Using the new metric called connectome harmonic decomposition (CHD), researchers have shown that psychedelics such as psilocybin, LSD, ketamine, and DMT cause a shift in energy in the brain from a low- to a high-frequency harmonic. A similar result was found when comparing meditative states to normal waking states of consciousness (Atasoy et al. 2017; 2018; Atasoy, Donnelly, and Pearson 2016; Luppi et al. 2020). Interestingly, the psychedelic states had the exact opposite signature of those found in patients with anesthesia, suggesting a continuous spectrum of consciousness that can potentially be measured by this new metric (Luppi et al. 2020). When focusing on brain regions, as the prior studies had done, it can be difficult to identify a continuum, which is why this new work is so important.

Taking a step back from all the research I had read, I realized that there was a pretty good understanding of the brain regions involved in experiencing a spiritual or mystical experience or altered states of consciousness. There were also good interpretations of the data within the framework of scientific materialism, meaning that there were proposed explanations that mapped the sensations of a spiritual or mystical experience onto a brain region and function. This is exactly the type of evidence I expected to find—a lot of data about the whirlpool, or to use the other metaphor, a lot of data about one of the personalities in DID.

After reading all that data, because some of us have definitely been trained to think this way, you might be thinking, if we know the neural correlates of these experiences, then doesn't that prove it is all in our brains? No, it does not. From a scientific materialist standpoint, these studies only show correlation. We technically cannot assume that brain activity is the cause of the experience, even though that is the implicit assumption in the field in the current day. William James, the "father of American psychology" and Harvard professor of psychology and philosophy, had even proposed a "transmission" model of consciousness that highlighted the fact that just because the brain is involved in consciousness does not necessarily mean that it *produces* it. Larry Dossey (Dossey 1999), M.D., described it like this:

> Consider your television set. Although you can damage it physically and destroy the picture on the screen, this does not prove that the TV set actually makes the picture. We know, rather, that the picture is due to electromagnetic signals originating outside the set itself and that the TV set receives, amplifies, and displays the signals; it does not produce them.

If the brain is not producing the experience, then where is it coming from? Before we discuss that, I need to take a psychedelic detour.

PSYCHEDELIC DETOUR

I can't go on to discuss models of the Universe without pausing to discuss psychedelics a little bit more. One hugely interesting thing about psychedelic substances is the profound and long-lasting effects on users, even from a one-time dose. This is evidenced by the number of participants who report that the mystical experience they underwent during the psychedelic session was one of the *most spiritual experiences of their lives* and caused positive behavior change in them. In one study, 71% of participants reported the experience as being one of the top five most spiritual experiences of their lives, and 33% reported it as being the most significant spiritual experience of their life (Griffiths et al. 2006).

Even fourteen months after the study, 67% of participants still reported the experience was one of the top five in their life, in line with birth of a child (Griffiths et al. 2006). That's incredible! Hardly any behavior-change techniques and therapies work that effectively, especially after just one session.

Earlier, I reviewed the most recent research with psychedelics that focus on the brain, but of course the exploration of psychedelic use has far predated research studies in Western research labs. Over the millennia, indigenous peoples on every continent have used psyche-delics for various purposes, many of them spiritual. While digging through those fascinating stories I found that psychedelic substances were often associated with paranormal experiences, and many times that was even the intention (Luke and Kittenis 2005; Stevens 1987; Devereux 1997)! The altered states from psychedelic use were thought to improve telepathy, precognition, clairvoyance, out-of-body travel, psychic healing, and spirit communication. This wasn't only true for indigenous peoples, either. Many of the academics who popular-ized the exploration of psychedelics in the twentieth century, such as Albert Hofman, Aldous Huxley, Timothy Leary, and Gordon Wasson, noticed the association as well (Wasson and Wasson, 1957; Schultes and Hofmann, 1980, 1992; Weil, Metzner, and Leary, 1965; Huxley, 1954; see Luke, 2012 for a comprehensive review). Stanislav Grof, the founder of transpersonal psychology and one of the pioneering psy-chiatrists who used psychedelics in conjunction with therapy, reported that events of precognition and remote viewing in his patients was so frequent that it became unextraordinary (Grof 1975; 2001). Other similar reports from therapy sessions have found patients reporting telepathic communication, extraordinary synchronicities and coin-cidences, precognition, and encounters with entities (Blewett and Chwelos 1959; Grof 2001; Harman 1963; Holzinger 1964; Stolaroff 2004; Abraham 1983; Luke and Kittenis 2005).

Descriptions of the entity encounters are intriguing in that they are reported as being a true experience with another sentient being rather than a hallucination. The entities have been described any number of ways including as spirit guides, angels, elves, plant spirits, aliens, helpers, and the divine (Luke and Kittenis 2005; Luke 2012). Although sometimes the encounters elicit fear, the most commonly reported feelings were love, joy, and kindness. Users have reported that they felt the entity was conscious, intelligent, and benevolent and lived in another dimension of reality that continued to exist after the encounter. Many report receiving messages or predictions about the future. In one study, over half of the participants who reported being atheists prior to the experience reported no longer being atheists after the session and rated the experience as being one of the most psychologically insightful, meaningful, and spiritual experiences of their lives (Davis et al. 2020)! It has even been recently suggested that there is value in exploring entity encounters through psychedelic use as a therapeutic (Lutkajtis 2021). That is a testament to how powerful these experiences can be.

Let's stop for a moment to really understand what this means. Through psychedelic use, you can perceive an entity or being that can give you enough insight to profoundly change your life. Is it your subconscious? Why is it in the form of an entity?

Some may brush off these experiences as simply odd things that happen to your brain on drugs. However, I want to highlight here that the transformative (and positive) effect on behavior by psychedelics is similar to the therapeutic effect of past life regression. Near-death experiences have also been known to cause powerful transformations for the better, with huge shifts in perception that have improved the person's appreciation of nature, tolerance for others, concern with social justice issues, and a sense that there is some inner meaning to life. Also, lest you think it's just the reorganization of brain networks by psychedelics that helps cause healing, it has been suggested that the subjective effects, or insightful and mystical experiences, of the psychedelic experience independently affect the desirable therapeutic outcome, such as the person reporting lower levels of depression or anxiety (Davis, Barrett, Griffiths, 2020; Yaden and Griffiths, 2021). In other words, if you were to be put under anesthesia and given a psychedelic, it's unclear whether you would see as much healing as you would if you were awake to go through the psychedelic trip and psychologically derive meaning from the experience.

Sure, a mystical or spiritual experience can be reduced to activation or deactivation of certain brain regions—but what's more interesting is the deep psychological and behavioral changes that emerge from these states that can improve a person's quality of life. Also, when you stay within the bounds of conventional neuroscience, you may think you've solved the mystery of this experience by identifying the brain regions involved. But once you step outside the bounds and consider that people undergoing these experiences can and do receive verifiable accurate information about other people, places, and times that they would otherwise have no knowledge of—what then of the neural correlate explanation? Ignoring parts of the experience prevents the construction of an accurate healing model.

My type A personality had never been interested in psychedelics before, but I was suddenly very curious. So I took a trip—an acid trip. The day I took LSD was one of the most profoundly magical and beloved days of my life. Oceanic love permeated my being, and truth was revealing itself to me in waves upon waves. With eyes closed, the doors of imagination were flung open, and wild, colorful panoramas folded and toppled into, onto, and through each other, leaving neon-streaked emotions in their wake. Electricity was sparkling up and down my spine and through my arms and legs. The energy was so intense that I *had* to get up and dance to release it. I felt like I was seeing reality for the very first time. The most profound part, though, was the instantaneous and clear answers that popped into my mind as I internally reflected on self-analysis questions I had prepared beforehand. The short answer? "You forgot to be weird." The underlying message was crystal clear: You project who you think you're supposed to be and forgot who you truly are; your true self has been a casualty. Then a montage of examples from my life flashed across my mind to really drive home the point and show me exactly how I had betrayed myself—e.g., desiring things I didn't actually want, striving for accomplishments to impress other people, suffocating my self-expression that wasn't deemed "productive," and more. Explaining the experience does not come one iota close to doing it justice. The insight wasn't solely logical or rational—I felt it and came to know it in every cell of my being, in mind, body, and spirit. Even with all the therapy and "work" I had been doing on myself, I was nowhere near coming to this insight that descended on me within 30 seconds during an LSD trip. The one disappointment from the trip was that, unfortunately, elves did not make an appearance, and neither did fairies—but there's always hope for next time!

It is important for us to understand how and why these experiences are so transformative, not only for the goal of better understanding the nature of our brains, consciousness, and the Universe, but also for leveraging and extending their dramatic healing effects. Okay, let's jump out of our psychedelic detour and back to consciousness.

WHAT IS THE THEORY OF EVERYTHING?

Quantum physics and physics are still incompatible. Everyone is still holding out hope that a grand unifying theory of everything will be discovered one day. In recent times, we've been seeing the re-emergence of the idea of consciousness being the true building block of the Universe because it seems to fit the data from contemporary physics (including quantum field theory) better and may be able to finally bridge the previously insurmountable gaps. I read many proposed philosophies and theories of existence (such as the ones I previously mentioned, idealism, dualism, and panpsychism, but also others such as simulation theory, which proposes we all live in a simulation) and consciousness (such as the integrated information theory, in which consciousness emerges as a property of physical matter, and Penrose-Hameroff Orch OR theory, in which consciousness emerges from quantum computations in the brain), but for simplicity, I will focus on just one that gives a proposed mechanism as an example.

Cosmopsychism is the idea that there exists one big field of consciousness "that serves as the ultimate bedrock of experiential reality"

(Shani 2015; Shani and Keppler 2018; Mathews 2011; Goff 2017; Nagasawa and Wager 2017; Keppler 2012; Kastrup 2018). The whirlpool and DID metaphors apply here. All people, memories, conscious states, objects, and experiences are derived from the field.

One interesting component of cosmopsychism is called "holism," or the idea that the Universe is a top-down or "holist" system. This is the complete opposite of what we're used to thinking. Our typical thinking goes that particles come together to form, say, my cherished stuffed animal horse. In a Holist Universe, however, the particles exist *because* of the existence of my stuffed animal horse. Existence isn't built up from parts but is instead derived from a whole. American philosopher Jonathan Schaffer suggests that this would more easily explain phenomena like entanglement in quantum physics, because it explains why two particles separated by a great distance act as one whole entity, rather than two separate entities (Schaffer 2009). *Agentive cosmopsychism* goes even further to suggest that the Universe might have the capacity to recognize, respond, and be aware of the consequences of its actions (Goff 2017), based off the observation that our Universe is fine-tuned for the emergence and existence of life, despite the fact that the conditions to enable life fall within an extremely narrow range and are extremely unlikely to have occurred by chance (Smolin 1999; Goff 2017). So is the Universe an intelligent, conscious, cosmic mind?

Now, I will admit that for a traditionally trained neuroscientist like me, this was a very difficult concept to wrap my mind around, accept, or even entertain. The idea that consciousness could be external to the body was too foreign to me and, frankly, unacceptable. It would take many books from many different authors with new perspectives to open my mind to the possibility that this could be reality.

It forced me to think about our materialist neuroscientific assumption that consciousness comes from the brain. We believe this because: (a) damage to certain parts of the brain correlates with changes in behavior and altered consciousness and (b) brain activity correlates with behavior. These seem like pretty reasonable assumptions. The problem is that this model falls apart if there are any cases or anomalies that question the model, and of course, those do indeed exist. One glaring example that I previously mentioned in passing is the case of savants who are born with skill sets and knowledge that they could not have possibly reasonably acquired through their five senses, such as Leslie Lemke, who was born a master musician but never took a music lesson in his life. There was also Kim Peek, the real Rain Man, who despite having poor motor skills and developmental disabilities could read two pages at once (one with the left eye and one with the right eye) in three seconds, remembered every piece of music he ever heard, and memorized over twelve thousand books! There are also the cases where brain injury can lead to savant-like abilities, such as photographic memory, musical genius, mathematical mastery, and—my favorite—expertise in a foreign language they had never before learned. Sometimes neuroscientists like to explain away these odd cases by invoking the concept of neuroplasticity, the ability of the nervous system to reorganize its structural or functional organization. Some have even suggested that maybe we are born with all these latent abilities that become uninhibited through brain injury, but that goes against our model of learning through the five senses. Also, if that's true, I hope someone figures it out soon so that I can paint like Degas without having to practice.

But there's more: Yet another phenomenon that questions scientific materialism's assumption that consciousness solely comes from the brain is *terminal lucidity*. Remarkable stories exist of patients who had significantly diminished cognitive capacity for many years from dementia, severe mental illness, or neurodegenerative disorders and who suddenly became fully lucid, as though nothing was amiss, a short time before their death (Nahm et al. 2012). One study found that of 227 dementia patients, approximately 10% exhibited terminal lucidity. That's a lot of cases for a phenomenon that is supposed to be impossible because of the damaged state of the patient's brain! There are cases of patients who have been deemed medically deceased with zero brain or heart activity for significant amounts of time who regain consciousness and report intensely vivid mental experiences, or near-death experiences, which I touched on earlier in this book. Some of the features of NDEs line up with altered brain activity in the temporoparietal junction—such as the sensation of leaving the body and being able to see it while floating above it and a sense of overwhelming peace, well-being, or absolute, unconditional love, but there is usually no brain activity in these patients to account for the experiences. These reports are often disregarded with rationalizations that there must have been residual brain activity that wasn't detected, even though we know that's not possible in most cases, such as during cardiac arrest when electrical brain activity measured by EEG flatlines after about fifteen seconds following cardiac arrest. In some of those cases, verifiable memories from the NDE occur in the time period between cardiac arrest and resuscitation, often many minutes long. Some of the cases even reported that the individual who was declared deceased had no heartbeat for twenty-five minutes before returning to life (Lommel et al. 2001; Kelly 2007). It doesn't make sense that people would report *more* intense and vivid experiences when the brain is producing no recordable electrical output. This is not one anomaly, but many! Regardless of whether something spiritual or anomalous is going on, the brain model must be incomplete.

I was beginning to think that it might be possible that consciousness doesn't come from the brain. I had found a large literature from well-trained and prominent physicians, neuroscientists, neurosurgeons, and a hodgepodge of other scientists that believed the brain was more like something through which consciousness is expressed. There is much work on this, but one of the strongest efforts to explore this theory has emerged from a consortium of scholars brought together by the Esalen Institute. The Esalen Institute, founded during the 1960s, is a nonprofit institute and retreat center in Big Sur, California, where the Human Potential Movement grew and new behavioral health practices, such as transpersonal psychology, were born. It is also where the phrase "spiritual but not religious" was popularized. In fact, the Esalen Institute's Center for Theory & Research has brought together a diverse group of scientists, scholars of religion, philosophers, and historians in a twenty-year collaboration to produce a commendable body of scholarship challenging the prevailing scientific worldview's position on brain and mind, while working toward a reconciliation of science and spirituality that doesn't recklessly abandon the reason and objectivity gained during the Enlightenment. The work has contributions from scholars at major academic universities, such as UC Berkeley and Rice University, and is published in three sweeping volumes: *Irreducible Mind: Toward a Psychology for the 21ˢᵗ Century* (Kelly et al., 2007), *Beyond Physicalism: Toward Reconciliation of Science and Spirituality* (Kelly, Crabtree, and Marshall, 2015), and *Consciousness Unbound: Liberating Mind from the Tyranny of Materialism* (Kelly and Marshall, 2021).

Even if you set aside philosophical theories like cosmopsychism, many prominent scientists and philosophers have come to question that consciousness could have evolved and emerged from the physical brain. Christof Koch (2012), a neuroscientist interested in consciousness and chief scientist of the Allen Institute for Brain Science, has said:

> I used to be a proponent of the idea of consciousness emerging out of complex nervous networks . . . but over the years, my thinking has changed. Subjectivity is too radically different from anything physical for it to be an emergent phenomenon. . . . I see no way for the divide between unconscious and conscious creatures to be bridged by more neurons.

Bringing back the whirlpool and stream metaphor, Bernardo Kastrup (2014) has said:

> While they may look different from other parts of the stream, the whirlpools are made of nothing more than water . . . to say that brain generates mind is as absurd as to say that a whirlpool generates water!

As it turns out, there exist many eminent scientists and scholars throughout history who were interested in or had direct experience with spiritual or mystical experiences and esoteric beliefs. You may be surprised to learn, as I was, that Sir Isaac Newton was one of them. It is difficult to think of someone more associated with the Age of Reason than Newton, as his three laws of physics have become part of the basis of scientific materialism, but Newton was an idealist. He believed that everything in the Universe was derived from consciousness and had intelligence, and that mind could influence matter (think the Law of Attraction) through a medium he called *sal nitrum* (Booth 2008). Sound familiar? It should (i.e., "The Force" in *Star Wars*). He used the sal nitrum concept when deriving his theory of gravity! Newton wasn't the only one either. Francis Bacon, best known for his Baconian scientific method, also believed in a similar intermediary etheric substance, as did Nikola Tesla.

Emanuel Swedenborg had an illustrious scientific career, dabbling in astronomy, physics, engineering, chemistry, geology, anatomy, physiology, and psychology. When he was fifty years old, he had a mystical experience and claimed that he had ongoing conversations with beings that he perceived to be angels (Booth 2008).

Pythagoras, the famous Greek mathematician and philosopher, claimed to be able to recall every one of his past lives, practiced divination, and is credited with pulling together different threads of knowledge to lay the foundation for the *perennial philosophy*, the philosophical and spiritual perspective that a single metaphysical truth is behind all the religions and esoteric knowledge in the world.

Plato was also an idealist. His Allegory of the Cave captures the philosophy well, describing a scene in which inside a cave, prisoners are chained and facing a wall, incapable of turning around. Reality to these prisoners is viewing the shadows on the wall that are cast by events occurring just outside the cave. Since the prisoners cannot turn around, they do not understand that the shadows are not the actual events. If one of the prisoners is broken free, comes out of the cave and into the light, takes in the wonders, and returns to the cave to tell his fellow men what he has seen, they don't believe him and think he is crazy because the wall and shadows are all they know of reality.

Well, it's one thing to suggest that we are all derived from one big ocean of consciousness, but *how* does that work mechanically?

Remember, I had already complained that this was my hang-up. While digging, I found a recently proposed model from Joachim Keppler, the ubiquitous field of consciousness theory, published in *Frontiers in Psychology,* that ties together findings from neuroscience and physics (Shani and Keppler 2018; Keppler and Shani 2020). This is a doozy to explain, so bear with me.

I'll start with the analogy and then breakdown the science for you below. The model proposes that the foundation of everything is one big field of consciousness. Every possible conscious state is held within the field, and let's say each conscious state has a different color. The field contains all the colors and is one big unordered mess. Let's say that the color of meditation (a conscious state) is blue. When the brain goes into a meditative state, it produces the color blue, but think of it as a blue key. The field responds by lining up a blue keyhole, causing a bond to form between the brain and field, and now the brain can download the phenomenal, or inner awareness of what a meditative state feels like, until the bond is broken. Because each moment is unique, your brain incorporates other colors of the present moment into the blue, changing the color, and then sends it up to the field to be stored. The brain and the field don't have to wait for special states to interact. They are interacting all the time—when you're zoned out, asleep, having ice cream, or telling a joke.

Put another way, an analogy offered by Keppler is to that of a tape recorder (remember those?), where the write-read head is the brain and the tape is the field. The write head uses magnetic alignment to generate ordered states on a magnetic tape that can be retrieved in the read mode.

So then what's the science? Let's start with quantum field theory. Quantum field theory proposes that the Universe comprises quantum fields (i.e., no particles and no waves, just fields). If you want to extract a particle from the field, you need to give energy to the field. When enough energy is given to the field, the particle can pop out and up to the next energy level. That's when you'd recognize it as a particle. It's similar to how water can go from ice to water to gas. According to the theory, all these quantum fields are contained within the zero-point field, an all-pervasive energy field that spans all of space (i.e., "The Force"). To ground the theory in classical physics, Keppler's model focuses on considering the electromagnetic background field as the zero-point field. The field is disordered and completely random, and particles or systems in the field are constantly interacting with it.

The way these systems or particles interact with the field is that they have inherent specific resonance frequencies and when the specific resonance frequency of the system becomes phase-locked with the zero-point field, an equilibrium state is achieved and the formerly disordered zero-point field becomes more ordered and, thus, has more information.

Keppler's model views the zero-point field as the field of consciousness that contains both a physical aspect (a spectrum of energetic oscillations) and an intrinsic aspect (phenomenology; i.e., the one we have trouble explaining). The field contains every possible state of consciousness, and each of them can be viewed as a specific frequency from the spectrum of all possible frequencies (Note: I'm using "frequency" here to simplify). When a specific frequency of the brain becomes phase-locked with the field, this coordination produces enough order in the previously disordered systems to create a temporary link, allowing the brain to download the phenomenal or conscious state from the field, or upload a state to the field.

Why would we think the brain is capable of linking to the field? Well, it is already thought that the neural correlates of consciousness are related to large-scale synchronization of brain activity. Since each part of the brain does something different, they have to coordinate, and they do that with long-range oscillations of electrical activity; in other words, the separate brain regions try to sync their rhythms to each other (Crick and Koch 2003; Desmedt and Tomberg 1994; Rodriguez et al. 1999; A. K. Engel and Singer 2001; Melloni et al. 2007; Doesburg et al. 2009; Gaillard et al. 2009; Singer et al. 2014). Keppler uses neuroscientific literature from memory and consciousness to propose the model. During memory formation and normal waking consciousness, the brain shows

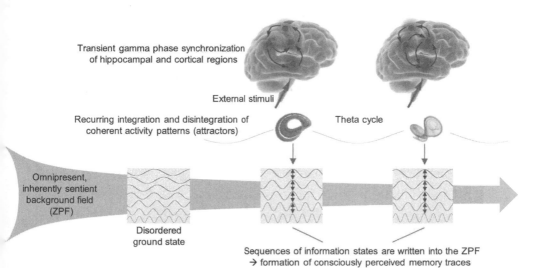

Transient gamma phase synchronization
of hippocampal and cortical regions

External stimuli

Recurring integration and disintegration of
coherent activity patterns (attractors)

Theta cycle

Omnipresent,
inherently sentient
background field
(ZPF)

Disordered
ground state

Sequences of information states are written into the ZPF
→ formation of consciously perceived memory traces

Figure 13.2. This illustration of Keppler's proposed model shows the "write" phase, where the brain exhibits increased gamma phase synchronization between cortical and hippocampal regions, and these activity patterns in the theta frequency cause phase-locking with the zero-point field (ZPF) that elicits a more ordered state. Reprinted from Keppler (2020)

increased gamma phase synchronization between cortical and hippo-campal regions, as well as the integration and disintegration of these activity patterns in the theta frequency. This state allows the brain to connect with the field and upload or "write" memory and conscious experiences (see figure 13.2). During self-referential consciousness and memory retrieval (i.e., when you're thinking about yourself), the brain shows increased gamma phase synchronization between default mode network and hippocampal regions, and the integration and disinte-gration of these activity patterns occurs in the alpha frequency. This state allows the brain to connect with the field and download or "read" memory and conscious experiences.

Keppler surmises that, under normal conditions, the brain is attuned to a limited spectrum of the field. He speculates that altered states of consciousness caused by psychedelics or meditation remove the restric-tions. He also proposes that the ongoing phase transitions that under-lie these neuronal processes can most likely be measured by photon emissions in the theta and alpha frequencies and should be tested.

In this book I have not reported on the brain studies that used psi research methods because I could not find a good meta-analysis or review. Brain data is especially noisy, so more research is needed to draw any conclusions on generalizable findings. Having said that, there have been a series of experiments conducted with a few exceptional intuitives, and those studies did find a prominence of alpha and theta waves from EEG recordings during the intuitives' "reading" states, aligning with the model from Keppler. This needs *far* more research and is highly speculative, so please don't get excited or carried away, but I felt the need to draw the comparison.

There was also overlap between the brain regions cited by Keppler (DMN, IPL, and temporoparietal junction) and those implicated in research with spiritual and mystical experiences, including psychedelic substances and meditation. So are these brain regions in charge of determining what state we are in and how we connect with the field?

Is the zero-point field what all the spiritual texts have been talking about for thousands of years? Could accessing the field explain mystical and spiritual experiences, as well as psi phenomena? It seems to me to be a completely ludicrous theory, until I pull in all the other data. If one is coming at it from a strictly materialist neuroscience perspective, they would have no reason to believe this theory because they would be staying in their narrow lane of neuroscience. They might believe consciousness comes from the brain, so there would be no need to look outside it. It is only when one pulls in observations and theories from clinical psychology and psychiatry, philosophy, physics, and spirituality that the previously unexplained evidence from psi research and reincarnation, past life regression and spiritual experiences becomes explainable and they might begin to see how it could *maybe* be possible.

14

Tying It Together . . . by Opening the Mind

The path towards transcendence is seeded by a noetic experience: an experience of receiving information in some way other than the traditional sensory or logical means. Although the experience can be initially denied or thought to be crazy, if we eventually accept the experience itself and its aftermath, the experience alters our worldviews and we are on the path to transcendence. This acceptance does not mean that we discard our logical capacities, just that we now have one more tool in our tool chests for understanding the world and making decisions.

JULIA MOSSBRIDGE

Again, this can all feel like a lot to absorb; I've been there. We've just reviewed a good amount of evidence and theories. If your mind is like mine, it won't stop debunking overnight or with just one book. Tying the evidence together can help with opening the mind. Consider the following: You can dismiss and justify an accurate intuitive reading as lucky guesses *or* argue that past life regression is the patient making up a fictional story that inexplicably becomes therapeutic *or* classify all the hundreds of researchers that find evidence of clairvoyance, precognition, and telepathy as frauds *or* believe that NDEs are residual brain activity (even though that goes against the evidence) *or* insist that the thousands of cases of children describing past lives with verifiable details are due to pure coincidence *or* explain away spiritual and mystical experiences as simply neural activity with no meaning, but . . . *all of them?* All the evidence together that spans millennia, continents, countries, cultures, and disciplines strongly suggests that our scientific models of reality need an update.

The evidence can seem disconnected and unrelated, but we can use cosmopsychism and some of the spiritual texts to build an architecture for understanding. Bear with me as I play with these ideas. Consider that the entire Universe is made of consciousness. This consciousness, or the zero-point field, could also be chi from Taoism, prana from yoga, or the Akashic records from the Yoga Sutras of Patanjali—which are the entire universal collection of all thoughts, actions, emotions, and events from the past, present, and future theorized to exist in a nonphysical plane of existence. This field is where all possibility lies. Maybe the field can mold into separate, but connected, beings/people (think back to the whirlpool example), within which brains are used as receivers of various states of consciousness from the field and minds are used to further separate the being from the field in order to fully experience life. The opening line of Hindu philosopher Patanjali's famous sutras says that "Yoga (becoming one with God) is mind-wave quieting" (can we take a moment to appreciate the fact that he knew about brain waves before electricity existed?!) (Targ 2012). He described how we can see the world and get in touch with our divine nature and the Akashic records by learning to stop our ongoing mental chatter and by becoming the records, with a "single-pointed focus of attention," which is strikingly similar to the way high-performer participants in psi research describe their methods and experience of successful trials. So maybe we can access different frequencies of the field by quieting the mind, which sometimes allows impressions from the field to enter the mind, such as those experienced in anomalous cognition.

Could holism explain the archetypes from Carl Jung's theory and the symbolic meaning of dreams and coffee grounds? Instead of reducing everything to atoms and particles, think of forms being born in the Universe with inherent symbolic meaning. Perhaps the thoughts, emotions, and actions of life become entangled with each being and are carried forward into existence even after bodily death, such as the *samskaras* from various schools of Indian philosophy, where a universal balancing force like karma attempts to reset the energetic scales. Perhaps altered states of consciousness provide such profound healing because they allow access to the field and permit an energetic reset of these scars, allowing the soul/consciousness to come closer to returning to its original burden-free nature.

I've been showing the *how* that links spirituality, philosophy, physics, quantum physics, and neuroscience. What all of this doesn't explain is the *why*. We still don't know why the Universe would have emerged to be this system and operate in this specific way. One possible explanation comes from the spiritual framework of reincarnation, karma, and soul lessons that explains that the cycles of life are for soul/consciousness evolution. Although this could easily be dismissed as just one of many possible spiritual explanations, I would argue it is an important one to consider, since this spiritual framework is described by individuals in relaxed states who neither consciously have knowledge of the spiritual framework nor believe in it, but nonetheless outline it.

Keppler's cosmopsychism model is by no means the only possible model that could work. Nevertheless, interaction with the field could explain all types of unexplained phenomena, so let's use this model as a framework to look at the evidence and list some additional questions that arise.

- Past Life Regression Hypnosis—This and any other hypnotic, ultrarelaxed altered state could put the brain in frequency alignment and allow access to the field and the subsequent download of past life information, allowing us to see what else our souls/consciousness have been up to.

How do we specifically access our past lives? Do we all have specific "frequencies"? Are our specific frequencies our souls/consciousness?

- Meditative States and Psychedelics—Quieting the mind, getting into a meditative state, or taking a psychedelic medicine could put you in a specific frequency alignment with the zero-point field that allows for the perception of the field, and thus the interconnectedness of everything and the timelessness and spacelessness of existence.

  Why don't we have conscious access to everything all the time? What's the deal with the beings or embodied consciousness appearing in these states?

- Savants, Terminal Lucidity, and NDEs—These all could be exceptional cases when access to the field occurs without a fully functioning brain; in other words, a properly working receiver for the field.

  Does this suggest there could be an alternate route of interacting with the field besides the brain? Or perhaps there exists an override function that bypasses the usual brain structures or states? What factors contribute to kicking the override function into gear?

- Souls—Souls could simply be consciousness that is a projection of a Holist Universe.

  What is the composition of souls and spirits? How can we become more aware of our interactions with other forms of disembodied consciousness more frequently? Can we make technology that allows better access? Can we make technology to embody disembodied consciousness?

- Energy Healing—This could occur by tapping into the zero-point field and facilitating a transfer of energy.

Is the field intelligent? How does this work mechanically? Is energy or information pulled from the field to help healing? Is it concentrated or funneled into a particular location? But how exactly?

- Divination Techniques—Perhaps the meaning from symbols in coffee fortune readings, dreams, and tarot exist in the field because of holism and are transmitted through the person doing the reading.

  But might the field also be interacting with matter (and not solely through the person), by shifting the grounds to be in a particular shape or pattern that multiple individuals can agree on? Or does it work by manipulating our perception of what we would consider matter?

- Universal Spirit, Archangels, Ascended Masters—Perhaps the field is intelligent, or sentient, and participatory and is perceived by people as higher level beings.

  Does the Universe know what you need because it is participatory? Does that intelligence manifest in various forms of consciousness that enter our awareness as stories of Universal Spirit, Archangels, Ascended Masters, and so on?

All told, no one needs to panic. Much of our current neuroscience is still valid, and none of this would invalidate it. Think back to the TV set analogy. We still need the brain for the functions to be expressed, and it is very useful to know how the brain does that. Moving forward, however, it would be great to investigate whether and how the brain and field interact and how consciousness is—to continue the TV metaphor—streamed.

Do I think cosmopsychism is the definitive model of the Universe? To be completely frank, I have no idea. There are plenty of other models of consciousness and the Universe trying to tie together the disparate sets of evidence from different disciplines. While I don't know which model is right, I do know that any model of the Universe that includes connection to a broader consciousness explains plenty more of human experience than does scientific materialism. A model simply cannot be correct when ignoring so many classes of data. Ignoring one line of outlying evidence is understandable, but overlooking many lines of evidence is just reckless disregard, and maybe even intentional ignorance. There are too many converging lines of evidence to think that all these findings are simply unimportant anomalies.

15
How Could I Have Missed This?

First, you know, a new theory is attacked as absurd; then, it is admitted to be true, but obvious and insignificant; finally, it is seen to be so important that its adversaries claim that they themselves discovered it.

WILLIAM JAMES

How could I have missed the holes in our current scientific worldview? I am just as guilty as anyone, and I have tried to show that here with this book, with 'old me.' I began this journey not expecting to find scientific evidence for my experiences, because the mainstream scientific materialist narrative suggests that evidence doesn't exist for unexplained phenomena, and to believe in these phenomena means you are either batty or stupid. Instead, I was searching for personal justification in being at least a little open to spiritual or metaphysical beliefs by speaking with other like-minded people. While I did find that (yay!), I also stumbled across a huge problem in scientific materialism: How could we hope to have a theory of everything when we so narrowly define what kind of evidence from which fields of knowledge can be included? To borrow Richard Tarnas's own language, he examines "the great philosophical, religious, and scientific ideas and movements that, over the centuries, gradually brought forth the world and world view we inhabit and strive within today." This is a worldview driven by the principles of the Scientific Revolution and the Age of Enlightenment that separated man from nature and emphasized reason above other human faculties, as you'll see in chapter 17. To refer to this worldview going forward, I use "society" for shorthand.

As I was delving into these various topics, I noticed the constant use of the word "pseudoscience" in media reports and on Wikipedia. I also found that Mark Boccuzzi of the Windbridge Research Center was correct: Google Scholar does not easily index articles from the peer-reviewed journals that investigate exploratory scientific topics, making them difficult to locate. Who decided that? I also read, frankly, many quite aggressive and condescending takedowns of anyone affiliated with ideas outside the dogma of scientific materialism. Again, this was *so* 'old me,' so I get it. As I educated myself, though, I realized how blindly the dogma was upheld—blindly, yet ferociously! It has been sewn so seamlessly into the fabric of society that I didn't see it, but I felt it when someone might try to pull the thread. I tried to think very hard about why this would be, putting myself back into my old shoes. Part of the reason is that I simply accepted what I heard from society: The Universe is random and meaningless, unexplained phenomena are impossible, and there's no evidence for a spiritual Universe. Go against this tenet and there will be mockery from many angles. 'Old me' most definitely would have retorted something along the lines of, "There's no evidence for that" to the idea of any of these alternative science topics—despite there being no way I could have known, since I had never bothered to look it up. Psychologist Imants Barušs and cognitive neuroscientist Julia Mossbridge list the commonly used strategies for discrediting exploratory research into unexplained and anomalous phenomena in their book *Transcendent Mind,* such as calling things "woo-woo," "pseudoscience," or "junk science." But here's the thing: I read the studies, and they rigorously used the scientific method. There was nothing "pseudo" about them; the topic of study was simply outside the arbitrary boundaries of research deemed acceptable by scientific materialism. So why are we perpetuating this false narrative?

It would be easy for me to blame Western society and mainstream science, but I also learned the importance of examining our own roles in our lives during this excruciating transformation. Yes, the message from society is that believing in unexplained or spiritual phenomena is irrational because these phenomena are impossible, but *I* believed that message. I believed that not only would I be foolish for believing, but, heaven forbid, others would view me as stupid, too. And there it is folks: The reason it was so challenging for me to accept spirituality without science was that science made me feel smart, and for whatever reason, I needed that for my self-worth. I betrayed myself and my experiences for who I thought I should be, and so that I would be regarded as valuable. The greatest unearthed treasure on my adventure was discovering that I have more to offer than purely my intelligence, logic, and capability to produce work, even though society suggests these are the most valuable traits I can offer. But in truth, compassion, kindness, and providing comfort for others are just as worthwhile.

Being a woman in science is already difficult. There are persistent worries of not being taken seriously by male colleagues, of how to dress, of how much makeup to wear, of how to speak, and more. Adding spiritual belief in the impossible to that list? Forget it. But ultimately, I got so tired of conforming to a fictional ideal that I prioritized being my authentic self. Who is the authentic me? Ah, well that is the point of the journey of life, the self-realization.

Our own fear and egos contribute to this myopic view held by mainstream science. Maybe, like me, other scientists like being perceived as smart. Maybe taboo research topics make scientists fear appearing *not* smart. I can see how that would elicit an emotional and defensive response. Or perhaps it is because they prefer having control over accepting mysteries (also like me)—maybe they are afraid of spirits and an unseen world! But I tell this personal story of identity transformation because the most likely explanation for pushback by scientists is inevitably because of the fear of loss of their own egos. Much of their identities are as materialist scientists, and those identities are tied up in a lifetime's worth of work, so the resistance is understandable. Not to mention that it is also tied to their livelihood and that there exist very real threats to that livelihood by associating with fringe science ideas and concepts. So we resist admitting being interested in socially unacceptable things.

But it turns out many scholars are interested in these topics and have personal experience. We know this for a fact because you can get scientists, psychologists, and physicians to share their miraculous, unexplained, and anomalous stories with you when you promise confidentiality, like I did for my project, or like Scott Kolbaba does in his book *Physicians' Untold Stories: Miraculous Experiences Doctors Are Hesitant to Share with Their Patients, or ANYONE!* (2016), or as Paul J. Leslie does in his book *Shadows in the Session: The Presence of the Anomalous in Psychotherapy* (2020). Sometimes it does take a personal experience to flip a scientist into believing in "impossible" things, as Jeffrey J. Kripal outlines in his excellent book *The Flip* (2019). Here, the classical materialist scientist can stop denying and erasing "so much of human experience to retain the illusion of the completeness of the materialist model." If you are a scientist looking for more validation, please read *The Flip*!

I believe that's how I missed the holes in my previous worldview.

ACADEMICS *ARE* INTERESTED IN IMPLICATIONS FOR SPIRITUALITY FROM UNEXPLAINED PHENOMENA

The prevailing attitude in intellectual circles is that no serious person believes, or is even interested, in unexplained or spiritual phenomena. That's simply not true. Many prominent scientists, physicians, philosophers, and writers throughout history have been interested in bridging spirituality and science, which has sometimes included studying unexplained phenomena. For example, William James was a member of the Society for Psychical Research (SPR)—a nonprofit started out of Cambridge University that still exists today and performs scientific investigation of extraordinary and unexplained phenomena. Other members included Nobel laureate and physiologist Charles Richet, Nobel laureate and physicist Sir J. J. Thomson, and Sir Arthur

Conan Doyle. The legendary psychologist Carl Jung and physicist Wolfgang Pauli had an entire dialogue around the relationship between mind and matter, synchronicity, and spirit, and it was partly to find an explanation for the Pauli effect, a phenomenon in which mind-over-matter effects manifested routinely around Pauli. Nobel laureate in physics Brian Josephson, who was interested in spiritual higher states of consciousness and psi phenomena, such as telepathy and psychokinesis, called the scientific community's dismissal of anything mystical or New Agey as "pathological disbelief." Marie Curie, the first woman to win a Nobel Prize, attended séances and studied the physics of paranormal phenomena. Francis Bacon performed divination, Galileo Galilei read horoscopes, Isaac Newton studied alchemy, and Albert Einstein wrote the preface to Upton Sinclair's book on telepathy, *Mental Radio* (1930).

It's not just prominent historical scientists, either. I wrote this sentence, thinking it to be true: "Generally, scientists tend to be atheists." Then I went to find a reference for it from the Pew Research Center. I was surprised to find that this statement was, in fact, not true. A 2009 Pew Research survey (Rosentiel 2009) of scientists who were members of the American Association for the Advancement of Science found that just over half of scientists (51%) believed in some kind of higher power (33% believed in "God," 18% believed in a universal spirit or higher power). Forty-one percent did not believe in any kind of higher power. That's almost a 50/50 split! I was blown away. Recognizing that my scientific colleagues and I rarely discussed spirituality was one of the reasons I started the project. I had assumed—probably erroneously based on this data—that they too are atheists or agnostics and were not interested in discussing such trivial topics. Welp, I was wrong.

The breakdown of believing scientists varies greatly from the American general population. A majority of Americans (24% believe in reincarnation [Pew Research Center 2009a], 95% believe in God or some higher power or spiritual force [Pew Research Center 2009b]), 46% believe in the existence of other supernatural beings (Ballard 2019), and 76% report having at least one paranormal belief (ESP being the most common at 41%) (Moore 2006).

Do scientists believe in the paranormal? Although a 1991 National Academy of Sciences survey of its members revealed that only 4% believed in ESP (McConnell and Clarke 1991), 10% believed it should be investigated. However, another study that anonymously surveyed 175 scientists and engineers found that 93.2% had at least one "exceptional human experience" (e.g., felt another person's emotions, had known something to be true that they would have no way of knowing, received important information through dreams, or seen colors or energy fields around people, places, or things) (Wahbeh et al. 2018). What an interesting discrepancy that under one set of circumstances, scientists deny believing in ESP, yet under another, they admit to having experiences of it. There could be many reasons for this, such as scientists being uncomfortable reporting their interest in ESP to a prestigious scientific institution and less uncomfortable doing so to a small, anonymous study. Or it could be because of the differences in wording used in the surveys, such as using "exceptional human experience" instead of "ESP," a much more stigmatized word in the intellectual community. If the latter is true, that would be an excellent example of the weight language carries in understanding and expressing our experiences. Very recently, over one hundred notable scientists have called for a post-materialist science where such topics are openly investigated, rather than quietly brushed under the rug ("The Manifesto for a Post-Materialist Science: Campaign for Open Science").

Dean Radin, Ph.D., chief scientist at the Institute of Noetic Sciences, who is trained in electrical engineering, physics, and psychology and who performs psi research, has hilariously described mainstream scientists' relationship with psi research in his book *Real Magic*. "If they are secretly interested in psi—and many are—they first swear everyone to secrecy, and then they approach it slowly while wearing a full hazmat suit, with multiple alibis set up in advance to provide plausible deniability"(Radin, 2018).

Based on his interactions with scientists at scientific meetings, such as those held at the U.S. National Academy of Sciences, in conjunction with the inquiries he receives, he states that his "impression is that the majority of scientists and scholars are personally interested in psi, but they've learned to keep their interests quiet. The same is true for many government, military, and business leaders. . . . The taboo is much stronger in the Western world (e.g., United States, Europe, Australia) than it is in Asia and South America" (Radin, 2018).

Through the dialogues I had with some of my neuroscience colleagues, I realized that they were much more open to nonmainstream scientific research topics than I had thought they would be. I even had a colleague who recounted to me how his brother, when he was under three years old, had shared memories that he could not have known from their grandmother's life in a country she had previously lived in before getting married. Another colleague, who had at one point been interested in psi research, had even bought dowsing rods to test them out. I had yet another colleague who, when I went to describe the research that I had been reading about telepathy, clairvoyance, and precognition, was already familiar with it and had read much of it himself. I'm not claiming that they're all believers but rather highlighting the fact that we were all interested in unconventional topics and didn't know that about each other. What fun conversations had we missed out on?!—I blame scientific materialism.

Because spiritual, mystical, or unexplained topics are taboo in mainstream science, it felt like my experiences were unique to me and I was alone in being curious about them. That's why I am making the point here that many, many academics are interested in spiritual and unexplained phenomena, or *typical human experiences,* as I now think of them. We're actually not alone at all. If more academics, and especially scientists, could shake off the invisible, but restrictive, shackles of culture and publicly admit their interest in unexplained mysteries, maybe we could explain the unexplainable.

WHAT ELSE ARE WE MISSING?

By excluding certain topics from scientific investigation, could we be missing other important findings in science?

If it's true that consciousness is fundamental and our minds interact with matter, what are the implications for the scientific method, which assumes an independent, objective observer/experimenter? What are we missing by ignoring this connection? What if when things come together, like an experimenter and a subject, they form a whole or a system and are no longer independent (think of how schools of fish swim or flocks of birds fly together)? And what about statistics? We colloquially and scientifically throw around the words "by chance." What force or law governs "chance"? Think of the bell curve, how it shows the majority of individuals in a population will fall in the middle of the curve for some trait (let's say altruism) and tapers off on the lower and higher ends. When we perform an experiment and recruit participants, we hope to find that in our study altruism among our participants falls along a bell curve indicating that we have a distribution that is representative of the general population. In fact, our statistical analysis can depend on it. But what force governs which subjects show up for your study enabling you to achieve that bell curve? Is there ever such a thing as something being truly due to chance? Thinking this way brings up a lot of questions around what we hold to be true in science.

Increasingly, society proposes that our beliefs and behaviors should be firmly planted in rock solid evidence and empirical data. Besides the glaring problem that humans clearly do not operate in this way, as evidenced by the entire history of humankind, during which many ill-advised and seemingly irrational leadership decisions have been made, there is another problem. The problem with that notion is the inherent assumption that humans have the technological or methodological means to measure and collect evidence and data on everything in the Universe, meaning that we have already discovered all properties of the world. If that assumption is not true, but we behave as if it were true, we will be potentially missing out on having a complete understanding of the Universe. Why would we do that?

In fact, Western society's recent overemphasis on "evidence-based" and "data-driven" criteria has me concerned, because evidence and data cost money. Let me explain. Clearly it is beneficial to have evidence proving something works as intended; for example, a medical device. The problem arises when we erroneously conclude that something doesn't work or doesn't exist simply because there is no available evidence to support it. This phrase, "There is no evidence to support that," is sometimes used by scientists and journalists in a disingenuous way. When the public hears that phrase, they assume the thing has been investigated and no evidence was found to support it, when in fact, what is usually meant is that the thing has *not been investigated*. So why not just say that? It is misleading and is constantly used to knock down anything not accepted by scientific materialism. Moreover, usually the lack of investigation is not typically due to lack of interest—it is usually because of lack of funding. The majority of science funding in the United States comes from the federal government. The research agendas of most research scientists at academic institutions across the country are determined by what the scientist believes will get funding. Further, federal legislation drives the themes of research for periods of time. For example, after many military personnel returned home from the long wars in the Middle East, an impressive amount of legislation and money was put toward research for traumatic brain injury (TBI), and for post-traumatic stress disorder (PTSD). A TBI is an injury that disrupts normal brain function, and PTSD is a disorder with a constellation of symptoms that develops in some people who have experienced a terrifying and traumatic event. Scientists then scrambled to find a way to frame their research as falling under these themes. Research funding for other topics can come from private foundations. However those funding streams are driven by the personal interests of the wealthy individuals who established the foundations. So please think of this when you hear someone throwing around the word "evidence-based." It would be really nice to have enough money for researchers to investigate anything they wanted and all the interesting questions in the Universe, but in reality, research agendas, and thus evidence and data, are dictated by money, the interests of the government, and wealthy individuals.

I want to take this one step further: What if there are things that can't be measured or explained by the scientific method itself? By deeming the scientific method the *only* important way to measure and understand the world around us, we are inherently saying that if something exists in the Universe that can't be measured by this method, then it is not important or worth knowing. There is a contradiction between believing that we only know for certain what we can measure and observe and the fact that we are using our brains to measure and observe. We know that both physics and quantum physics are true, but we can't reconcile them, and yet we persist in declaring that the scientific method is *the* method.

The limitation of the scientific method is something I encountered on my journey that helped me accept personal proof in addition to scientific proof, and it is also the reason consciousness itself is so hard to study. *There are just some things about the human experience that are hard to quantify and that aren't replicable.* Science can't measure those experiences, and they are usually delegated to the humanities—but then there is no communication between the humanities and science when developing theories about the Universe. We don't experience life in two dimensions, with separate scientific and humanities experiences; it's just one life experience. We need to include both the sciences and the humanities in constructing theories of this stunning, horrid, blissful, cruel thing we call life.

A MEANINGFUL AND MYSTICAL UNIVERSE

Had I stumbled across all of this information years ago while I was still in graduate school, or even when I had just graduated, I don't think I would have ever written this book. The series of life events that unfolded for me—the power of my mother's readings and predictions and an existential crisis—were all needed to open me up to new modes of thinking. Maybe it all happened in "divine timing," as the intuitives say.

Understanding that consciousness could be the foundation of the Universe reframed my thinking in such a way that unexplained phenomena did not seem extraordinary any longer. It all seemed really simple, actually, and not a big deal. Based on scientific and personal proof,

I now thought it possible that our souls/consciousness reincarnate, carry karma, and evolve by learning lessons. I took this spiritual framework for a test drive and was dazzled at the way it reshaped my interaction with life. When I moved outside the scientific literature into the suggested reading from "the people who know," I learned that the Greeks used the word *Cosmos* to describe the Universe as an orderly system. This is an ancient idea found in most cultures across the world since the beginning of the emergence of humanity. At the confluence of science and spirituality, a new worldview emerged for me: The Universe has meaning and there exists a spiritual and mystical dimension to life. Believing that we are interwoven with the Cosmos and that there is no true distinction between mind and matter, outside and inside, or you and me, has actually been the foundation of reality longer than it hasn't.

16
Pulling Back the Curtain
Science Is Not Enough

We need more than just science to understand the Cosmos and human experience. I hope there is no doubt about how much I love the scientific method—I did cite scientific research extensively throughout this book! But like anything else, it has its limitations. I discussed a few in the previous chapter, such as how funding drives research topics and not everything about human experience can be measured by the scientific method. Let's pull the curtain back even farther and dig in a bit more by examining scientific assumptions and politics.

SCIENCE AND THE ACADEMY

By the time I left graduate school I knew that science, and we as a society, most definitely did not have all the answers (although, as I have already mentioned, I was an inductee into the Science Cult and a true believer). When a science experiment is wrapped up, published, and presented to the public, we usually have to summarize the findings in a neat and tidy way that the ordinary public can understand. In actuality, though, biological systems and the natural world are incredibly complex systems that have multiple overlapping and dependent variables. We design studies to the best of our ability to isolate variables so that we can examine causes and effects. We have advanced statistical methods to ascertain the certainty of what we have observed in the experiments, but our statistical thresholds are somewhat arbitrary, and we can sometimes leave unexplained variance within our results in the dust. For each decision made in an experiment, there were plenty of different options to choose from. That means that there are many branch points in the design and analysis of scientific studies, and if you had made a different decision along the way, the results of the study could have turned out completely differently—and they often do, contributing to the "replication crisis" I mentioned earlier.

While it is true that we have good reasons for making the decisions that we do in experiments most of the time, I want to highlight that a lot of the decisions are based on assumptions. In neuroscience in particular, we *assume* that personality traits can be accurately captured and classified by surveys. We *assume* that blood flow in a particular part of the brain indicates that the brain is working in that area and is correlated with behavior. We *assume* that brains across a population are similar enough that we can generalize findings. We *assume* researchers are independent, objective, unbiased components of an experiment who have no effect on the outcome of the experiment. And of course, and this one is important, we *assume* consciousness is produced by the brain. In scientific materialism, as already mentioned, we assume that the physical world is independent of our perceptions, that physical laws can be discovered and described, and that these laws are constant throughout the Cosmos. I make this point because, in order for our results to be accurate, all of those assumptions that we make need to be true.

I go into detail here to convey the complexity of performing scientific research. To be clear, the scientific method is an exceptional tool for investigating and expanding our understanding of the Cosmos. There are many things we learn by using the scientific method, and there are many practical applications of science. Science has aided humanity in finally understanding cause and effect, which has propelled our advancements in medicine and technology, and humans are, albeit arguably, better off now than in centuries before. I'm grateful for the advancement every single morning when I wake up to an automatically ready cup of coffee and an Instagram inbox full of cute animal videos to watch from my friends. Using the pandemic as another example, I appreciate that technology enabled communication during our "two weeks to flatten the curve" that turned into a year-long quarantine. It was scientific progress that provided many beneficial treatments for diseases. Again, I have and will always have profound respect for the scientific process and the advancements it has brought us. Despite this, if any of our assumptions about the Cosmos are wrong—such as that time flows in one direction and that we are independent observers of reality—which they appear to be according to quantum physics—then the models need to be updated.

From a place of appreciation for science and what it has done for humanity, I am going to pull the curtain back a bit farther, because after having gone through this journey I find a tad bit comical the pedestal that science is held upon, especially having been exposed for so long to the incredibly narrow, petty, and infantile reality of the academic scientific world. Reputations and careers are sustained by publishing papers—for which researchers are not compensated—and the sentiment is captured perfectly by the popular phrase "publish or perish." Publications—the currency of a scientist's livelihood—are peer reviewed by scientific competitors (yes, those exist). Can you imagine a venture fund consulting a CEO from a competitor company to review your product (like Nike reviewing Adidas) and making a recommendation on an investment?

The system rewards incremental innovation and staying in line—not earth-shattering, unorthodox, contrarian thinking. Max Planck captured the sentiment well, saying, "Science advances one funeral at a time." We are so narrowly trained and *specialized* that, even within the field of neuroscience, an experimenter studying individual neurons may not even know the different lobes of the human brain! They are brilliant, beautiful, earnest people trapped in a broken system.

So despite science being invaluable, many fundamental limitations and practical constraints prevent it from being the only method capable of helping us understand the Cosmos and human experience. Mainstream science encourages curiosity and open thinking, but you know, not *too* open, not *too* curious.

17

Moving Toward a
Meaningful Cosmos

*Our psyche is set up in accord with the structure of the universe,
and what happens in the macrocosm likewise happens in the
infinitesimal and most subjective reaches of the psyche.*

C. G. JUNG

Continuing to explore other fields of knowledge, I came to realize that
although the modern Western worldview is quite dominant in the present
day, it has only existed for a sliver of human existence. Many of its
foundational philosophies were birthed during the Scientific Revolution
and the Age of Enlightenment. Before those two movements, religion
provided an understanding of the world and, by providing a reason for
existence, supplied meaning to life. From the rational and physicalist
beliefs of the Enlightenment, the Cosmos eventually came to be viewed
as inherently random and meaningless. As scientific advancements
provided increasing control over nature, and previous mysteries of the
world became explainable, a deep reverence for science, and the skepticism we see exhibited by scientific materialism, emerged. It was believed
that scientific progress was limitless and, eventually, everything could
be explained by scientific methods.

It's true we have seen miraculous progress, but it's also true that *many many* things in the world remain mysterious, and instead of trying to explore these mysteries, scientific materialism has decided to ignore them. The benefits of the West's view of the world have come at significant costs, some being manifested as modern-day society's increased existential and mental health crises. Let's look at some of the differences between worldviews and how the Western worldview may not be working out for us as hoped, after all.

WESTERN VS. ANIMA MUNDI WORLDVIEWS

The boundary between self and other, subject and object, and human and nature are different between the modern Western worldview and the holistic and ecological worldview characteristic of traditional indigenous cultures (as well as the ancient Greeks, medieval scholastics, Renaissance humanists, and many more). In the latter worldview, the entire world and Cosmos are viewed as having a soul, an anima mundi. For simplicity, I will refer to this as the anima mundi worldview. Everything—humans, plants, animals, the Earth, stars, planets—are connected in a living matrix that is naturally embedded with meaning. These cultures find meaning in everything, including the patterns of weather, the activity of animals, and the movement of stars. To them, the world is intelligent, intentional, spiritual, meaningful, alive, and purposeful, and it communicates through symbols and archetypes. The human psyche is viewed as part of the Cosmos, and the Cosmos is part of the human psyche, because we are a microcosm of the macrocosm (Tarnas 2006). In this system, it is believed humans can access this intelligent matrix with their own subconscious minds through altered states of consciousness that can be achieved through dance, chanting, substances, and other methods. Typically, individuals will be selected and trained in these spiritual and mystical practices to heal, perform divination, or control events, such as in shamanism. Cultures that subscribe to the anima mundi worldview are mindful of balance with nature because they believe they are intimately and divinely connected to it.

This worldview is in sharp contrast to the modern Western worldview that sees humankind as completely separate from its surroundings; in other words, as a subject separate from objects, including all living and nonliving things. Meaning is created solely from the human mind and should not be projected onto the external world or the Cosmos, which are inherently random, mechanistic, and purposeless. With this ideology and its advancement in science, humans have aimed to control and dominate nature as a resource to be owned and utilized for the benefit of humankind. This patriarchal worldview prioritizes rationality, logic, reason, productivity, individuality, hierarchies, and domination over emotion, intuition, compassion, equality, sustainability, and partnership. Anything not aligned with the tenets is denigrated.

The thing is, though, as depth psychologist Richard Tarnas (2006) puts it, the anima mundi ". . . cosmos was universally *experienced*, for countless millennia, as tangibly self-evidently alive and awake— pervasively intentional and responsive, informed by ubiquitous spiritual presences, animated throughout by archetypal forces and intelligible meanings."

IT'S NOT WORKING OUT

There are countless ways the modern Western worldview has failed us, and I will expand on a few here that most pertain to spiritual and mystical experiences. In particular, I'll look at how the ideology has harmed us as an integrated society trying to understand life, as well as on an individual existential level.

The Western worldview, naturally, asserts itself as the dominant view of the world and condescendingly refers to other types of thinking or ways of being that challenge its foundational ideas as irrational, primitive, inferior, or undeveloped. It excludes countering narratives from mainstream culture with derision, makes those who are different feel their ideas and cultures are wrong, and causes pressure for conformity. Insisting and asserting that the Western worldview is the best and only respectable one is one way the West has demeaned and marginalized all other cultures and peoples. Women, too, have long been sidelined by the patriarchal West. Think of women being stereotyped as having greater intuition, an internal state that operates independently of reason. Is it a mere coincidence that we are then trained to be untrustworthy of that intuition (Rosenbaum 2011; Baruš and Mossbridge 2017)? The real kicker, though, is that scientific evidence shows that some of the tenets that we celebrate from the Age of Enlightenment are actually much more complicated than is generally believed, such as the finding that relying on unconscious processing of information, or intuition, can be advantageous in certain circumstances, such as decision making (Dijksterhuis et al. 2006; Voss, Lucas, and Paller 2012; Voss, Baym, and Paller 2008). Yet still, belief in things that the West deems impossible are referred to derogatorily as irrational, delusional, crazy, and magical thinking, despite the fact that the people usually espousing such beliefs are none of those things.

The experience of entire groups of people, such as those who experience subtle energy and unexplained phenomena, is also discounted. But we saw from the Cardeña (2018) meta-analysis that there is scientific evidence; and we can even see one possible mechanism for transcendental experience and subtle energy perception from the accounts from neuroscientist Dr. Bolte Taylor, whose brain's left hemisphere, the one responsible for reasoning, essentially went off-line after a stroke. She showed us that the right hemisphere does perceive subtle energy dynamics in a way that our left hemisphere does not.

She writes:

I hope your level of discomfort about such things as energy dynamics and intuition has decreased as you have increased your understanding about the fundamental differences in the way our two hemispheres collaborate to create our single perception of reality. . . . Our right hemisphere is designed to perceive and decipher the subtle energy dynamics we perceive intuitively. Since the stroke, I steer my life almost entirely by paying attention to how people, places, and things feel to me energetically.

She also writes:

Our right brain perceives the big picture and recognizes that everything around us, about us, among us, and within us is made up of energy particles that are woven together into a universal tapestry. Since everything is connected, there is an intimate relationship between the atomic space around and within me, and the atomic space around and within you—regardless of where we are.

The power that drives our nervous system and keeps our heart beating is just energy. Our senses receive energy signals that our brains translate. If you ever need a reminder, think of how humans appear on infrared cameras. Is it, then, still woo-woo to think that some people's brains are wired in such a way that the subtle energy detection ability of the right hemisphere is enhanced, as it was for Dr. Bolte Taylor following her stroke? It's entirely possible.

Terrence McKenna (1992), an ethnobotanist, wrote that when he visited the Amazon, he carried the Western world's assumptions that science could prove everything and that belief in magic, divination, or spiritual healing, the kind performed by Amazonian shamans, was naive. But after a few psychedelic trips, he wrote, "I was initially appalled at what I found: the world of shamanism, of allies, shape shifting, and magical attack are far more real than the constructs of science can ever be, because these spirit ancestors and their other world can be seen and felt, they can be known, in the nonordinary reality."

McKenna also believed that our disconnection from our unconscious minds and the anima mundi, living matrix, nature, and spiritual dimension—and the zero-point field?—have propelled humanity into the crisis of meaningless existence in which it now finds itself. I now happen to agree. Our society would have us believe we are birthed into an uncaring, indifferent world and we should nurture our sense of abandonment ourselves. A search is undertaken by the modern person to fill the missing hole, but they find nothing but anguish, frustration, shallow moments of joy, disappointment, and deep unfulfillment. No wonder the United States has a mental health crisis in which one in five Americans lives with a mental health condition (according to the National Alliance on Mental Illness), and there exists an alarming shortage of behavioral health practitioners. We can't find the missing pieces of ourselves, or our connection to the sacred, in a new Xbox, a Balenciaga gown, or a larger house.

I would include scientists in this group of people afflicted by mental health conditions. Let's even assume momentarily that the evolutionary theories are true about religious and spiritual belief systems having evolved to protect humans from the suffering of life by building meaning into events. Why do skeptics, believing they are upholding Western values, try so hard to squash that if it has a purported evolutionary purpose? Will we disadvantage the species in some way by doing so? As we saw earlier, scientists are split down the middle in whether they believe in a higher power, but those who do believe have reported feeling uncomfortable expressing their views to their colleagues. Why are we so inauthentic? Are we surprised about the high rates of mental health issues when scientists' livelihood requires them to think there is no meaning behind life? On the one hand, the scientific world condescendingly argues that stories of religion and spirituality are mechanisms of comfort and coping to help make it through the hellish existence of human life on Earth, and then we deprive scientists of having that comfort at the fear of ostracism and stigma? I wish I had known that before I went to graduate school!

I also believe the pushback on ideas, phenomena, or modalities that are not aligned with Western values is justified by the patriarchy with a narrative of "protection," especially when it comes to medicine and healing—which is a whole nother can of worms. Usually when people say something doesn't have evidence, they mean it could actually harm you. Those fears are not unjustified. I am keenly aware that belief can sometimes move people away from science in dangerous ways. Modern science and medicine have also, however, failed us in some ways. For physical and mental healing, in particular, I believe Western medicine comes up short. But rather than admit its weaknesses, we see the suppression of decentralized, alternate, and unconventional ideas with arrogance through patriarchal and hierarchical structures. Since the Western worldview prioritizes external, objective data, patients can struggle to be heard by their health care practitioners—a well-known consequence of this being the historic dismissal of the subjective experiences of women patients in Western medicine. Patients may feel judged by their health care practitioners when disclosing the use of healing remedies from their own non-Western cultures. I think people should be supported in seeking all healing modalities, especially when Western medicine has failed them. While protection from harm is important, shouldn't there also be room in health care for compassion, understanding, and inclusivity? As we saw from the meta-analysis of the noncontact healing studies, energy medicine has some budding scientific support. It also has significant anecdotal personal support from countless individuals, which may not be enough for statistically minded fields but could mean everything for a person in pain.

In summary, certain aspects of the Western worldview are not working for us, such as prioritizing reason and empirical evidence over intuition and personal experience, thereby denying the mystical and spiritual aspects of the world and that the world has meaning. The effects are seen in the way people and groups with different perspectives feel marginalized and inferior; this is creating a disintegrated society, as well as the existential and mental health crises of our society and limitations to the ways we heal.

MOVING FORWARD

I didn't write this book to just complain about my existential crisis and transformation. I really believe there is great potential in broadening our worldview by incorporating the evidence of spiritual and unexplained phenomena, because it hints at a radiantly interlaced reality where we are more supported than we think. Here are some implications I see for moving forward.

IMPLICATIONS FOR HEALING

What most caught my attention from the past life regression literature, and then again later in the psychedelic work, was the surprising and extensive mental and physical healing that resulted from the practice. This is *the* most important implication, in my opinion. Not only did the extensive literature on altered states of consciousness reveal effective resolution of chronic mental and physical issues, but I also personally experienced the dramatic healing effects. As mentioned above, Western medicine, psychiatry, and psychology leave much to be desired, and is it any wonder when they are using incomplete models of the Cosmos derived from only one worldview? I am grateful that there are a number of formally trained health practitioners recognizing this problem and working to incorporate more healing modalities to address trauma, such as Drs. Dan Siegel, Gabor Maté, Peter Levine, and Bessel Van der Kolk. But we need much more than a small cohort of broad-minded thinkers. Our society is plagued with mental health issues and unresolved trauma, and we take our issues out into the world with us. Instead of focusing on healing ourselves—arguably the most important thing one can do—our society is focused on acquiring material success. It's time to change that. It's time to combine the scientific accomplishments since the Enlightenment, the developments in psychology from the past 150 years, and other worldviews in addition to the West's to heal ourselves and find purpose.

IMPLICATIONS FOR SCIENCE

Science needs to cross into interdisciplinary territory to tackle the gigantic questions of fully comprehending the Cosmos and human experience—and I mean *way* across the aisle. All scientists need to seek knowledge from other disciplines to help place scientific materialism into a larger human historic context. Many subfields of the humanities, such as anthropology, the history of non-Western cultures, and ethnobotany, to name just a few, can potentially provide new ways of thinking about systems and cycles of nature. Philosophy can help supply the subjective component of understanding consciousness that science cannot address. While neuroscience has been enormously informative about the underlying biological mechanisms of behavior, especially in animal studies, clinical psychology can provide insight into what actually truly works on shaping human behavior and healing trauma and interpersonal issues in the real world, as opposed to in the lab. In fact, while the majority of psychedelic research of the current day has come from neuroscience labs, the initial extensive, comprehensive, and groundbreaking work of using psychedelics for personal healing has come from transpersonal psychology. If you really want to have your mind blown, read anything written by Stanislav Grof, one of the founders of transpersonal psychology. Also, depth psychology, particularly Carl Jung's work, provides unique observations and theories about synchronicities and how the human psyche is inextricably linked to the Cosmos.

Now that we have scientific and philosophical models that help explain spiritual and mystical experiences, as well as the experiences of intuitives, mediums, and energy healers, would it be too wild to suggest that we also include metaphysics in the conversation? Maybe we should listen more closely to people who claim to be sensitive to subtle energy because their descriptions of how things work might lead us to more answers? For example, when reviewing the neuroscientific findings earlier, I found descriptions of the new brain metric, CHD, that showed a spectrum of consciousness from anesthesia up to psychedelics with increasing frequency harmonics. When reading the finding, I immediately thought about how people who subscribe to New Age thought always seem to be talking about keeping your vibrations high to access the higher levels of consciousness, and how that enables you to be in flow with the Universe. Maybe that kind of elevated state truly does allow you to connect to the zero-point field better (I can't believe I'm saying this). Of course, this is a huge jump, and I'm just using this example to demonstrate how the phenomenological experiences of unexplained phenomena could be useful in moving forward with scientific theory. As yet another example, Keppler suggested measuring phase transitions in the brain with photons. Maybe that's why intuitives and mediums use the words "light energy" when describing mystical things. I used to roll my eyes at those words, but now I have seen an actual scientific model proposing such a thing in a peer-reviewed scientific journal. I know this is a blasphemous suggestion, and I'm imagining some scientists recoiling at the thought of respectfully engaging with spiritual or metaphysical people. I'd tell them what many of the intuitives I went to see (embarrassingly) told me: *Get off your high horse.* There's already a bit of progress with labs, like the COPE Project at Yale, taking seriously the claims of individuals that see and hear more things than others (i.e., intuitives, mediums, mystics, and those with visual and auditory "hallucinations") and investigating the differences between these individuals, who are capable of living normal and healthy lives, and those with serious mental illness who are not. But imagine what else we can learn!

If we take the model of cosmopsychism, as just one example, and ask whether mental illness is perhaps a broken connection with the zero-point field, as Keppler ponders, we can study how this might be solved with a new technology or therapeutic practice. Or perhaps we could identify the override function from savants and terminal lucidity and extend the application to TBI, stroke, and dementia patients. Maybe by using newly developed methods of more easily tapping into the zero-point field we will find greater insight into the inner working of the Universe, providing inspiration for new scientific breakthroughs. The possibilities are endless. It's not science fiction; I believe it could be the future of science.

It is important to continue doing traditional science research because it does have benefits, but it is also imperative that we invest in research supporting models other than scientific materialism to begin filling the holes in our incomplete model. Ultimately, whether consilience between the fields is obtainable is open to debate, but it is imperative that we work as though it is.

One more thing: If you are a scientist reading this and have never experienced anything mystical or spiritual, I want to invite you to try. Is meditation too demanding? Get a metaphysical reading of any kind, whether energy or intuitive or astrological or whatever. If you approach it with an open mind, you just might be surprised. I'm not promising you will be astonished because, as I have outlined in this book, there are many unknown factors that influence these interactions. But what do you have to lose? Thirty minutes of your time? Or maybe an hour and a half of your time if you get three different readings (which I recommend) to really get a good sample. You might come away with a completely new understanding of one (common) type of human experience.

IMPLICATIONS FOR SPIRITUALITY

I was vehemently anti-spiritual until my worldview failed me to the point that I wished I didn't exist. Although I was flirting with the idea that some kind of meaning structured the Cosmos by getting intuitive readings, I didn't use any spiritual framework to rethink my perspective of life until I was repeatedly confronted with the reincarnation and karma spiritual framework, and especially from clinical psychology and psychiatry. Because my mind works best with mechanisms, the scientific evidence for psi and the consciousness theories of the Cosmos helped bridge personal experience with spirituality. I am now comfortable accepting that I believe that meaning creates the Cosmos and that there is indeed a spiritual and mystical component. For me, the idea of a meaningful Cosmos immediately reduced my suffering. Adding on the framework of reincarnation, karma, and soul lessons was a bonus, creating a narrative for understanding my life's events.

If this is not our one and only life, and we truly carry karma over into the next ones, shouldn't we be behaving better? I know that for me, personally, reading all this material has changed the way I think about life and the way I behave. I am definitely not perfect by any means, but I try to be more cognizant of the way I think about situations, how I treat people, and how consciously I make decisions that align with my values. As cliché as it sounds, I try to lead with love and understanding. I fail a ton, but I try. That's why it's called a spiritual *practice*. We can start working together more effectively as a global population, say to address social justice and climate change issues, by seeing the truth: that we are one interconnected consciousness. Let's take seriously the results of the Global Consciousness Project that showed, when mass consciousness and attention were sharply focused on one event, random number generators behaved nonrandomly. As we improve our inner worlds, we also can improve the outer world. Feeling that deep interconnectedness among us can help shift our attention from the differences between us to the common issues that face us all, such as social justice, climate change, and the economy.

Personal experiential proof is important, too. If 5% of the human population experienced something like, say, their eyes turning purple for ten seconds every time they reached their max heart rate, but a study to quantify and document the effect was never conducted, would that mean the effect doesn't exist? Of course not. The purple eye syndrome would be very real for the 5% of people who experience it, and it shouldn't be discounted. Unfortunately, Western culture has made us question our own experiences, but they're important, too!

In summary, the implications range from poetic to practical. I brought you on my long journey in this book because trying to tie together unexplained phenomena, spirituality, science, and altered states of consciousness healing techniques at the outset would have been a challenge, not only to understand, but to accept—for both you and me! I hope I have laid a groundwork that more easily shows the connections and implications of these interrelated topics. If you choose to launch a personal exploration, you can start your own journey. I would even go so far as to say, after my own journey into the topic, that you might try to unbind your consciousness, soar through the oceanic Cosmos, touch the divine, and bring back a bit of magic to your everyday life. You might find a piece of yourself that you didn't know had been hiding. As a society, we should support internal flights through altered states of consciousness because of the dramatic healing that can arise. I also hope we can bridge fields of knowledge to exponentially advance our understanding of the Cosmos and, as a natural consequence, be more inclusive of the experiences and beliefs of others, because, even if it's not always obvious, we are one splendid labyrinth of glittering consciousness.

18

Sometimes Things Need to Die

You are not a drop in the ocean. You are the entire ocean in a drop.

R U M I

The death of your ego, your old life, your old self happens one thousand times—being only slightly less painful each passing. Similarly, healing happens bit by bit, one thousand more times.

As I said in the preface, I wished this had never happened and that I never had to write this book. In time, though, I have come to see this experience as a gift. Hopefully, this happens eventually for all of us with all experiences, but this shift in perspective began emerging for me unexpectedly from an interview I heard of Stephen Colbert by Anderson Cooper (Cooper 2019). Anderson Cooper had just lost his beloved mother, Gloria Vanderbilt, and asked Stephen Colbert, who lost his father and two brothers in a plane crash when he was ten years old, about how he previously had said that he had come to learn to "love the thing that I most wish had not happened." The rest of the exchange is below:

"You went on to say, 'What punishments of God are not gifts?' Do you really believe that?" Cooper asked.

"Yes," Colbert said. "It's a gift to exist and with existence comes suffering. There's no escaping that. What do you get from loss? You get awareness of other people's loss, which allows you to connect with that other person, which allows you to love more deeply and to understand what it's like to be a human being, if it's true that all humans suffer."

One reason I decided to write this book is that the journey was so mentally difficult for me—with so much belief and disbelief and uncertainty and revisiting of evidence. I saw firsthand within myself what it took to overthrow, or adjust, a belief system—even when faced with compelling evidence from decades of research from many labs, scientists, and other scholars. It was *damn* hard. My old beliefs went kicking and screaming, leaving scars in their wake. As my old beliefs tore away from me, they wrapped their tendrils around some of my self-illusions and forced me to *very reluctantly* face myself. Then I saw that it wasn't the beliefs I was attached to. It was the self-worth I thought I could earn through the beliefs.

My own existential crisis truly was a gift because it helped me to understand the broader range of human emotions, like despair and intense, unrelenting anger. I hope it has made me a more understanding and compassionate person. The image that comes to mind when I think of the crisis is a shattered mirror. Watching the broken pieces come back together in slow-motion rewind through my healing efforts has been surprisingly gratifying.

As for my intellectual journey, years of scientific training were no joke. The concepts and skepticism were so deeply ingrained in me that, no matter the vigor with which I tried to erase them, there still remained remnants of the pencil marks on the page. There was a lasting impression that continuously resurfaced, just when I thought I found new beliefs or turned the page. The new beliefs could, it seemed, so easily be overturned or, in the least, have a pin put in them for further consideration. For a return look. For a repeat tumble through the skepticism dryer. What would it take to finally accept a new belief system? Or was the identity so deeply ingrained that it wasn't possible?

It's just an identity, though. An ethereal concept. Something solid but ever changing, and something that can (apparently) cause a lot of inner turmoil. Or it's the attachment to the identity that causes the suffering. In thinking about this, it occurred to me that I'd have to grieve for my former self in some way to really accept the new version of myself that is open to ideas that are not yet accepted by scientific materialism. This book is part of that grieving process. In the end it was such a lovely gift to become more open minded to alternative views of the world, where I am the Cosmos and the Cosmos is me. Personal transformation is difficult because of our deep-seated identities and embodied beliefs, but it is possible to transform with hard work, surrendering, and asking, "What if I'm wrong?" Through my transformation, I eventually realized that I was only losing the identity of the person I *thought I should be*. One way I think about the process is as death and rebirth. When one identity dies, I let go, grieve, and let something new come in; this allows for a new identity to be born. Or I think of it as an unearthing of additional parts of myself. Each newly discovered part fuses with the previous parts to form a new whole, a new identity. Through it all, we can have compassion for ourselves for the experience. I have been intensely and thoroughly humbled in my ego's death and rebirth, and I hope to keep this humility with me as I continue moving through this life.

In reading esoteric texts, I found elegant knowledge and symbolism for the cycles of life: birth and death, light and dark, activity and rest, beginnings and endings, happiness and sadness, joy and despair. An understanding that sometimes things need to die to be replaced by better things could alleviate fear of transformation and help us all face ourselves.

At the beginning of this journey, I could not see what was causing my personal darkness, my dark night. A broken heart? Dissatisfaction with my career? That I didn't have a $20 million house in Bel Air? It turns out it was something far broader: my worldview. Living without meaning and purpose in a random, dead Universe was not working out for me, but I never would have come to this understanding by myself. I was lucky to have a series of coincidences lead me to spiritual exploration and self-actualization, which I now believe are parts of the purpose of life.

I now consider myself a spiritual scientist, and it fills me with indescribable light and joy to say that. It was, after all, a hard-earned destination. Finally, a semblance of peace has floated into my day-to-day existence. It's not that life got easier; it's just that my perspective changed. I still find myself having all the human trappings of desiring things, wanting specific outcomes, and reaching for some sort of control, but I practice letting go whenever I can. Believing that things happen for a reason and that maybe—*just maybe*—I chose these specific challenges for myself prior to this lifetime helps me take a step back, calm down, and not see myself as a victim of life. Honestly, whether I ever find out if the spiritual framework is true or not, I wouldn't trade this journey for anything.

One of my best friends told me that the ultimate test of my evolution would be my answer to the question, "Do you believe in God?" After a lifetime of flipping the bird to the word "God," it was admittedly hard to accept any kind of intelligence behind the Universe. That is the concept with which I have the most trouble. Reading the literature from physics and cosmology, though, and seeing that the odds of the emergence of the Universe and life were so slim that even physicists and cosmologists are amazed, did make me pause. Wondering whether we would ever be able to prove such a thing, it occurred to me that if there truly was an intelligence who was orchestrating things, then it would in no way be obligated to bow to our scientific method. Heck, if I were the intelligence behind everything and I was watching my human babies try to measure me, catch me, prove me, I would *most definitely* have some fun with it!

I don't know as a definitive fact that the spiritual framework involving soul lessons, karma, and reincarnation is true, but I can say that there is compelling scientific and personal evidence, and I can *choose* to believe it. Anything is possible! It is definitely worth investigating.

As for research into unexplained phenomena, if we hold it to the same standard as other fields of science, the results are very strongly in support of its existence. Personally, I have also had far too many out-of-this-world accurate intuitive readings and direct personal experiences to question the phenomena any longer. Sure, there is no *agreed-upon* mechanism. But what's so controversial about that? We don't know how the placebo effect works, either, but we accept that it does. So let's find out, and if everything truly is one field of interconnected consciousness (and that's where I'm leaning right now), then the phenomena are not anomalous at all—they're simply tapping into our broader consciousness.

It was comforting to know that many people had experiences similar to that of mine and my mother's. In fact, I now believe we are the majority, not the minority. The dominance of scientific materialism and rationalism have constituted but a mere few hundred years of human existence, while the idea of being enmeshed with something greater than ourselves, an ensouled and meaningful Universe, has existed and served humans for thousands of years and still exists in many, if not most, (non-Western) cultures around the world. What we have come to readily mock in Western civilization as complete and utter nonsense and magical thinking has been used by humans around the world to guide purposeful, fulfilling lives for millennia. We may yet find that this theory of scientific materialism and the Western worldview that some of us currently use as the foundation of our version of reality does not in fact serve our best interests and can be replaced with something better. What I do know is that our current scientific models are not enough to accommodate my personal experiences—nor those of countless others—and that the evidence for expanded consciousness provides a more likely explanation thus far.

I continue to periodically have intuitive readings, but this is no longer out of desperation or need for control, but rather because they help me with more deeply knowing myself. I find intuitive readings to be healing. Maybe it is because they can actually see so many layers of me and my energy. Maybe it's because I can unburden my heavy heart. Or maybe, like one of the mystics I spoke with suggested, intuitives, psychic mediums, energy healers, and mystics create space for you to heal yourself—because at the end of the day, no one can heal you but you. The signs of a spiritual experience can be subtle, and you have to be cognizant. Also, if you have a brain like mine that is adamant on being kept peace-free, the skepticism floats up to hammer out any magic. I imagine it would take years of belief retraining to rewire those neural circuits of mine, and I am not sure that would even be for the best. A healthy dose of skepticism is necessary for the modern world.

Having said that, I'll tell you the one piece of evidence that knocked me off my feet. Before I had jumped into my interview project and had only begun reading the past life regression literature, I read somewhere that you could ask the Universe or your spirit guides, or whatever you believed in, for a sign. I had sort of been trying this off and on, but I was choosing signs that were not that specific, and most of the time I would forget what sign I had even chosen. Since I was unreliable, one day I thought I would try one last time and put the responsibility on the Universe by asking it for a sign so big that even I couldn't miss, meaning that it couldn't be something like a butterfly or a bird. It had to be something significant to me, but since I was bad at choosing signs, I left it up to the Universe as to what that should be. Two nights later I was in an Uber going to meet my friends to celebrate a birthday. On the way to the restaurant one of them called me and asked how far away I was from the restaurant. I told her I was about five minutes away and asked why. She said, "You are not going to believe who is here! CHELSEA HANDLER!" I got chills from head to toe. Are. You. Kidding. Me?!?!?! I knew this was my sign.

I got to the restaurant, and there she was in all her vintage-tee-wearing glory with family and friends eating dinner. It was none other than the woman whose podcast interview with Laura Lynne Jackson had led me to Brian Weiss's book and, ultimately, this whole crazy ride! She also so deeply inspired me with her own transformation story and gave me strength to embrace the change. The Universe could not have possibly chosen a more meaningful sign for me, and I was in awe—but also still a bit intimidated by the Universe! I felt like I was in conversation with the Universe, and I was tingling. I did not want to bother

Chelsea while she was at dinner, but as we left the restaurant at the same time, I did make sure to tell her that I loved her book and podcast. Yes, it is LA, and we run into celebrities now and again, as I'm sure the skeptics would like to point out. But it certainly isn't daily, and I have never seen her before or since. The meaningfulness of that night still gives me goose bumps. We may never be able to prove whether the meaning we construct from personal events like the one I had that night are a gift from the Universe or spirit world, or rather just internally generated from my coincidence-detector brain—but it doesn't change the fact that meaning existed in that moment, and I was reminded of how the Universe could sparkle for us.

Yes, sparkle *for us*. That means you, too. Because as I came to find in my review of the literature, theories from both physics and philosophy leave a door open for a participatory Universe. If we live in a participatory Universe, it matters how you show up for yourself and for others. Whether you show up with positivity or negativity *matters*. I now try to move through life being more awake, always assessing whether things align with my values, and trying to be conscious. What if our brains seek patterns and meaning because there are patterns and meaning to be found? I liked the way Mark Booth put it in *The Secret History of the World:* "Cicero and Newton were idealists. They experienced life as meaningful, and the cosmos as meant. They believed, then, that something like human qualities, indeed something like human consciousness, is built into the structure of the cosmos."

Now, as I wrap up this book, I am still devouring as much knowledge as I can—and I imagine this will continue until the end of my time. Although this experience started with following what I deemed the only worthy kind of evidence—scientific—into the world of the mysterious, I am now open to all types of knowledge and understand that, to truly begin to grasp the nature of the world and our experience of it, we must reach across and through different fields and types of thought. You will not get the answers from just science, or from any other single field.

How do I decide what to read and study next? I try to take, as my friend Royce says, "inspired action." I follow my intuition and what excites me. I imagine being in one of those long hallways, the type you might find in an old English manor, and moving down past the doors until I feel the pull to enter a doorway.

As of this current moment, I am diving into Western astrology (the full birth chart analysis type, not the popular magazine sun sign horoscopes), which is, again, another field of study I never believed in and that society, on the whole, doesn't bother to understand on a deeper level. The jury is still out for me on the effectiveness of astrology in guiding or understanding the events of life, but I did find it to be profoundly useful as a psychological tool that can elicit many personal insights. Recently, it left me with yet another experience of wonder. I was reading about my lunar phase, which is the phase of the moon under which you were born and which allegedly tells about your soul purpose or mission. My moon phase happens to be a disseminating moon, represented by the archetypes of the pilgrim, teacher, servant, mystic, Virgo type. These archetypes even fit 'old me,' as someone who was asking questions and seeking knowledge. As my life unfolded, these questions became more complex, and that led me to look beyond science and, ultimately, to blend science and spirituality in my own life. Let me explain this in more detail.

Those born under this moon phase purportedly are drawn toward intellectual pursuits of discovering universal truths through experience, but with the ultimate purpose of then disseminating—hence the name of the phase—all the knowledge they have gained in a practical way to society in order for it to be helpful. Another motif associated with this lunar phase is death and rebirth. People born under this lunar phase can come to question the meaning of their lives through the confrontation of suffering and undergo a "spiritual conversion midway through life—a symbolic death and rebirth where they leave their old life behind and completely change direction" (Thurman 2016). I chuckled out loud when I read this description because that has been exactly my experience, as a scientist-turned-spiritual believer, and I hope to share it with others through writing this book in order to be helpful to anyone else who finds themself in a position similar to mine. At least I am in good company, as some examples of other disseminating moons include Ram Dass, Alan Watts, Alan Ginsberg, Aldous Huxley, Albert Einstein, and even the guitarist from my favorite band, The Beatles, George Harrison.

I came to think of my prior self as someone living in a cave (a smart person in a nice, comfortable cave, but limited nonetheless). I thought of (what I am now considering) my life crisis as an earthquake that caused the domed rock of the cave to crack wide open, allowing sunlight to pour in. The cave was nice before, but the shimmering daylight is incomparably exquisite with its illuminating warmth. I never want to step out of the sun again.

From that image of warmth and light, I want to leave you with this: What would you research, read, or begin learning next to further your life experience for the better? I invite you to get personally acquainted with the enchanted and numinous dimensions of life in whatever way you choose! This is your invitation from the Cosmos.

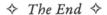

✧ *The End* ✧

Recommended Reads

CONSCIOUSNESS

Baruš, Imants, and Julia Mossbridge (2017) *Transcendent Mind: Rethinking the Science of Consciousness*. Washington, D.C.: American Psychological Association.

Dossey, Larry (2014) *One Mind: How Our Individual Mind Is Part of a Greater Consciousness and Why It Matters*. Carlsbad, Calif: Hay House Inc.

Gober, Mark (2018) *An End to Upside Down Thinking*. Hampshire, UK: Waterside Press.

Kelly, Edward F., Adam Crabtree, and Paul Marshall (Eds.) (2015) *Beyond Physicalism: Toward Reconciliation of Science and Spirituality*. Lanham, Md.: Rowman & Littlefield.

Kelly, Edward F., Emily Williams Kelly, Adam Crabtree, Alan Gauld, and Michael Grosso (Eds.) (2007) *Irreducible Mind: Toward a Psychology for the 21st Century*. Lanham, Md.: Rowman & Littlefield.

Kelly, Edward F., and Paul Marshall (Eds.) (2021) *Consciousness Unbound: Liberating Mind from the Tyranny of Materialism*. Lanham, Md.: Rowman & Littlefield.

Kripal, Jeffrey J. (2019) *The Flip: Epiphanies of Mind and the Future of Knowledge*. New York: Bellevue Literary Press.

Sheldrake, Rupert (2018) *Science and Spiritual Practices: Transformative Experiences and Their Effects on Our Bodies, Brains, and Health*. Berkeley, Calif: Counterpoint Press.

Tart, Charles (2009) *The End of Materialism: How Evidence of the Paranormal*

Is Bringing Science and Spirit Together. Oakland, Calif: New Harbinger Publications.

PAST LIFE REGRESSION

Newton, Michael (2010) *Destiny of Souls: New Case Studies of Life Between Lives.* Woodbury, Minn.: Llewellyn Worldwide.

Newton, Michael (1994) *Journey of Souls: Case Studies of Life Between Lives.* Woodbury, Minn.: Llewellyn Publications.

Webber, John (2020) *The Red Chair.* Carlsbad, Calif: Balboa Press.

Weiss, Brian L. (1988) *Many Lives, Many Masters.* New York: Simon & Schuster.

Weiss, Brian L. (1992) *Through Time Into Healing.* New York: Simon & Schuster.

Woolger, Roger J. (1988) *Other Lives, Other Selves: A Jungian Psychotherapist Discovers Past Lives.* New York: Bantam Books.

SPIRITUALITY

Dass, Ram (1971) *Be Here Now.* New York: Three Rivers Press.

Salzberg, Sharon (1999) *A Heart as Wide as the World: Stories on the Path of Loving Kindness.* Boulder, Colo.: Shambhala Publications.

Satchidananda, S. (1984) *The Yoga Sutras of Patanjali: Translation and Commentary by Sri Swami Satchidananda.* Buckingham, Va.: Integral Yoga Publications.

Singer, Michael A. (2007) *The Untethered Soul: The Journey Beyond Yourself.* Oakland, Calif: New Harbinger Publications.

PSYCHEDELICS

Fadiman, James (2011) *The Psychedelic Explorer's Guide: Safe, Therapeutic, and Sacred Journeys.* New York: Simon & Schuster.

Leary, Timothy, Ralph Metzner, and Richard Alpert (1964) *The Psychedelic Experience: A Manual Based on the Tibetan Book of the Dead.* New York: University Books.

McKenna, Terence (1999) *Food of the Gods: The Search for the Original Tree of Knowledge: A Radical History of Plants, Drugs and Human Evolution.* New York: Random House.

Pollan, Michael (2019) *How to Change Your Mind: What the New Science of*

Psychedelics Teaches Us about Consciousness, Dying, Addiction, Depression, and Transcendence. New York: Penguin Books.

NEW TO PSI RESEARCH

Carpenter, J. C. (2015) *First Sight: ESP and Parapsychology in Everyday Life.* Lanham, Md.: Rowman & Littlefield.

Dossey, Larry (2014) *One Mind: How Our Individual Mind Is Part of a Greater Consciousness and Why It Matters.* Carlsbad, Calif: Hay House Inc.

Gober, Mark (2018) *An End to Upside Down Thinking.* Hampshire, UK: Waterside Press.

Jacobsen, Annie (2017) *Phenomena: The Secret History of the U.S. Government's Investigations into Extrasensory Perception and Psychokinesis.* New York: Little, Brown and Company.

Kean, Leslie (2017) *Surviving Death: A Journalist Investigates Evidence for an Afterlife.* New York: Crown Archetype.

Radin, Dean (2013) *Supernormal: Science, Yoga, and the Evidence for Extraordinary Psychic Abilities.* La Jolla, Calif.: Deepak Chopra Books.

Targ, Russell (2012) *The Reality of ESP: A Physicist's Proof of Psychic Abilities.* Wheaton, Ill.: Theosophical Publishing House.

MEDIUMSHIP/PSYCHIC/INTUITIVE

Beischel, Julie (2014) *From the Mouths of Mediums.* Vol. 1: *Experiencing Communication.* Tucson, Ariz.: Windbridge Institute, LLC.

Beischel, Julie (2015) *Investigating Mediums: A Windbridge Institute Collection.* San Francisco: Blurb.

Beischel, Julie (2013) *Meaningful Messages: Making the Most of Your Mediumship Reading.* Tucson, Ariz.: Windbridge Institute, LLC

Jackson, Laura Lynne (2016) *The Light Between Us: Stories from Heaven. Lessons for the Living.* New York: Spiegel & Grau.

Jackson, Laura Lynne (2020) *Signs: The Secret Language of the Universe.* New York: Random House.

Russo, Kim (2017) *The Happy Medium: Life Lessons from the Other Side.* New York: HarperOne.

Russo, Kim (2020) *Your Soul Purpose: Learn How to Access the Light Within.* New York: HarperOne.

PSI RESEARCH/PARAPSYCHOLOGY

Cheung, Theresa, Julia Mossbridge, Loyd Auerbach, and Dean Radin (2018) *The Premonition Code: The Science of Precognition, How Sensing the Future Can Change Your Life*. London: Watkins Publishing.

Radin, Dean (2018) *Real Magic: Ancient Wisdom, Modern Science, and a Guide to the Secret Power of the Universe*. New York: Harmony Books.

Radin, Dean (2013) *Supernormal: Science, Yoga, and the Evidence for Extraordinary Psychic Abilities*. La Jolla, Calif.: Deepak Chopra Books.

SURVIVAL/REINCARNATION RESEARCH

Fontana, David (2005) *Is There An Afterlife?: A Comprehensive Overview of the Evidence*. Winchester, UK: Iff Books.

Holden, Janice Miner, Bruce Greyson, and Debbie James (Eds.) (2009) *The Handbook of Near-Death Experiences: Thirty Years of Investigation*. Westport, Conn.: Praeger.

Horn, Stacy (2010) *Unbelievable: Investigations into Ghosts, Poltergeists, Telepathy, and Other Unseen Phenomena, from the Duke Parapsychology Laboratory*. New York: Ecco.

Kean, Leslie (2017) *Surviving Death: A Journalist Investigates Evidence for an Afterlife*. New York: Crown Archetype.

Rock, Adam J. (2014) *The Survival Hypothesis: Essays on Mediumship*. Jefferson, N.C.: McFarland & Co.

Tucker, Jim B., and Ian Stevenson (2008) *Life Before Life: Children's Memories of Previous Lives*. New York: St. Martin's Publishing Group.

Bibliography

Abraham, Henry David (1983) "Visual Phenomenology of the LSD Flashback." *Archives of General Psychiatry* 40 (8): 884–89.

Aglioti, S., N. Smania, M. Manfredi, and G. Berlucchi (1996) "Disownership of Left Hand and Objects Related to It in a Patient with Right Brain Damage." *NeuroReport* 8 (1): 293–96.

Alderson-Day, B. (2016) "The Silent Companions." *Psychologist* 29 (4): 272–75.

Anchisi, Davide, and Marco Zanon (2015) "A Bayesian Perspective on Sensory and Cognitive Integration in Pain Perception and Placebo Analgesia." Edited by Jean Daunizeau. *PLOS One* 10 (2): e0117270.

Arzy, S., and R. Schurr (2016) "'God Has Sent Me to You': Right Temporal Epilepsy, Left Prefrontal Psychosis." *Epilepsy & Behavior* 60: 7–10.

Atasoy, Selen, Gustavo Deco, Morten L. Kringelbach, and Joel Pearson (2018) "Harmonic Brain Modes: A Unifying Framework for Linking Space and Time in Brain Dynamics." *Neuroscientist*. SAGE Publications Inc.

Atasoy, Selen, Isaac Donnelly, and Joel Pearson (2016) "Human Brain Networks Function in Connectome-Specific Harmonic Waves." *Nature Communications* 7 (January).

Atasoy, Selen, Leor Roseman, Mendel Kaelen, Morten L. Kringelbach, Gustavo Deco, and Robin L. Carhart-Harris (2017) "Connectome-Harmonic Decomposition of Human Brain Activity Reveals Dynamical Repertoire Re-Organization under LSD." *Scientific Reports* 7 (1).

Atlas, Lauren Y., and Tor D. Wager (2012) "How Expectations Shape Pain." *Neuroscience Letters* 520 (2): 140–48.

Aviezer, Hillel, Shlomo Bentin, Veronica Dudarev, and Ran R. Hassin (2011)

"The Automaticity of Emotional Face-Context Integration." *Emotion* 11 (6): 1406–14.

Balcetis, Emily, and David Dunning (2006) "See What You Want to See: Motivational Influences on Visual Perception." *Journal of Personality and Social Psychology* 91 (4): 612–25.

Balcetis, Emily, David Dunning, and Yael Granot (2012) "Subjective Value Determines Initial Dominance in Binocular Rivalry." *Journal of Experimental Social Psychology* 48 (1): 122–29.

Balestrini, S., S. Francione, R. Mai, L. Castana, G. Casaceli, Daniela Marino, Leandro Provinciali, Francesco Cardinale, and Laura Tassi (2015) "Multimodal Responses Induced by Cortical Stimulation of the Parietal Lobe: A Stereo-Electroencephalography Study." *Brain* 138 (9): 2596–2607.

Ballard, Jamie (2019, October 21) "Many Americans Believe Ghosts and Demons Exist." YouGov America.

Baptista, Johann, Max Derakhshani, and Patrizio Tressoldi (2015) "Explicit Anomalous Cognition: A Review of the Best Evidence in Ganzfeld, Forced-Choice, Remote Viewing and Dream Studies." *Parapsychology: A Handbook for the 21st Century.* Edited by Etzel Cardeña, John Palmer, and David Marcusson-Clavertz. Jefferson, N.C.: McFarland & Company, Inc. 192–214.

Barreiro, Julio T. (2011) "Environmental Effects Controlled." *Nature Physics* 7 (12): 927–28.

Barušs, Imants, and Julia Mossbridge (2017) *Transcendent Mind: Rethinking the Science of Consciousness.* Washington, D.C.: American Psychological Association.

Battelli, L., A. Pascual-Leone, and P. Cavanagh (2007) "The 'When' Pathway of the Right Parietal Lobe." *Trends in Cognitive Sciences* 11 (5): 204–10.

Bear, David M., and Paul Fedio (1977) "Quantitative Analysis of Interictal Behavior in Temporal Lobe Epilepsy." *Archives of Neurology* 34 (8): 454–67.

Behrendt, R. P. (2013) "Hippocampus and Consciousness." *Reviews in the Neurosciences* 24 (3): 239–66.

Beischel, J., C. Mosher, and M. Boccuzzi (2017) "Quantitative and Qualitative Analyses of Mediumistic and Psychic Experiences." *Threshold: Journal of Interdisciplinary Consciousness Studies* 1 (2).

Bell, John S. (1964) "On the Einstein Podolsky Rosen Paradox." *Physics Physique Fizika* 1 (3): 195.

Bem, Daryl J. (2011) "Feeling the Future: Experimental Evidence for Anomalous

Retroactive Influences on Cognition and Affect." *Journal of Personality and Social Psychology* 100 (3): 407–25.

Bem, Daryl J., and Charles Honorton (1994) "Does Psi Exist? Replicable Evidence for an Anomalous Process of Information Transfer." *Psychological Bulletin* 115 (1).

Bem, Daryl J., Patrizio Tressoldi, Thomas Rabeyron, and Michael Duggan (2016) "Feeling the Future: A Meta-Analysis of 90 Experiments on the Anomalous Anticipation of Random Future Events." *F1000Research* (4).

Berkovich-Ohana, A., M. Harel, A. Hahamy, A. Arieli, and R. Malach (2016) "Data for Default Network Reduced Functional Connectivity in Meditators, Negatively Correlated with Meditation Expertise." *Data in Brief* 8: 910–14.

Berlucchi, G., and S. Aglioti (1997) "The Body in the Brain: Neural Bases of Corporeal Awareness." *Trends in Neurosciences* 20 (12): 560–64.

Blanke, O., T. Landis, L. Spinelli, and M. Seeck (2004) "Out-of-Body Experience and Autoscopy of Neurological Origin." *Brain* 127 (2): 243–58.

Blanke, Olaf, Christine Mohr, Christoph M. Michel, Alvaro Pascual-Leone, Peter Brugger, Margitta Seeck, Theodor Landis, and Gregor Thut (2005) "Linking Out-of-Body Experience and Self Processing to Mental Own-Body Imagery at the Temporoparietal Junction." *Journal of Neuroscience* 25 (3): 550–57.

Blanke, O., S. Ortigue, T. Landis, and M. Seeck (2002) "Stimulating Illusory Own-Body Perceptions." *Nature* 419 (6904): 269–70.

Blewett, D. B., and N. Chwelos (1959) "Handbook for the Therapeutic Use of LSD-25: Individual and Group Procedures." Multidisciplinary Association for Psychedelic Studies.

Blom, Jan Dirk (2010) *A Dictionary of Hallucinations*. New York: Springer.

Booth, Mark (2008) *The Secret History of the World*. New York: The Overlook Press.

Bösch, Holger, Fiona Steinkamp, and Emil Boller (2006) "Examining Psychokinesis: The Interaction of Human Intention With Random Number Generators—A Meta-Analysis." *Psychological Bulletin* 132 (4): 497.

Brugger, P. (2006) "From Phantom Limb to Phantom Body: Varieties of Extracorporeal Awareness." *Human Body Perception from the Inside Out*. Edited by G. Knoblich, I. M. Thornton, M. Grosjean, and M. Shiffrar. Oxford: Oxford University Press: 171–209.

Buckner, Randy L., Jessica R. Andrews-Hanna, and Daniel L. Schacter (2008)

"The Brain's Default Network Anatomy, Function, and Relevance to Disease." *Annals of the New York Academy of Sciences* 1124: 1–38.

Bueti, Domenica, and Vincent Walsh (2009) "The Parietal Cortex and the Representation of Time, Space, Number and Other Magnitudes." *Philosophical Transactions of the Royal Society B: Biological Sciences* 364 (1525): 1831–40.

Cardeña, Etzel (2014) "A Call for an Open, Informed Study of All Aspects of Consciousness." *Frontiers in Human Neuroscience* 8 (January): 17.

Cardeña, Etzel (2018) "The Experimental Evidence for Parapsychological Phenomena: A Review." *American Psychologist* 73 (5): 663–77.

Cardeña, Etzel, John Palmer, and David Marcusson-Clavertz, eds. (2015) *Parapsychology: A Handbook for the 21st Century*. Jefferson, N.C.: McFarland & Company, Inc.

Carhart-Harris, Robin L, David Erritzoe, Tim Williams, James M. Stone, Laurence J. Reed, Alessandro Colasanti, Robin J. Tyacke, et al. (2012) "Neural Correlates of the Psychedelic State as Determined by fMRI Studies with Psilocybin." *National Academy of Sciences* 109 (6): 2138–43.

Carhart-Harris, R., R. Leech, and E. Tagliazucchi (2014) "How Do Hallucinogens Work on the Brain?" *Journal of Psychophysiology* 71 (1): 2–8.

Carney, Dana R., Amy J. C. Cuddy, and Andy J. Yap (2010) "Power Posing." *Psychological Science* 21 (10): 1363–68.

Cavanna, A. E., and M. R. Trimble (2006) "The Precuneus: A Review of Its Functional Anatomy and Behavioural Correlates." *Brain* 129 (3): 564–83.

Center for Humane Technology (2021, February 11) "A Renegade Solution to Extractive Economics." Your Undivided Attention.

Chalmers, David J. (1995) *The Conscious Mind. In Search of a Fundamental Theory*. Oxford: Oxford University Press.

Chalmers, David J. (2003) "Consciousness and Its Place in Nature." *The Blackwell Guide to Philosophy of Mind*. Hoboken, NJ: Blackwell Publishing Ltd.: 102–42.

Cheyne, J. A. (2001) "The Ominous Numinous: Sensed Presence and 'Other' Hallucinations." *Journal of Consciousness Studies* 8 (5–6): 133–50.

Cleary, T. (1993) *The Flower Ornament Scripture: A Translation of the Avatamsaka Sutra*. Boulder, Colo.: Shambhala Publications.

Cohen, Jacob. (1992) "A Power Primer." *Psychological Bulletin* 112 (1): 155–59.

Cohen, Jacob. (2013) *Statistical Power Analysis for the Behavioral Sciences. Statistical Power Analysis for the Behavioral Sciences*. Cambridge: Academic Press.

Cole, Shana, Emily Balcetis, and David Dunning (2013) "Affective Signals of Threat Increase Perceived Proximity." *Psychological Science* 24 (1): 34–40.

Colloca, Luana (2018) "Preface: The Fascinating Mechanisms and Implications of the Placebo Effect." *International Review of Neurobiology*. Cambridge: Academic Press.

Cook, C. M., and M. A. Persinger (1997) "Experimental Induction of the 'Sensed Presence' in Normal Subjects and an Exceptional Subject." *Perceptual and Motor Skills* 85 (2): 683–93.

Cooper, Anderson (2019, August 16) "Interview of Stephen Colbert." *Anderson Cooper 360°*.

Cranston, S., and C. Williams (1984) *Reincarnation: A New Horizon In Science, Religion And Society*. New York: Julian Press.

Crescentini, C., M. Di Bucchianico, F. Fabbro, and C. Urgesi (2015) "Excitatory Stimulation of the Right Inferior Parietal Cortex Lessens Implicit Religiousness/Spirituality." *Neuropsychologia* 70: 71–79.

Crescentini, C., C. Urgesi, F. Campanella, Roberto Eleopra, and Franco Fabbro (2014) "Effects of an 8-Week Meditation Program on the Implicit and Explicit Attitudes toward Religious/Spiritual Self-Representations." *Consciousness and Cognition* 30: 266–80.

Crick, Francis, and Christof Koch (2003) "A Framework for Consciousness." *Nature Neuroscience*. Nature Publishing Group.

Daltrozzo, Jerome, Boris Kotchoubey, Fatma Gueler, and Ahmed A. Karim (2016) "Effects of Transcranial Magnetic Stimulation on Body Perception: No Evidence for Specificity of the Right Temporo-Parietal Junction." *Brain Topography* 29 (5): 704–15.

Damisch, Lysann, Barbara Stoberock, and Thomas Mussweiler (2010) "Keep Your Fingers Crossed! How Superstition Improves Performance." *Psychological Science* 21 (7): 1014–20.

Davis, Alan K., Frederick S. Barrett, and Roland R. Griffiths (2020) "Psychological Flexibility Mediates the Relations between Acute Psychedelic Effects and Subjective Decreases in Depression and Anxiety." *Journal of Contextual Behavioral Science* 15: 39–45.

Davis, Alan K., John M. Clifton, Eric G. Weaver, Ethan S. Hurwitz, Matthew W. Johnson, and Roland R. Griffiths (2020) "Survey of Entity Encounter Experiences Occasioned by Inhaled N,N-Dimethyltryptamine: Phenomenology, Interpretation, and Enduring Effects." *Journal of Psychopharmacology* 34 (9): 1008–20.

Davisson, C., and L. H. Germer (1927) "The Scattering of Electrons by a Single Crystal of Nickel." *Nature* 119 (2998): 558–60.

Decety, J., and C. Lamm (2007) "The Role of the Right Temporoparietal Junction in Social Interaction: How Low-Level Computational Processes Contribute to Meta-Cognition." *The Neuroscientist* 13 (6): 580–93.

Denny, Bryan T., Hedy Kober, Tor D. Wager, and Kevin N. Ochsner (2012) "A Meta-Analysis of Functional Neuroimaging Studies of Self- and Other Judgments Reveals a Spatial Gradient for Mentalizing in Medial Prefrontal Cortex." *Journal of Cognitive Neuroscience* 24 (8): 1742–52.

De Ridder, Dirk, Koen Van Laere, Patrick Dupont, Tomas Menovsky, and Paul Van de Heyning (2007) "Visualizing Out-of-Body Experience in the Brain." *New England Journal of Medicine* 357 (18): 1829–33.

Desmedt, John E., and Claude Tomberg (1994) "Transient Phase-Locking of 40 Hz Electrical Oscillations in Prefrontal and Parietal Human Cortex Reflects the Process of Conscious Somatic Perception." *Neuroscience Letters* 168 (1–2): 126–29.

Devereux, Paul (1997) *The Long Trip: A Prehistory of Psychedelia*. New York: Penguin Arkana.

Diekhof, Esther K., Hanne E. Kipshagen, Peter Falkai, Peter Dechent, Jürgen Baudewig, and Oliver Gruber (2011) "The Power of Imagination: How Anticipatory Mental Imagery Alters Perceptual Processing of Fearful Facial Expressions." *NeuroImage* 54 (2): 1703–14.

Dijksterhuis, Ap, and Henk Aarts (2003) "On Wildebeests and Humans: The Preferential Detection of Negative Stimuli." *Psychological Science* 14 (1): 14–8.

Dijksterhuis, Ap, Maarten W. Bos, Loran F. Nordgren, and Rick B. Van Baaren (2006) "On Making the Right Choice: The Deliberation-without-Attention Effect." *Science* 311 (5763): 1005–7.

Doesburg, Sam M., Jessica J. Green, John J. McDonald, and Lawrence M. Ward (2009) "Rhythms of Consciousness: Binocular Rivalry Reveals Large-Scale Oscillatory Network Dynamics Mediating Visual Perception." *PLOS One* 4 (7): 6142.

Dossey, Larry (1999) *Reinventing Medicine: Beyond Mind-Body to a New Era of Healing*. San Francisco: Harper Collins.

Ducasse, C. J. (1960) " How the Case of The Search for Bridey Murphy Stands Today." *The Journal of the American Society for Psychical Research* 54 (January): 3–22.

Duggan, Michael, and Patrizio Tressoldi (2018) "Predictive Physiological Anticipatory Activity Preceding Seemingly Unpredictable Stimuli: An Update of Mossbridge et al's Meta-Analysis." *F1000Research* (7): 407.

Dunne, Brenda J., and Robert G. Jahn (2003) "Information and Uncertainty in Remote Perception Research." *Journal of Scientific Exploration* 17 (2): 207–41.

Dunning, Jonathan P., Muhammad A. Parvaz, Greg Hajcak, Thomas Maloney, Nelly Alia-Klein, Patricia A. Woicik, Frank Telang, Gene-Jack Wang, Nora D. Volkow, and Rita Z. Goldstein (2011) "Motivated Attention to Cocaine and Emotional Cues in Abstinent and Current Cocaine Users: an ERP Study." *European Journal of Neuroscience* 33 (9): 1716–23.

Eagleman, David (2011) *Incognito: The Secret Lives of the Brain*. New York: Pantheon.

Eastwood, John D., Daniel Smilek, and Philip M. Merikle (2001) "Differential Attentional Guidance by Unattended Faces Expressing Positive and Negative Emotion." *Perception and Psychophysics* 63 (6): 1004–13.

Eimer, Martin, and Amanda Holmes (2002) "An ERP Study on the Time Course of Emotional Face Processing." *NeuroReport* 13 (4): 427–31.

Engel, Andreas K., and Wolf Singer (2001) "Temporal Binding and the Neural Correlates of Sensory Awareness." *Trends in Cognitive Sciences* 5 (1): 16–25.

Engel, G. S., T. R. Calhoun, E. L. Read, T. K. Ahn, T. Mančal, Y. C. Cheng, R. E. Blankenship, and G. R. Fleming (2007) "Evidence for Wavelike Energy Transfer through Quantum Coherence in Photosynthetic Systems." *Nature* 446 (7137): 782–86.

Fallon, Nicholas, Carl Roberts, and Andrej Stancak (2020) "Shared and Distinct Functional Networks for Empathy and Pain Processing: A Systematic Review and Meta-Analysis of fMRI Studies." *Social Cognitive and Affective Neuroscience* 15 (7): 709–23.

Feynman, Richard (1967) *The Character of Physical Law*. Cambridge, Mass.: MIT Press.

Fiore, Edith (1978) *You Have Been Here before: A Psychologist Looks at Past Lives*. New York: Coward, McCann & Geoghegan.

Fox, K. C. R., M. L. Dixon, S. Nijeboer, M. Girn, J. L. Floman, M. Lifshitz, M. Ellamil, P. Sedlmeier, and K. Christoff (2016) "Functional Neuroanatomy of Meditation: A Review and Meta-Analysis of 78 Functional Neuroimaging Investigations." *Neuroscience & Biobehavioral Reviews* 65: 208–28.

Fox, Michael D., Abraham Z. Snyder, Justin L. Vincent, Maurizio Corbetta,

David C. Van Essen, and Marcus E. Raichle (2005) "The Human Brain Is Intrinsically Organized into Dynamic, Anticorrelated Functional Networks." *Proceedings of the National Academy of Sciences* 102 (27): 9673–78.

Friedrich, Alena, Barbara Flunger, Benjamin Nagengast, Kathrin Jonkmann, and Ulrich Trautwein (2015) "Pygmalion Effects in the Classroom: Teacher Expectancy Effects on Students' Math Achievement." *Contemporary Educational Psychology* 41 (April): 1–12.

Gaillard, Raphaël, Stanislas Dehaene, Claude Adam, Stéphane Clémenceau, Dominique Hasboun, Michel Baulac, Laurent Cohen, and Lionel Naccache (2009) "Converging Intracranial Markers of Conscious Access." Edited by Leslie Ungerleider. *PLOS Biology* 7 (3): e1000061.

Gazzaniga, Michael S. (2005) "Forty-Five Years of Split-Brain Research and Still Going Strong." *Nature Reviews Neuroscience* 6: 653–659.

Gazzaniga, Michael S. (1970) *Neuroscience Series.* Vol. 2: *The Bisected Brain.* New York: Appleton-Century-Crofts.

Geschwind, Norman (1983) "Interictal Behavioral Changes in Epilepsy." *Epilepsia* 24: S23–30.

Goff, Philip (2017) *Consciousness and Fundamental Reality.* Oxford: Oxford University Press.

Goff, Philip (2018, February 8) "Cosmopsychism Explains Why the Universe Is Fine-Tuned for Life." Aeon.

Goleman, Daniel, and Richard J. Davidson (2017) *Altered Traits: Science Reveals How Meditation Changes Your Mind, Brain, and Body.* New York: Avery Publishing.

Good, Thomas L., Natasha Sterzinger, and Alyson Lavigne (2018) "Expectation Effects: Pygmalion and the Initial 20 Years of Research1." *Educational Research and Evaluation* 24 (3–5): 99–123.

Griffiths, R. R., W. A. Richards, U. McCann, and R. Jesse (2006) "Psilocybin Can Occasion Mystical-Type Experiences Having Substantial and Sustained Personal Meaning and Spiritual Significance." *Psychopharmacology* 187 (3): 268–83.

Grof, S. (1988) *The Adventure of Self-Discovery: Dimensions of Consciousness and New Perspectives in Psychotherapy and Inner Exploration.* Albany: State University of New York Press.

Grof, S. (2001) *LSD Psychotherapy.* 3rd ed. Sarasota, Fla.: Multidisciplinary Association for Psychedelic Studies.

Grof, S. (1975) "Varieties of Transpersonal Experiences: Observations from LSD

Psychotherapy." *Psychiatry and Mysticism*. Edited by SR Dean. Chicago: Nelson-Hall: 311–45.

Gronau, Quentin F., Sara Van Erp, Daniel W. Heck, Joseph Cesario, Kai J. Jonas, and Eric Jan Wagenmakers (2017) "A Bayesian Model-Averaged Meta-Analysis of the Power Pose Effect with Informed and Default Priors: The Case of Felt Power." *Comprehensive Results in Social Psychology* 2 (1): 123–38.

Haidich, A. B. (2010) "Meta-Analysis in Medical Research." *Hippokratia* 14 (Suppl 1): 29-undefined.

Handler, Chelsea (2019) *Life Will Be the Death of Me*. New York: The Dial Press.

Handler, Chelsea (2019, September 25) "People on the Other Side with Laura Lynne Jackson." *Life Will Be the Death of Me*. iHeart.

Harman, Willis W. (1963) "Some Aspects of the Psychedelic-Drug Controversy." *Journal of Humanistic Psychology* 3 (2): 93–107.

Head, Joseph, and Sylvia L. Cranston (1977) *Reincarnation: The Phoenix Fire Mystery: An East-West Dialogue on Death and Rebirth from the Worlds of Religion, Science, Psychology, Philosophy, Art, and and Literature, and from Great Thinkers of the Past and Present*. New York: Julian Press.

Herbet, Guillaume, Gilles Lafargue, Nicolas Menjot de Champfleur, Sylvie Moritz-Gasser, Emmanuelle Le Bars, François Bonnetblanc, and Hugues Duffau (2014) "Disrupting Posterior Cingulate Connectivity Disconnects Consciousness from the External Environment." *Neuropsychologia* 56: 239–44.

Hermle, Leo, Matthias Fünfgeld, Godehard Oepen, Hanno Botsch, Dieter Borchardt, Euphrosyne Gouzoulis, Rose A. Fehrenbach, and Manfred Spitzer (1992) "Mescaline-Induced Psychopathological, Neuropsychological, and Neurometabolic Effects in Normal Subjects: Experimental Psychosis as a Tool for Psychiatric Research." *Biological Psychiatry* 32 (11): 976–91.

Hoffman, Donald (2019) *The Case Against Reality: Why Evolution Hid the Truth from Our Eyes*. New York: W. W. Norton & Company.

Holt, Nicola J., Deborah L. Delanoy, and Chris A. Roe (2004) "Creativity, Subjective Paranormal Experiences and Altered States of Consciousness." *The Parapsychological Association, 47th Annual Convention*: 433–36.

Holzinger, Rudolf (1964) "LSD-25, A Tool in Psychotherapy." *The Journal of General Psychology* 71 (1): 9–20.

Honorton, C., and D. C. Ferrari (1989) "'Future Telling': A Meta-Analysis of Forced-Choice Precognition Experiments, 1935–1987." *Journal of Parapsychology* 53: 281–308.

Humphreys, G. F., and M. A. Lambon Ralph (2015) "Fusion and Fission of Cognitive Functions in the Human Parietal Cortex." *Cerebral Cortex* 25 (10): 3547–60.

Huxley, Aldous (1954). *The Doors of Perception*. London. Chatto & Windus.

Hyman, Ray (1995) "Evaluation of Program on Anomalous Mental Phenomena." *Journal of Scientific Exploration* 10 (1): 31–58.

Hyman, Ray (1985) "The Ganzfeld Psi Experiment: A Critical Appraisal." *The Journal of Parapsychology* 49 (1): 3-undefined.

Ionta, Silvio, Roger Gassert, and Olaf Blanke (2011) "Multi-Sensory and Sensorimotor Foundation of Bodily Self-Consciousness: an Interdisciplinary Approach." *Frontiers in Psychology* 2 (December): 383.

Ionta, S., L. Heydrich, B. Lenggenhager, M. Mouthon, Eleonora Fornari, Dominique Chapuis, Roger Gassert, and Olaf Blanke (2011) "Multisensory Mechanisms in Temporo-Parietal Cortex Support Self-Location and First-Person Perspective." *Neuron* 70 (2): 363–72.

Jacobsen, Annie (2017) *Phenomena: The Secret History of the U.S. Government's Investigations into Extrasensory Perception and Psychokinesis*. New York: Little, Brown and Company.

Johanson, Mika, Olli Vaurio, Jari Tiihonen, and Markku Lähteenvuo (2020) "A Systematic Literature Review of Neuroimaging of Psychopathic Traits." *Frontiers in Psychiatry* 10 (February): 1027.

Josipovic, Zoran (2010) "Duality and Nonduality in Meditation Research." *Consciousness and Cognition* 19 (4): 1119–21.

Josipovic, Zoran, Ilan Dinstein, Jochen Weber, and David J. Heeger (2012) "Influence of Meditation on Anti-Correlated Networks in the Brain." *Frontiers in Human Neuroscience* 5 (January): 1–11.

Kahneman, Daniel (2011) *Thinking, Fast and Slow*. New York: Macmillan.

Kahneman, Daniel., Dan Lovallo, and Olivier Sibony (2011) "Before You Make That Big Decision." *Harvard Business Review* 89 (6): 50–60.

Kaptchuk, Ted J., Elizabeth Friedlander, John M. Kelley, M. Norma Sanchez, Efi Kokkotou, Joyce P. Singer, Magda Kowalczykowski, Franklin G. Miller, Irving Kirsch, and Anthony J. Lembo (2010) "Placebos without Deception: A Randomized Controlled Trial in Irritable Bowel Syndrome." Edited by Isabelle Boutron. *PLOS One* 5 (12): e15591.

Kastrup, Bernardo (2018) "The Universe in Consciousness." *Journal of Consciousness Studies* (25): 5–6.

Kastrup, Bernardo (2014) *Why Materialism Is Baloney: How True Skeptics Know There Is No Death and Fathom Answers to Life, the Universe, and Everything.* Hampshire, U.K.: John Hunt Publishing.

Kastrup, Bernardo, Adam Crabtree, and Edward F. Kelly (2018, June 18) "Could Multiple Personality Disorder Explain Life, the Universe and Everything?" *Scientific American Blog Network.* (June) *Scientific American.*

Kelley, W. M., C. N. Macrae, C. L. Wyland, S. Caglar, S. Inati, and T. F. Heatherton (2002) "Finding the Self? An Event-Related fMRI Study." *Journal of Cognitive Neuroscience* 14: 785–94.

Kelly, Edward F., Adam Crabtree, and Paul Marshall (Eds.) (2015) *Beyond Physicalism: Toward Reconciliation of Science and Spirituality.* Lanham, Md.: Rowman & Littlefield.

Kelly, Edward F., Emily Williams Kelly, Adam Crabtree, Alan Gauld, and Michael Grosso, eds. (2007) *Irreducible Mind: Toward a Psychology for the 21st Century.* Lanham, Md.: Rowman & Littlefield.

Kelly, Edward F., and Paul Marshall, eds. (2021) *Consciousness Unbound: Liberating Mind from the Tyranny of Materialism.* Lanham, Md.: Rowman & Littlefield.

Kelly, Emily Williams (2007) "Unusual Experiences Near Death and Related Phenomena." *Irreducible Mind: Toward a Psychology for the 21st Century.* Edited by E. F. Kelly, E. W. Kelly, A. Crabtree, A. Gauld, and M. Grosso. Lanham, Md.: Rowman & Littlefield.

Keppler, Joachim (2012) "A Conceptual Framework for Consciousness Based on a Deep Understanding of Matter." *Philosophy Study* 2 (10): 689–703.

Keppler, Joachim, and Itay Shani (2020) "Cosmopsychism and Consciousness Research: A Fresh View on the Causal Mechanisms Underlying Phenomenal States." *Frontiers in Psychology* 11 (March) 371.

Kim, Yoon Ho, Rong Yu, Sergei P. Kulik, and Marlan O. Scully (2000) "Delayed 'Choice' Quantum Eraser." *Physical Review Letters* 84 (1): 1–5.

King, Lester S. (1975) "Cases of the Reincarnation Type, Vol. 1: Ten Cases in India." *JAMA: The Journal of the American Medical Association* 234 (9): 978.

Koch, Christof (2012) *Consciousness: Confessions of a Romantic Reductionist.* Cambridge, Mass.: MIT Press.

Kolbaba, Scott J. (2016) *Physicians' Untold Stories: Miraculous Experiences*

Doctors Are Hesitant to Share with Their Patients, or ANYONE! Scotts Valley, Calif.: Createspace Independent Publishing Platform.

Kometer, Michael, Thomas Pokorny, Erich Seifritz, and Franz X. Volleinweider (2015) "Psilocybin-Induced Spiritual Experiences and Insightfulness Are Associated with Synchronization of Neuronal Oscillations." *Psychopharmacology* 232 (19): 3663–76.

Kometer, Michael, André Schmidt, Lutz Jäncke, and Franz X. Vollenweider (2013) "Activation of Serotonin 2A Receptors Underlies the Psilocybin-Induced Effects on α Oscillations, N170 Visual-Evoked Potentials, and Visual Hallucinations." *Journal of Neuroscience* 33 (25): 10544–51.

Kominis, Iannis K. (2015) "The Radical-Pair Mechanism as a Paradigm for the Emerging Science of Quantum Biology." *Modern Physics Letters B* 29 (1): 1530013.

Kripal, Jeffrey J. (2019) *The Flip: Epiphanies of Mind and the Future of Knowledge.* New York: Bellevue Literary Press.

Kubit, Benjamin, and Anthony Ian Jack (2013) "Rethinking the Role of the RTPJ in Attention and Social Cognition in Light of the Opposing Domains Hypothesis: Findings from an ALE-Based Meta-Analysis and Resting-State Functional Connectivity." *Frontiers in Human Neuroscience* 7 (June): 323.

Kurzweil, Ray (2013) *How to Create a Mind: The Secret of Human Thought Revealed.* New York: Penguin Books.

Lamont, Ruth A., Hannah J. Swift, and Dominic Abrams (2015) "A Review and Meta-Analysis of Age-Based Stereotype Threat: Negative Stereotypes, Not Facts, Do the Damage." *Psychology and Aging* 30 (1): 180–93.

Leslie, Paul J. (2019) *Shadows in the Session: The Presence of the Anomalous in Psychotherapy.* Path Notes Press.

Leucht, Stefan, Bartosz Helfer, Gerald Gartlehner, and John M. Davis (2015) "How Effective Are Common Medications: A Perspective Based on Meta-Analyses of Major Drugs." *BMC Medicine* 13 (October): 253.

Lick, D. J., A. L. Alter, and J. B. Freeman (2018) "Superior Pattern Detectors Efficiently Learn, Activate, Apply, and Update Social Stereotypes." *Journal of Experimental Psychology* 147 (2): 209–27.

Lommel, P. Van, R. Van Wees, V. Meyers, and I. Elfferich (2001) "Near-Death Experience in Survivors of Cardiac Arrest: A Prospective Study in the Netherlands." *The Lancet* 358 (9298): 2039–45.

Long, Jeffrey, and Jody Long (1999) "Near Death Experience (NDE) Overview." Near-Death Experience Research Foundation.

Luhrmann, Tanya M. (2012) *When God Talks Back: Understanding the American Evangelical Relationship with God*. New York: Knopf Doubleday Publishing Group.

Luke, David P. (2012) "Psychoactive Substances and Paranormal Phenomena: A Comprehensive Review." *International Journal of Transpersonal Studies* 31 (1): 97–156.

Luke, David P., and Marios Kittenis (2005) "A Preliminary Survey of Paranormal Experiences with Psychoactive Drugs." *The Journal of Parapsychology* 69 (2): 305.

Luppi, Andrea I., Jakub Vohryzek, Morten L. Kringelbach, Pedro A. M. Mediano, M. M. Craig, Ram Adapa, R. L. Carhart-Harris, et al. (2020) "Connectome Harmonic Decomposition of Human Brain Dynamics Reveals a Landscape of Consciousness." *bioRxiv* (August 10): 244459.

Lutkajtis, Anna (2021) "Entity Encounters and the Therapeutic Effect of the Psychedelic Mystical Experience." *Journal of Psychedelic Studies* 4 (3): 171–78.

Lutz, A., H. A. Slagter, J. D. Dunne, and R. J. Davidson (2008) "Attention Regulation and Monitoring in Meditation." *Trends in Cognitive Sciences* 12 (4): 163–69.

Maner, Jon K., Matthew T. Gailliot, D. Aaron Rouby, and Saul L. Miller (2007) "Can't Take My Eyes off You: Attentional Adhesion to Mates and Rivals." *Journal of Personality and Social Psychology* 93 (3): 389–401.

Manning, A. G., R. I. Khakimov, R. G. Dall, and A. G. Truscott (2015) "Wheeler's Delayed-Choice Gedanken Experiment with a Single Atom." *Nature Physics* 11 (7): 539–542.

Mathews, Freya (2011) "Panpsychism as Paradigm." *The Mental as Fundamental: New Perspectives on Panpsychism*. Edited by M. Blamauer. Heusenstamm, Ger.: Ontos Verlag: 141–56.

May, Edwin C., Jessica M. Utts, Virginia V. Trask, Wanda W. Luke, Thand J. Frivold, and Beverley S. Humphrey (1989) "Review of the Psychoenergetic Research Conducted at SRI International (1973–1988)." *Menlo Park* 33: 1–25.

McConnell, R. A., and T. K. Clarke (1991) "National Academy of Sciences' Opinion on Parapsychology." *Journal of the American Society for Psychical Research* 85 (4): 333–65.

McKenna, Terence (1999) *Food of the Gods: The Search for the Original Tree of Knowledge: a Radical History of Plants, Drugs and Human Evolution*. New York: Random House.

Melloni, Lucia, Carlos Molina, Marcela Pena, David Torres, Wolf Singer, and Eugenio Rodriguez (2007) "Synchronization of Neural Activity across Cortical Areas Correlates with Conscious Perception." *Journal of Neuroscience* 27 (11): 2858–65.

Mertens, Gaëtan, and Iris M. Engelhard (2020) "A Systematic Review and Meta-Analysis of the Evidence for Unaware Fear Conditioning." *Neuroscience and Biobehavioral Reviews* 108: 254–268.

Mills, A., E. Haraldsson, and H. J. Keil (1994) "Replication Studies of Cases Suggestive of Reincarnation by Three Independent Investigators." *Journal of the American Society for Psychical Research* 88 (3): 207–19.

Mills, Antonia and Jim B. Tucker (2015) "Reincarnation: Field Studies and Theoretical Issues Today." *Parapsychology: A Handbook for the 21st Century*. Edited by Etzel Cardeña, John Palmer, and David Marcusson-Clavertz. Jefferson, N.C.: McFarland & Company, Inc., Publishers: 314–326.

Milton, J. (1997) "Meta-Analysis of Free-Response ESP Studies without Altered States of Consciousness." *The Journal of Parapsychology* 61 (4): 279.

Milton, Julie, and Richard Wiseman (1999) "Does Psi Exist? Lack of Replication of an Anomalous Process of Information Transfer." *Psychological Bulletin* 125 (4): 387.

Moore, David W. (2005, June 16) "Three in Four Americans Believe in Paranormal." Gallup Poll News Service.

Mossbridge, Julia (2016) "Designing Transcendence Technology." *Psychology's New Design Science and the Reflective Practitioner*. Edited by Susan Imholz, and Judy Sachter. River Bend, N.C.: LibraLab Press.

Mossbridge, Julia, Patrizio Tressoldi, and Jessica Utts (2012) "Predictive Physiological Anticipation Preceding Seemingly Unpredictable Stimuli: A Meta-Analysis." *Frontiers in Psychology* 3 (October): 390.

Mossbridge, Julia A., Patrizio Tressoldi, Jessica Utts, John A. Ives, Dean Radin, and Wayne B. Jonas (2014) "Predicting the Unpredictable: Critical Analysis and Practical Implications of Predictive Anticipatory Activity." *Frontiers in Human Neuroscience* 8: 146.

Muthukumaraswamy, Suresh D., Robin L. Carhart-Harris, Rosalyn J. Moran, Matthew J. Brookes, Tim M. Williams, David Errtizoe, Ben Sessa, et al. (2013) "Broadband Cortical Desynchronization Underlies the Human Psychedelic State." *Journal of Neuroscience* 33 (38): 15171–83.

Nagasawa, Yujin, and K. Wager (2017) "Panpsychism and Priority Cosmopsychism." *Panpsychism: Contemporary Perspectives*. Edited by

G. Brüntrup and L. Jaskolla. Oxford: Oxford University Press: 113–29.

Nahm, Michael, Bruce Greyson, Emily Williams Kelly, and Erlendur Haraldsson (2012) "Terminal Lucidity: A Review and a Case Collection." *Archives of Gerontology and Geriatrics* 55 (1): 138–42.

Nash, Jonathan D., and Andrew Newberg (2013) "Toward a Unifying Taxonomy and Definition for Meditation." *Frontiers in Psychology* 4 (November): 806.

National Alliance on Mental Illness. "Mental Health Conditions." NAMI. Accessed on January 10, 2022.

Nelson, Roger (2020) "Formal Analysis September 11, 2001." The Global Consciousness Project.

Newberg, A., A. Alavi, M. Baime, M. Pourdehnad, J. Santanna, and E. d'Aquili (2001) "The Measurement of Regional Cerebral Blood Flow during the Complex Cognitive Task of Meditation: A Preliminary SPECT Study." *Psychiatry Research: Neuroimaging* 106 (2): 113–22.

Newberg, Andrew B., and Eugene G. d'Aquili (2000) "The Neuropsychology of Religious and Spiritual Experience." *Journal of Consciousness Studies* 7 (11–12): 251–66.

Newton, Michael (2010) *Destiny of Souls: New Case Studies of Life between Lives*. Woodbury, Minn.: Llewellyn Worldwide.

Northoff, G., A. Heinzel, M. De Greck, F. Bermpohl, H. Dobrowolny, and J. Panksepp (2006) "Self-Referential Processing in Our Brain: A Meta-Analysis of Imaging Studies on the Self." *Neuroimage* 31 (1): 440–57.

Öhman, Arne, Anders Flykt, and Francisco Esteves (2001) "Emotion Drives Attention: Detecting the Snake in the Grass." *Journal of Experimental Psychology: General* 130 (3): 466–78.

Open Science Collaboration (2015) "Estimating the Reproducibility of Psychological Science." *Science* 349 (6251).

Open Sciences. "The Manifesto for a Post-Materialist Science: Campaign for Open Science." Open Sciences. Accessed on April 8, 2021.

Overbye, Dennis (2021, April 7) "A Tiny Particle's Wobble Could Upend the Known Laws of Physics." *The New York Times*.

Pasricha, S., and I. Stevenson (1987) "Indian Cases of the Reincarnation Type Two Generations Apart." *Journal of the Society for Psychical Research* 54 (809): 239–246.

Persinger, Michael A. (1989) "Geophysical Variables and Behavior: LV. Predicting the Details of Visitor Experiences and the Personality of Experiments: The Temporal Lobe Factor." *Perceptual and Motor Skills* 68 (1): 55–65.

Pierre, L. S, and M. A. Persinger (2006) "Experimental Facilitation of the Sensed Presence Is Predicted by the Specific Patterns of the Applied Magnetic Fields, Not by Suggestibility: Re-Analyses of 19 Experiments." *International Journal of Neuroscience* 116 (9): 1079–96.

Pew Research Center (2009a) "Eastern, New Age Beliefs Widespread Many Americans Mix Multiple Faiths." Pew Forum.

Pew Research Center (2009b) "Religion and Science in the United States." Pew Forum.

Puthoff, Harold E., and Russell Targ (1976) "A Perceptual Channel for Information Transfer over Kilometer Distances: Historical Perspective and Recent Research." *Proceedings of the IEEE* 64 (3): 329–54.

Rabeyron, Thomas (2020) "Why Most Research Findings About Psi Are False: The Replicability Crisis, the Psi Paradox and the Myth of Sisyphus." *Frontiers in Psychology* 11 (September): 2468.

Radin, Dean (2018) *Real Magic: Ancient Wisdom, Modern Science, and a Guide to the Secret Power of the Universe.* New York: Harmony Books.

Raichle, Marcus E., Ann Mary MacLeod, Abraham Z. Snyder, William J. Powers, Debra A. Gusnard, and Gordon L. Shulman (2001) "A Default Mode of Brain Function." *Proceedings of the National Academy of Sciences of the United States of America* 98 (2): 676–82.

Raichle, M. E., and A. Z. Snyder (2007) "A Default Mode of Brain Function: A Brief History of an Evolving Idea." *Neuroimage* 37 (4): 1083–90.

Ramster, P. (1994) "Past Lives and Hypnosis." *Australian Journal of Clinical Hypnotherapy and Hypnosis* 15 (2): 67–91.

Renes, R. A., N. E. M. van Haren, H. Aarts, and M. Vink (2015) "An Exploratory fMRI Study into Inferences of Self-Agency." *Social Cognitive and Affective Neuroscience* 10 (5): 708–12.

Riba, Jordi, Peter Anderer, Francesc Jané, Bernd Saletu, and Manel J. Barbanoj (2004) "Effects of the South American Psychoactive Beverage Ayahuasca on Regional Brain Electrical Activity in Humans: A Functional Neuroimaging Study Using Low-Resolution Electromagnetic Tomography." *Neuropsychobiology* 50 (1): 89–101.

Riba, Jordi, Peter Anderer, Adelaida Morte, Gloria Urbano, Francesc Jané, Bernd Saletu, and Manel J. Barbanoj (2002) "Topographic Pharmaco-EEG Mapping of the Effects of the South American Psychoactive Beverage Ayahuasca in Healthy Volunteers." *British Journal of Clinical Pharmacology* 53 (6): 613–28.

Riccio, Matthew, Shana Cole, and Emily Balcetis (2013) "Seeing the Expected, the Desired, and the Feared: Influences on Perceptual Interpretation and Directed Attention." *Social and Personality Psychology Compass* 7 (6): 401–14.

Richard, F. D., Charles F. Bond, and Juli J. Stokes-Zoota (2003) "One Hundred Years of Social Psychology Quantitatively Described." *Review of General Psychology* 7 (4): 331–63.

Ritz, T. (2011) "Quantum Effects in Biology: Bird Navigation." *Procedia Chemistry* 1: 262–75.

Ritz, T., R. Wiltschko, P. J. Hore, C. T. Rodgers, K. Stapput, P. Thalau, C. R. Timmell, and W. Wiltschko (2009) "Magnetic Compass of Birds Is Based on a Molecule with Optimal Directional Sensitivity." *Biophysical Journal* 96 (8): 3451–57.

Rodriguez, Eugenio, Nathalie George, Jean Philippe Lachaux, Jacques Martinerie, Bernard Renault, and Francisco J. Varela (1999) "Perception's Shadow: Long-Distance Synchronization of Human Brain Activity." *Nature* 397 (6718): 430–33.

Roe, C. A, C. Sonnex, and E. C. Roxburgh (2015) "Two Meta-Analyses of Noncontact Healing Studies." *Explore* 11 (1): 11–23.

Rosenbaum, Ruth (2011) "Exploring the Other Dark Continent: Parallels between Psi Phenomena and the Psychotherapeutic Process." *Psychoanalytic Review* 98 (1): 57–90.

Rosentiel, Tom (2009) "Public Praises Science; Scientists Fault Public, Media." Pew Research.

Rouder, Jeffrey N., Richard D. Morey, and Jordan M. Province (2013) "A Bayes Factor Meta-Analysis of Recent Extrasensory Perception Experiments: Comment on Storm, Tressoldi, and Di Risio (2010)." *Psychological Bulletin* 139 (1): 241–247.

Rovelli, Carlo (1996) "Relational Quantum Mechanics." *International Journal of Theoretical Physics* 35 (8): 1637–78.

Sarraf, Matthew, Michael A. Woodley of Menie, and Patrizio Tressoldi (2020) "Anomalous Information Reception by Mediums: A Meta-Analysis of the Scientific Evidence." *Explore* 17 September-October (5): 396–402.

Satchidananda, Swami (1984) *The Yoga Sutras of Patanjali: Translation and Commentary by Sri Swami Satchidananda.* Buckingham, Va.: Integral Yoga Publications.

Schaffer, Jonathan (2009) "Spacetime the One Substance." *Philosophical Studies* 145 (1): 131–48.

Schmidt, Stefan (2015) "Experimental Research on Distant Intention Phenomena." *Parapsychology: A Handbook for the 21st Century*. Edited by Etzel Cardeña, John Palmer, and David Marcusson-Clavertz. Jefferson, N.C.: McFarland & Company, Inc.: 244–57.

Scholz, Jonathan, Christina Triantafyllou, Susan Whitfield-Gabrieli, Emery N. Brown, and Rebecca Saxe (2009) "Distinct Regions of Right Temporo-Parietal Junction Are Selective for Theory of Mind and Exogenous Attention." *PLOS One* 4 (3): e4869.

Schrödinger, Erwin (1935) "Discussion of Probability Relations Between Separated Systems," *Mathematical Proceedings of the Cambridge Philosophical Society* (31): 555–563.

Schultes, Richard Evans, and Albert Hofmann (1979) *Plants of the Gods: Origins of Hallucinogenic Use*. London: Hutchinson.

Schultes, Richard Evans, and Albert Hofmann (1992) *Plants of the Gods: Their Sacred, Healing, and Hallucinogenic Powers*. Rochester, Vt.: Healing Arts Press.

Schwarz, Katharina A., Roland Pfister, and Christian Büchel (2016) "Rethinking Explicit Expectations: Connecting Placebos, Social Cognition, and Contextual Perception." *Trends in Cognitive Sciences* 20 (6): 469-480.

Schwarz, Katharina A., Matthias J. Wieser, Antje B. M. Gerdes, Andreas Mühlberger, and Paul Pauli (2013) "Why Are You Looking like That? How the Context Influences Evaluation and Processing of Human Faces." *Social Cognitive and Affective Neuroscience* 8 (4): 438–45.

Shani, Itay (2015) "Cosmopsychism: A Holistic Approach to the Metaphysics of Experience." *Philosophical Papers* 44 (3): 389–437.

Shani, Itay, and Joachim Keppler (2018) "Beyond Combination: How Cosmic Consciousness Grounds Ordinary Experience." *Journal of the American Philosophical Association* 4 (3): 390–410.

Simons, Daniel J., and Christopher F. Chabris (1999) "Gorillas in Our Midst: Sustained Inattentional Blindness for Dynamic Events." *Perception* 28 (9): 1059–74.

Sinclair, Upton (1930) *Mental Radio*. Charlottesville, Va.: Hampton Roads Publishing Company.

Singer, Wolf, Thomas Metzinger, Johannes Gutenberg, and Jennifer M. Windt (2014) "The Ongoing Search for the Neuronal Correlate of Consciousness." Open MIND.

Smolin, Lee (1999) *The Life of the Cosmos*. Oxford: Oxford University Press.

Solov'Yov, Ilia A., Henrik Mouritsen, and Klaus Schulten (2010) "Acuity of a Cryptochrome and Vision-Based Magnetoreception System in Birds." *Biophysical journal* 99 (1): 40-49.

Steele, Claude M., and Joshua Aronson (1995) "Stereotype Threat and the Intellectual Test Performance of African Americans." *Journal of Personality and Social Psychology* 69 (5): 797–811.

Stevens, Jay (1987) *Storming Heaven: LSD and the American Dream*. New York: Grove Press.

Stevenson, Ian (1977) "The Explanatory Value of the Idea of Reincarnation." *The Journal of Nervous and Mental Disease* 164 (5): 305–26.

Stilwell, Blake (2018, April 2) "The US Military Once Successfully Used a Psychic to Locate a Lost Plane." We Are the Mighty.

Stolaroff, Myron. J. (2004) *The Secret Chief Revealed: Conversations with a Pioneer of the Underground Psychedelic Therapy Movement*. San Jose, Calif: Multidisciplinary Association for Psychedelic Studies.

Storm, Lance, and Suitbert Ertel (2001) "Does Psi Exist? Comments on Milton and Wiseman's (1999) Meta-Analysis of Ganzfield Research." *Psychological Bulletin* 127 (3): 424–33.

Storm, L., P. E. Tressoldi, and L. Di Risio (2012) "A Meta-Analysis of ESP Studies, 1987–2010: Assessing the Success of the Forced-Choice Design in Parapsychology." *Journal of Parapsychology* 76: 243–73.

Storm, Lance, Patrizio E. Tressoldi, and Lorenzo Di Risio (2010) "A Meta-Analysis With Nothing to Hide: Reply to Hyman (2010) On the Words Used to Describe Evidence for Psi." *Psychological Bulletin* 136: 491–94.

Svoboda, E., M. C. McKinnon, and B. Levine (2006) "The Functional Neuroanatomy of Autobiographical Memory: A Meta-Analysis." *Neuropsychologia* 44 (12): 2189–2208.

Tagliazucchi, Enzo, Robin Carhart-Harris, Robert Leech, David Nutt, and Dante R. Chialvo (2014) "Enhanced Repertoire of Brain Dynamical States during the Psychedelic Experience." *Human Brain Mapping* 35 (11): 5442–56.

Tagliazucchi, Enzo, Leor Roseman, Mendel Kaelen, Csaba Orban, Suresh D. Muthukumaraswamy, Kevin Murphy, Helmut Laufs, et al. (2016) "Increased Global Functional Connectivity Correlates with LSD-Induced Ego Dissolution." *Current Biology* 26 (8): 1043–50.

Tarazi, L. (1990) "An Unusual Case of Hypnotic Regression with Some Unexplained Contents." *Journal of the American Society for Psychical Research* 84 (4): 309–44.

Targ, Russell (2012) *The Reality of ESP: A Physicist's Proof of Psychic Abilities.* Wheaton, Ill: Theosophical Publishing House.

Targ, Russell (2019) "What Do We Know about Psi? The First Decade of Remote-Viewing Research and Operations at Stanford Research Institute." *Journal of Scientific Exploration* 33 (4): 569–92.

Targ, Russell, and Harold Puthoff (1974) "Information Transmission under Conditions of Sensory Shielding." *Nature* 251 (5476): 602–7.

Tarnas, Richard (2006) *Cosmos and Psyche: Intimations of a New World View.* New York: Penguin Books.

Thompson, C. (1982) "Anwesenheit: Psychopathology and Clinical Associations." *The British Journal of Psychiatry* 141 (6): 628–30.

Thurman, Michael (2016) "The Lunar Phases: Archetypes of the Soul." Mountain Astrologer.

Tracey, Irene (2010) "Getting the Pain You Expect: Mechanisms of Placebo, Nocebo and Reappraisal Effects in Humans." *Nature Medicine* 16 (11): 1277–83.

Tressoldi, Patrizio E. (2011) "Extraordinary Claims Require Extraordinary Evidence: The Case of Non-Local Perception, a Classical and Bayesian Review of Evidences." *Frontiers in Psychology* 2 (June): 117.

Tucker, Jim B. (2000) "A Scale to Measure the Strength of Children's Claims of Previous Lives: Methodology and Initial Findings." *Journal of Scientific Exploration* 14 (4): 571–81.

Turin, Luca (1996) "A Spectroscopic Mechanism for Primary Olfactory Reception." *Chemical Senses* 21 (6): 773–91.

Urgesi, Cosimo, Salvatore M. Aglioti, Miran Skrap, and Franco Fabbro (2010) "The Spiritual Brain: Selective Cortical Lesions Modulate Human Self-Transcendence." *Neuron* 65 (3).

Utts, Jessica (1996) "An Assessment of the Evidence for Psychic Functioning." *Journal of Scientific Exploration* 10 (1): 3–30.

Van Veluw, Susanne J., and Steven A. Chance (2014) "Differentiating between Self and Others: An ALE Meta-Analysis of fMRI Studies of Self-Recognition and Theory of Mind." *Brain Imaging and Behavior* 8 (March) 1: 24–38.

Vogt, B. A., and S. Laureys (2005) "Posterior Cingulate, Precuneal and Retrosplenial Cortices: Cytology and Components of the Neural Network Correlates of Consciousness." *Progress in Brain Research* (150): 205–17.

Vollenweider, Franz X., and Mark A. Geyer (2001) "A Systems Model of Altered

Consciousness: Integrating Natural and Drug-Induced Psychoses." *Brain Research Bulletin* 56 (November) 5: 495–507.

Vollenweider, F. X., K. L. Leenders, C. Scharfetter, P. Maguire, O. Stadelmann, and J. Angst (1997) "Positron Emission Tomography and Fluorodeoxyglucose Studies of Metabolic Hyperfrontality and Psychopathology in the Psilocybin Model of Psychosis." *Neuropsychopharmacology* 16 (5): 357–72.

Voss, Joel L., Carol L. Baym, and Ken A. Paller (2008) "Accurate Forced-Choice Recognition without Awareness of Memory Retrieval." *Learning and Memory* 15 (6): 454–59.

Voss, Joel L., Heather D. Lucas, and Ken A. Paller (2012) "More than a Feeling: Pervasive Influences of Memory without Awareness of Retrieval." *Cognitive Neuroscience* 3 (3–4): 193–207.

Wahbeh, Helané, Dean Radin, Julia Mossbridge, Cassandra Vieten, and Arnaud Delorme (2018) "Exceptional Experiences Reported by Scientists and Engineers." *Explore* 14 (5): 329–41.

Wasson, R. Gordon, and Valentina Pavlovna Wasson (1957) *Mushrooms, Russia, and History*. 2 vols. New York: Pantheon.

Watt, Caroline, and Marleen Nagtegaal (2004) "Reporting of Blind Methods: An Interdisciplinary Survey." *Journal of the Society for Psychical Research, 68* (875)[2]: 105–14.

Webber, John (2020) *The Red Chair*. Carlsbad, Calif: Balboa Press.

Weil, Gunther M., Ralph Metzner, and Timothy Leary, eds. (1965) *The Psychedelic Reader*. New York: University Books.

Weiss, Brian L. (1988) *Many Lives, Many Masters*. New York: Fireside Books.

Weiss, Brian L. (1992) *Through Time Into Healing*. New York: Fireside Books.

Wheeler, John Archibald (1973) "From Relativity to Mutability." *The Physicist's Conception of Nature*. Dordrecht, Neth: Springer: 202–47

Williams, B. J. (2011) "Revisiting the Ganzfeld ESP Debate: A Basic Review and Assessment." *Journal of Scientific Exploration* 25 (4): 639–undefined.

Yaden, David B., and Roland R. Griffiths (2021) "The Subjective Effects of Psychedelics Are Necessary for Their Enduring Therapeutic Effects." *ACS Pharmacology and Translational Science* 4 (2), 568–72.

Zdrenka, Marco, and Marc S. Wilson (2017) "Individual Difference Correlates of Psi Performance in Forced-Choice Precognition Experiments: A Meta-Analysis (1945–2016)." *The Journal of Parapsychology* 81 (1): 9–32.

Index

Page numbers in *italics* refer to illustrations.